Schooled on Fat

Schooled on Fat explores how body image, social status, fat stigma and teasing, food consumption behaviors, and exercise practices intersect in the daily lives of adolescent girls and boys. Based on nine months of fieldwork at a high school located near Tucson, Arizona, the book draws on social, linguistic, and theoretical contexts to illustrate how teens navigate the fraught realities of body image within a high school culture that reinforced widespread beliefs about body size as a matter of personal responsibility while offering limited opportunity to exercise and an abundance of fattening junk foods. Taylor also traces policy efforts to illustrate where we are as a nation in addressing childhood obesity and offers practical strategies schools and parents can use to promote teen wellness. This book is ideal for courses on the body, fat studies, gender studies, language and culture, school culture and policy, public ethnography, deviance, and youth culture.

Nicole Taylor is an anthropologist who explores contemporary social issues related to education and health through the analytic lens of language practices. She is Director of Scholar Programs at the School for Advanced Research, and an adjunct faculty member in the Department of Anthropology at the University of New Mexico.

Innovative Ethnographies

Series Editor: Phillip Vannini, Royal Roads University

The purpose of this series is to use the new digital technology to capture a richer, more multidimensional view of social life than was otherwise done in the classic, print tradition of ethnography, while maintaining the traditional strengths of classic, ethnographic analysis.

Available

Ferry Tales: Mobility, Place, and Time on Canada's West Coast by Phillip Vannini

Digital Drama: Teaching and Learning Art and Media in Tanzania by Paula Uimonen

Concrete and Dust: Mapping the Sexual Terrains of Los Angeles by Jeanine Marie Minge and Amber Lynn Zimmerman

Water in a Dry Land: Place Learning Through Art and Story by Margaret Somerville

My Father's Wars: Migration, Memory, and the Violence of a Century by Alisse Waterston

Off the Grid: Re-Assembling Domestic Life by Phillip Vannini and Jonathan Taggart

Schooled on Fat: What Teens Tell Us About Gender, Body Image, and Obesity by Nicole Taylor

Schooled on Fat

What Teens Tell Us About Gender, Body Image,
and Obesity

Nicole Taylor

Routledge
Taylor & Francis Group

NEW YORK AND LONDON

Please visit the companion website at
www.innovativeethnographies.net/schooledonfat/

First published 2016
by Routledge
711 Third Avenue, New York, NY 10017

and by Routledge
2 Park Square, Milton Park, Abingdon, Oxon, OX14 4RN

Routledge is an imprint of the Taylor & Francis Group, an informa business

Library of Congress Cataloging-in-Publication Data
Taylor, Nicole.
Schooled on fat : what teens tell us about gender, body image, and obesity /
by Nicole Taylor. — 1 Edition.
pages cm. — (Innovative ethnographies)
Includes bibliographical references and index.
1. Body size—Arizona—Juvenile literature. 2. Body image—Arizona—Juvenile
literature. I. Title.
RC569.B65.T39 2015 (2016)
616.3'98—dc23
2015023357

ISBN: 978-1-138-92420-8 (hbk)
ISBN: 978-1-138-92421-5 (pbk)
ISBN: 978-1-315-68450-5 (ebk)

Typeset in Adobe Caslon Pro and Copperplate
by FiSH Books Ltd, Enfield

For David and Oliver

CONTENTS

PREFACE

When people ask me about my research and I explain that I am a linguistic anthropologist who studies body image and obesity, the next question is almost always, "What does language have to do with body image or obesity?" To which I answer, "A lot." Language is powerful—it shapes our worldview, our perception of reality. It is a primary means through which humans relate to each other and make sense of the world around us. Everyday conversation among people in communities all over the world has the capacity to soothe, hurt, connect or divide people, and influence how we think, behave, interact with others, and interpret our experiences.

Think back to a time when you were teased by someone, a classmate, friend, romantic partner, family member, or complete stranger. Perhaps you were teased for being too fat or too thin, having dark skin, wearing glasses, being gay, having acne, or wearing clothes that weren't cool enough. Maybe you were teased to your face, or perhaps you were gossiped about behind your back and you later found out about it. Close your eyes and recall how those words felt at the moment of impact. It still stings, doesn't it?

I grew up white among white people in middle-class suburbs throughout the South and West. In seventh grade, I attended a middle school in Littleton, Colorado, where, for the first time in my life, I was teased for the way I looked, specifically for the color of my skin. One day, while I was walking alone to class, three boys encircled me and began chanting "Taco! You're such a taco!" I don't remember much about those boys except that they were white with blond hair and blue eyes and wore stylish, expensive-looking clothes, all markers of the popular crowd. They seemed to materialize out of nowhere to taunt me that day. We did not have any classes together or share any friends or acquaintances that I was aware of. At the time I had no idea what their words meant, but I understood that I was being insulted by the tone of their voices and the way they sneered. In that moment I felt confusion, shame, embarrassment, anger, and fear.

The boys did not stop there. For weeks, they continued to taunt me, calling me "taco" when they passed me in the hallway or saw me at recess. One day they stood near me outside my classroom, and one boy said to another, "Hey, would you ever go out with that taco?" The boy yelled in response, "No way. I wouldn't touch her with a ten-foot pole." His words resonated throughout the hallway and caught the attention of nearby students, who stopped talking with their friends to stare. My face burned hot and glowed red with embarrassment. I wanted to curl up into myself and disappear. Then just as suddenly as those boys had materialized one day they vanished never to bother me again. I can only assume they grew bored with me and moved on to their next victim.

For months I thought about the incidents and wondered what they meant. And since it occurred before the Internet, I couldn't simply "Google" it. My feelings of shame and fear kept me from asking my parents or a trusted teacher what the insult meant. What if being a taco was something truly horrible, worse than anything I could imagine? Besides, I was already a shy, socially anxious preteen who hated getting attention, positive or negative. Knowing what the insults meant could have pushed me further into my shell and I did not want to take the risk.

Only recently have I learned about my Choctaw heritage on my father's side. That, combined with my mom's Scandinavian ancestry, explains my brownish red complexion. Because my family had always lived among white, middle-class people who, for the most part, accepted and treated me as one of their own, it had never occurred to me to question my racial heritage or how it was related to my appearance.

In retrospect, I remember other, more subtle instances when people had questioned my ethnicity and judged me based on my skin tone. For example, at the private, all-white elementary school I attended in Shreveport, Louisiana a teacher once asked me, "How did you get so dark over the summer?" Her tone was a bit accusatory, which confused and frightened me, making me wonder if I was in trouble. I tentatively replied, "I played outside in the sun every day," hoping that was the right answer. She stood before me for a moment, scrutinizing my face, before replying, "Hmph" and walking away. I was so relieved to be off the hook that I did not even care to reflect on what her question really meant.

These personal stories illustrate the power of language in shaping our experience with the world around us and emphasize the importance of interpreting language in context. In both examples, even though I did not understand the meaning of their words at the time, I was able to surmise their intention by reading intonation, facial expressions, and body language.

Regardless of the descriptive accuracy of what the teacher in Louisiana or the boys in Colorado had said about me, their words deeply affected me. Face-to-face communication is complex and dynamic precisely because words spoken acquire meaning through context and it is often the context that aids most in interpreting the true meaning of discourse.

Sociolinguist Dell Hymes was among the first to emphasize the importance of context in understanding language interaction, developing a model that takes into account setting (e.g., school playground), purpose or goals of the utterances (e.g., to insult or lower social status), sequence (e.g., rhetorical question and response—"Would you go out with that taco? No way!"), tone (e.g., playful or serious), style (e.g., informal or formal), social norms that structure the interaction (e.g., rules governing who is allowed to insult whom publicly), and genre (e.g., insult or joke).[1]

In the example of the teasing boys, without taking context into account it is impossible to make sense of someone calling another person a "taco," which normally refers to a type of food people eat. It is the sociocultural and situational context that makes such an utterance meaningful. If you had been an observer on that playground when the boys teased me, to understand what the interaction meant you would need to have some knowledge of the relationship between me and the boys; you would need to pay attention to their intonation and body language as well as my response; you would need to have a basic understanding of the social hierarchy at the school and how each of us fit into it; you would need to have a sense of racial relations at the school, and you would need to understand that "taco" has multiple meanings, depending on the context in which the word is used.

Sociolinguist John Gumpertz identified a set of "contextualization cues" that help those communicating with each other to signal and interpret the content and meaning of what is being said, determine how the content should be understood, and figure out how parts of the interaction relate to the whole.[2] Contextualization cues can operate at multiples levels of speech production, including prosody (e.g., intonation, stress, and pitch), voice quality (e.g., breathy or creaky voice), speech tempo (e.g., pauses), and turn-taking (e.g., interruptions). In the example I described of the teacher and me, her question was so cryptic that the contextualization cues were essential to interpreting meaning. The content of her question alone seemed innocuous—"How did you get so dark over the summer?" It was the disapproving, scrutinizing look on her face, the judgmental tone of her voice, the way she leaned her body in, narrowed her eyes, and pursed her lips while saying "Hmph" after a prolonged pause that later helped me interpret the interaction.

Fortunately, I do not have any substantive examples of being teased for how my body looked during my teen years and beyond. I inherited my mother's fast metabolism and cultivated a lifelong love of exercise that has kept me pretty lean and fit. Additionally, I spent my teen years in the San Joaquin Valley of southern California, where loose-fitting clothing that camouflaged body shape was in style for both boys and girls at that time. I wore comfortable-fitting jeans or cutoff shorts and baggy T-shirts to school most days, threw my hair back into a ponytail, and did not bother with makeup. This casual style was the typical look for girls, including those who were popular.

Consequently, as a teen I was not socialized by my peer culture to obsess about the details of my appearance. Additionally, we did not have cable TV at my house and the Internet did not yet exist. So unlike most teens these days I did not have the constant input from my friends, peers, and the media about the need for concern about how my body looked. It wasn't until my sophomore year of college, when I transferred from California Polytechnic University to a university in central Texas, that I was introduced to an environment of hyperawareness about body image and socialization and enforcement of female beauty norms. There for the first time guys I dated chastised me for wearing sandals with unpainted toenails, going without makeup, and wearing jeans and T-shirts to parties. Girls I befriended fretted over the way their bodies looked, standing in front of mirrors scrutinizing themselves in different outfits, pinching the fat on the insides of their thighs and around their waist, and obsessing over how their food choices might impact their weight.

Thus the transition from California to Texas schools represented a major culture shock for me. I was fascinated daily as I watched girls wearing high heels, panty hose, dresses, and gobs of makeup trudge up the steep hills of campus in the oppressive Texas heat. Meanwhile, guys walked around in shorts, T-shirts, and flip-flops. I could not make sense of what I was seeing and experiencing. But at the time I remained rather nonchalant about it; when my date would ask me to change into something more formal for a keg party or tell me I needed to wear more makeup, I found it amusing. I would laugh and say, "Whatever."

When I graduated and began teaching high school English in a rural area outside of Austin, I saw an earlier stage in this process of girls becoming preoccupied with appearance and body image. Small groups of ninth-grade middle-class white girls who attended the school would come into my classroom daily just before class and engage in "fat talk,"[3] taking turns calling themselves fat and assuring each other they are not fat. What I found even more interesting than girls' engagement in fat talk was boys' daily conversations among themselves about how girls looked. Similar to my experiences in college, boys at the high school felt entitled to evaluate girls' appearance. I would hear boys discussing how good this or that girl looked in her outfit, critiquing every little ripple that appeared beneath her clothing.

Fortunately, by the time I had encountered this culture of hyperawareness around appearance and the expectation that girls twist themselves into pretzels to look perfect I had already developed into a confident young woman and was mostly unaffected by it. However, watching these gendered socialization processes play out at the high school angered me. To my perception, these girls were developing into young women who thought they weren't pretty enough or good enough, messages that were reinforced daily by male classmates and the local culture, not to mention media influences.

My experiences in Texas as a college student and high school teacher are what sparked my interest in the topic of teens, body image, the power of language to shape beliefs and perceptions about appearance and how vastly different appearance standards are for boys and girls. I saw the cumulative effect of seemingly trivial, harmless conversations about body image that took place among teens at the high school where I taught. I saw the potential long-term impact of everyday discourse about body image on girls' self-esteem and became concerned about it. I wanted to better understand what I was experiencing and ultimately raise awareness about the consequences of this type of ongoing commentary about body image.

Because this book addresses topics that appear regularly in news media and have tangible social impacts, such as bullying and teasing in schools, the "obesity epidemic," the ubiquity of junk food in US schools, and youth's focus on body image, I intend it to appeal to individuals interested in important social issues. I draw on research from anthropology, sociology, developmental psychology, education, public health, and gender studies and hope that scholars in these fields will find the book useful both in teaching and informing their own work. I imagine that school administrators, counselors, parents, and anyone who works with youth might find the book of interest as well. I hope my book provides new insights into the social dynamics of teens concerning body image and highlights potential positive changes in outlook and policies that could be implemented to improve the lives of teens and others.

Schooled on Fat is an in-depth, ethnographic account exploring how body image, social status, fat stigma and teasing, food consumption behaviors, and exercise practices intersect in the daily lives of adolescent girls and boys from their perspectives. It is based on nine months of ethnographic fieldwork at a high school I call Desert Vista located near Tucson, Arizona. The book draws on social, linguistic, and theoretical contexts to illustrate how teens negotiated and sometimes got caught in the middle of competing public obesity narratives that were often at odds with the realities of their school environment.

Notes

1. Hymes, 1974.
2. Gumpertz, 1982a, 1982b, 1992.
3. Nichter, 2000.

ACKNOWLEDGMENTS

It's true what they say about book projects being a team effort and this endeavor was no exception. First I thank the students at Desert Vista High School who shared their experiences with me. Additionally, the steadfast support of teachers and administrators who provided unlimited access to students and places around the school enabled me to collect meaningful data on sensitive topics.

My dissertation committee members, Norma Mendoza-Denton, Mimi Nichter, Mark Nichter, and Jane Hill, helped guide the initial versions of this work and continue to offer mentorship and friendship. Even earlier in my intellectual development Mary Bucholtz was instrumental in bringing this book to fruition by introducing me to anthropology when I felt adrift in an English department and had only the kernel of an idea but no strategy for developing it into something tangible. Thanks also to Susan U. Philips for teaching me foundational theories of language, self, and society, which influenced my approach to this project.

I am grateful to others who have critiqued the manuscript at various and, in some cases, multiple stages, including David Schachter, David E. Stuart, Luther Wilson, Ellen Kleiner and her editing team, Mimi Nichter, and the anonymous reviewers. Their feedback has moved my work forward in ways I could not have achieved alone. In addition, colleagues who have offered insights and perspectives that have shaped my thinking on this project include Marina Merrill and participants in the School for Advanced Research (SAR) seminar "Obesity, Upward Mobility, and Symbolic Body Capital in a Rapidly Changing World": Eileen Anderson-Fye, Monica Casper, Anne Becker, Sarah Trainer, Alexander Edmonds, Stephanie McClure, Daniel Hruschka, Alexandra Brewis Slade, and Rebecca Lester. I further appreciate SAR scholars who provided comments on Chapter 3 – Elana Resnick, William Nomikos, Joseph Aguilar, Severin Fowles, and

Michael Brown – and Mike Agar for sharing publishing stories and serving as a sounding board for some of my ideas.

Thanks also to Sabra Mwaura for helping me identify fieldwork stories to share on the companion website as well as to the high school students who contributed artwork, poetry, music, and essays and teachers who facilitated the process. I am grateful Pattie Christianson for reaching out to me during a low point in the project by sharing a deeply personal story about her teenage daughter. This experience motivated me to keep writing.

Thanks to the following reviewers for their valuable feedback:

Elroi Windsor, Salem College
Donna King, University of North Carolina Wilmington
Laurie Schaffner, Univeristy of Illinios at Chicago
Ginny Garcia-Alexander, Portland State University
Zoe Newman, York University
Nicholas Rattray, Indiana University—Purdue University Indianapolis
Kimberly Fox, Bridgewater State University
Elise Lake, the University of Mississippi
Shira Tarrant, California State University, Long Beach
Mimi Nichter, the University of Arizona

I thank Samantha Barbaro, my Routledge editor, for her enthusiastic support of the project as well as Innovative Ethnographies Series editor Phillip Vannini, who helped me think through important aspects of the companion website, and Sarah Abbott, who constructed the website. Margaret Moore, Andrew Acuff, and the Routledge production and marketing teams were wonderful to work with as well. SAR provided time to write and research funds, without which this book would not have been possible. I especially appreciate the support of Scholar Programs staff Laura Holt, Cynthia Geoghegan, and Maria Spray. Thanks also to the School of Anthropology at the University of Arizona and the American Association of University Women for providing grants and fellowships to support my research.

Last, but not least, I am eternally grateful to my family—Mom, Dad, Jason, and Becky—for always believing in me and helping me through the difficult times. My deepest gratitude goes to my husband, David, who has encouraged and supported me throughout this process by providing feedback on my writing, engaging with me in countless hours of discussion as ideas for the book developed, keeping me updated on relevant current events, proudly sharing my work with students, colleagues, and anyone who would listen, and taking on additional childcare and household responsibilities so I could have uninterrupted blocks of time to write and think.

1

INTRODUCTION

During the past fifteen or twenty years, obesity has taken center stage in the popular media as one of the most pressing health problems of the new millennium. For example, the *New York Times* reportedly published more than 750 articles on obesity between 1990 and 2001, with the majority appearing after 1997.[1] This media bombardment brought awareness of obesity as a problem into just about every American household and shaped people's ideas about what it means to be obese and why the average person should care about this issue.

High rates of obesity, and by extension, fat people are often blamed for rising health-care costs and a weakening of national security. For example, in a series of speeches that received repeated national news coverage in 2004 US Surgeon General Richard Carmona stated that obesity represents as great a threat to Americans as weapons of mass destruction, referring to obesity as "the terror within" and emphasizing personal responsibility in the "war" on obesity.[2]

More recently, First Lady Michelle Obama has embraced the fight against obesity, encouraging families to engage in physical activity and eat healthfully as part of her "Let's Move" campaign. She has also expressed concern about the potential impact of obesity on national security, repeatedly citing 2012 reports by military officials that obesity is the primary reason why young adults who want to join the military do not qualify.[3]

Public obesity discourses in the United States, where the dominant body-image ideal is thin and fat free, have constructed a perceptual reality wherein it seems no one is safe from becoming fat. The frantic tenor of obesity-crisis rhetoric suggests that the problem is urgent, out of our control, and that we must address it before it cripples the US health-care system, economy,

1

and military. Because obesity is framed as a major threat to our national well-being, the central underlying question in popular obesity-crisis rhetoric is: "Who is responsible?" and by extension, "Who should be held accountable for changing behavior resulting in obesity?" The most common answer to that question is that fat people are to blame. In the next section I discuss the historical and cultural context of how fat bodies have become so politicized and stigmatized in the US and the broader implications of this dominant anti-fat belief system.

The Backstory and the Big Picture

The social meaning of body weight and shape in the United States has shifted throughout history.[4] Feminist philosopher Susan Bordo notes that during the mid-nineteenth century corpulence symbolized economic prosperity for the bourgeoisie, whereas by the end of the century, "Social power had come to be less dependent on the sheer accumulation of material wealth and more connected to the ability to control and manage the labor resources of others."[5] At the same time, corpulence began to be associated with poor moral character and a lack of willpower.

Early in the twentieth century, the concept of health and body image norms were introduced through the medical practice of measuring, weighing, and documenting individuals' body size and weight. During World War I, excess fat was seen as a sign of greed in the context of national fears about food shortages. Historian Helen Zoe Veit writes, "Because patriotic food conservation supposedly resulted quite naturally in a healthfully trim weight, patriotism was visible in a way it had never been before."[6] Fat stigma became pervasive, as people who displayed excess body weight were thought of as lazy, greedy, selfish, and unpatriotic. Veit argues that the widespread condemnation of excess body fat continued to thrive postwar as dieting culture gained in popularity, converging with Progressive values of self-control and sacrifice and the mainstream thin beauty ideal that took hold during the late 1910s.[7]

By the mid-1900s, insurance companies were using biomedical standards of height and weight to assess morbidity risk in individuals.[8] American Studies professor Charlotte Biltekoff traces the concept of obesity as a national health crisis to the early1950s when Metlife published a study linking body weight to mortality and legitimizing the concept of a healthy, ideal weight.[9] It was at this point that major media outlets began referring to obesity as a health threat and associating body size with lifestyle choices.

According to Biltekoff, in the 1960s another pivotal moment added institutional legitimacy to the developing national narrative framing obesity as a public health crisis and highlighting individual responsibility in the personal management of health / body weight. In 1969 the White House Conference on Food, Nutrition, and Health focused on health issues of the affluent, highlighting the Metlife study findings that linked obesity with high rates of mortality. Health experts concluded that poor food choices were the cause of obesity, further institutionalizing a normative standard for body weight, as well as the ranking of individuals according to their adherence to this standard.[10]

Then in the 1990s two reports published by the Centers for Disease Control showed a dramatic increase in adult obesity rates, which intensified national concern about obesity.[11] Critics of the reports challenged statistical methods used and noted that the increase in obesity rates coincided with the release of new weight guidelines in 1998 by the National Institutes of Health. These challenges did not garner the same level of media attention as the reports themselves, resulting in a full scale governmental double down on efforts to shrink the waistlines of Americans. Biltekoff notes that shortly thereafter, in 2001, the US government officially declared obesity a national epidemic and by 2011 the problem of obesity had become a sixty-billion-dollar-a-year industry.[12]

Women have long been judged for the way their bodies look. In the latter half of the nineteenth century, an S-curve figure highlighting a very slim waistline became popular for women and required the wearing of tightly cinched corsets, which restricted movement and circulation, often resulting in fainting spells.[13] Fashion and media of the 1920s promoted an overall slender image of the female body, and a postwar shift in attitude from conservative to carefree prompted women to replace the outward constraint of the corset with the internal constraint of dieting.[14] Movies and fashion magazines began encouraging girls to constantly "try on new identities" through clothing, makeup, and hairstyles. As fashionable clothing for women continued to become more revealing, baring a woman's midriff and thighs, women's obsession with body image intensified.[15]

In the 1980s, as diet and fitness industries expanded along with mass-media advertisements selling slimming products, consumers were increasingly considered responsible for managing their own weight, an ideology that was deeply embedded in the consciousness of the teens who participated in my study. Youth I interviewed grappled with their beliefs about personal responsibility as they faced the reality of junk food environments that made self-control and management of body weight nearly impossible. As a result of the dominant personal responsibility narrative, overweight bodies increasingly represent laziness, weakness, and a lack of control, while thin, toned bodies reflect discipline and willpower, as well as access to exercise as a leisure activity.[16]

The emphasis on managing body fat that gained momentum during the latter half of the twentieth century increased pressures for boys and men to achieve a certain body type as well.[17] Subsequent chapters will illustrate that boys and girls in my study were both concerned with how their bodies looked. What differed the most for boys and girls were their body-image goals and the social consequences associated with failing to achieve those gendered goals.

This historical shift toward the idealization of slimness and stigmatization of being overweight "provided the basis for the moral model of fatness, which suggests that fat people are responsible for their condition and should be punished as a means of social control for being fat."[18] Embedded within popular obesity discourses focusing on individual responsibility is the belief that body size is a choice.[19] Susan Bordo argues that mass-media messages reinforce the belief about body size as a personal choice through advertisements for dieting products, body-shaping lingerie, exercise equipment, and plastic surgery, leading American consumers to perceive the body's capacity for physical transformation as limitless.[20] For students I interviewed, the consequences of this deeply held conviction that body size is a choice included food-related guilt, low self-esteem, and harsh judgment of their peers' bodies that resulted in fat teasing.

Competing public obesity discourses in the United States tend to place blame on either overweight individuals or environmental factors, such as built environments, cultural norms that encourage sedentary lifestyles, and the prevalence of junk foods. In popular media, obesity is alternately framed as a public health crisis, an issue of individual and moral responsibility, and a social justice issue.[21] Discourses that frame obesity as an issue of personal responsibility and a public health crisis remain predominant, obscuring the everyday realities of discrimination, social inequality, and the pressure to conform faced by those who are labeled overweight and obese.[22]

Popular obesity discourses focusing on individual responsibility normalize the moral model of fatness that sociologist Jeffrey Sobal[23] writes about and perpetuate negative stereotypes and social stigma associated with obesity. *Schooled on Fat* explores the modern-day intersection between body-image ideology and obesity-related issues, such as fat stigma, ideas about personal responsibility, engagement in and attitudes toward exercise, food-consumption behaviors, and social relationships among teens. I found that these issues converged in unexpected ways. For example, teens, even those who were overweight, were critical of fat people and harshly scrutinized the eating habits of others, despite the fact that they ate junk food almost daily.

Although dominant body-image ideologies in the United States favor slenderness and stigmatize excess body fat, not everyone has historically agreed with, or strived to achieve, the mainstream beauty ideal. Social science research has suggested that body-image ideals among African-American and Latina women may be more flexible than those of white women. Anthropologist Mimi Nichter and her colleagues reported that African-American teenage girls were more satisfied with their bodies than white girls and defined beauty in terms of one's attitude, the way one moves, and one's ability to create a personal style that "works" and is unique.[24] Similarly, a study based on analysis of focus-group data reported that African-American and Latina women challenged the mainstream beauty ideal of slenderness by embracing an ethic of self-acceptance and nurturance.[25]

More recent body image research suggests that the slender ideal has begun to influence non-white girls and women who increasingly want to rid their bodies of excess fat and achieve a toned physique.[26] Along these lines, anthropologist Stephanie McClure found a range of body-image satisfaction among African-American girls, reporting that their experience with fitness and physicality shaped the way they felt about and presented their bodies.[27] McClure's findings emphasize the importance of recognizing diverse body-image ideologies within ethnic groups.

Beyond the United States, body-image ideals vary cross-culturally depending on the symbolic value placed on body size.[28] For example, anthropologist Eileen Anderson-Fye found that in Belize women thought body size was God-given and therefore unchangeable. They emphasized body shape and adornment over size, believing that an hourglass "Coca-Cola" figure was most attractive and that, regardless of one's shape, personal style was key in determining attractiveness.[29] Anthropologists have similarly reported that larger body sizes, which are considered both aesthetically pleasing and symbolic of individual health and a thriving community, have traditionally been valued in Jamaica[30] and Fiji,[31] for example.

Most recently, anthropological research suggests a global shift in body-image ideals toward a preference for slenderness coupled with the spread of fat stigma among some non-Western cultures that have traditionally valued larger body sizes. For example, anthropologist Sarah Trainer found that modern college women in the United Arab Emirates had embraced Western body-image ideals and reported higher rates of body dissatisfaction than women in their mothers' and grandmothers' generations.[32] Because the processes of this cultural shift are complex and highly dependent upon local contexts, researchers do not yet understand the underlying causal factors.[33] However, studies suggest rapid social and economic change, industrialization, and increasing exposure to US media are likely influences.[34]

Research on cross-cultural and global variation in body-image ideals gives a broad contextual backdrop to in-depth ethnographic studies, such as mine, that focus on a single community. These kinds of studies provide a window into other ways of perceiving and interpreting body size and shape. Findings from cross-cultural body-image research can be incorporated into media-literacy curricula for teens in the United States to prompt critical thinking about the dominant and ubiquitous media messages that idealize slenderness and stigmatize fat. They can provide a research-based counter message to the dominant US narratives about body image, body fat, the meaning of food, and how these ideas are shaped by cultural context, including beliefs about health, beauty, and the role of community. In the next section I briefly summarize what has been written on obesity and body image so far to situate my book within the broader literature and clarify what I bring to the conversation.

The Skinny on Obesity

Given all the media hype about obesity, it is not surprising that several noteworthy books on the topic have recently been published. They provide an additional sociocultural backdrop for my in-depth ethnographic account of how teens understood fat and how their perceptions influenced sense of self, willingness or motivation to participate in physical activity, food-consumption behaviors, and relationships with classmates. These books generally examine various ways in which obesity is constructed as a problem in US public discourses (e.g., news media, public health service announcements, popular diet plan ads) and offer a bird's-eye view of widely held assumptions about fatness that have consequences for people in everyday life.

Sociologist Natalie Boero, for example, explores the world of weight-loss programs through interview data with individuals participating in them, as well as content analysis of *New York Times* articles and a series of government reports on obesity.[35] She traces the historical processes by which obesity came to be seen as a health epidemic, suggesting that the "war" on obesity is really a moral attack on fat people. Boero discusses the disconnect between dominant discourses that frame obesity as a costly public health epidemic and the experiences of fat people who face social and economic barriers in their day-to-day lives because of their body size. She examines the broader political and economic backdrop of the obesity epidemic, noting, for example, that the current moralistic focus on individual responsibility has taken hold during a time when social service spending is low and the income gap is high.

Sociologists Samantha Kwan and Jennifer Graves deconstruct the ways in which obesity is framed in the popular media.[36] Their analytic premise is that no objective truth about obesity exists; instead, various "claims makers" with competing interests socially construct realities. The authors explore these competing claims through in-depth discourse analysis of four organizations that address obesity: the Centers for Disease Control (focus on obesity as a public health issue), the Center for Consumer Freedom (neoliberal focus on the importance of protecting individual choice), the National Association to Advance Fat Acceptance (focus on obesity as a civil rights and social justice issue), and the Fashion-Beauty Complex (consumerist focus on obesity as an aesthetic issue). Based on survey data, they conclude the most culturally resonant beliefs about obesity are that fat is ugly (Fashion-Beauty Complex frame), obesity is a serious health concern (Center for Disease Control frame), and individuals are responsible for their body size (present in all but the National Association to Advance Fat Acceptance frame).

Sociologist Abigail Saguy similarly explores the ways in which obesity is framed as a medical, moral, and public health problem, as well as frames that promote fatness as healthy and beautiful.[37] Saguy discusses the politics of why some frames become foregrounded and popularized while others remain marginalized. She argues that frames are powerful because they impact public policy, body-image ideals, self-esteem, and the way people are treated in day-to-day life based on their body size. Saguy draws on a wide variety of data including interviews with scientists and activists, participant observation in fat acceptance meetings and online weight-loss forums, text analysis of American and French obesity-related media coverage, and scientific studies. Like Kwan and Graves,[38] Saguy found that frames depicting fat as a problem are more dominant than those promoting health and beauty at every size and that obesity is primarily framed as an issue of personal responsibility. She concludes bullying and fat stigma are serious consequences of these dominant obesity narratives.

Political scientist Eric Oliver questions the widely held belief that obesity is a problem by examining the oft-cited medical and public health research that frames it as such.[39] Oliver challenges scientific studies claiming that health outcomes commonly associated with obesity, such as hypertension, diabetes, and high cholesterol, are the direct result of excess weight. He argues that the US public health establishment, backed by funding from the drug and weight-loss industry, is the driving force behind scientific research that links health outcomes with excess weight and the resultant obesity-crisis narrative. Oliver also explores body-image ideals and fat stigma among Americans, arguing that our hatred of fat is related to social status, race, and sex, but not health. Oliver concludes with a discussion of obesity policy and argues that it is ineffective in reducing obesity rates and the real problem is pervasive, harmful perceptions about weight, not the weight itself. He advocates for conflict of interest rules that disallow obesity researchers to be funded by the diet and weight-loss industry and development of programs to fight obesity stigma.

Anthropologist Alexandra Brewis delves beneath the surface of "obesity-crisis" rhetoric to examine adaptive, ecological, and cultural perspectives on obesity; discuss what we can learn from prevention and intervention efforts that have consistently failed; and suggest methods for moving beyond the limitations of statistics and cultural theorizing to better understand the complexities of obesity.[40] Her research on body image and nutrition, conducted during the past twenty years in the Pacific Islands, the United States, and Mexico, is discussed in conjunction with other similarly focused studies to explore historical and cross-cultural variation in obesity rates, risk, and beliefs about body size. Brewis addresses such critical questions as whether obesity is a disease, an illness, or a moral panic; why minority and poor urban populations are most at risk; why obesity remains stigmatized when the majority of people are overweight or obese; and whether or not obesity is inherently unhealthy.

Any of these books would serve as a useful companion to my close ethnography. They address broad political, social, economic, biological, and historical forces that shape pervasive, taken-for-granted beliefs about fat whereas I focus on the day-to-day consequences of how one group of teens are influenced by and operate within that broader context.

Additionally, hundreds of academic articles and edited volumes on obesity examine the issue from all angles, including the causes, treatment, and social, economic, and political effects of being fat. Scholars from medicine, public health, psychology, sociology, political science, economics, and anthropology have examined food environments, eating behaviors, attitudes toward exercise, the impact of built environments on exercise, and obesity stigma across age ranges, ethnicities, socioeconomic status, gender, and social and institutional contexts.

The vast majority of this research is quantitative, based on surveys that provide information about self-reported trends in attitudes and behaviors related to obesity for relatively large groups or communities. Findings from quantitative studies give us the broad brush-strokes (e.g., how attitudes about, and participation in, physical activity vary by region, ethnicity, gender, and socioeconomic status). But it is qualitative research, like my ethnographic study, that helps us understand those broad trends, why issues differ for males and females, people of different ethnic identities or socioeconomic backgrounds, and those who live in different types of environments. The relatively few published qualitative studies on obesity tend to rely on a handful of focus-group interviews written up as a single article.

Schooled on Fat is an in-depth ethnography of body image and obesity that foregrounds the voices of those who are being studied, emphasizes the social context to allow for a deeper understanding of the findings, and embraces the topic's complexity by examining the interrelated nature of multiple issues connected to obesity and body image. In contrast, the existing body of work on obesity, both quantitative and qualitative, tends to examine obesity-related issues in relative isolation, looking at food environments, engagement in physical activity, obesity stigma, or body esteem but not exploring how all of these pieces fit together in the puzzle of real people's lives.

To date, only one ethnographic monograph exists on teen body image—anthropologist Mimi Nichter's *Fat Talk: What Girls and Their Parents Say about Dieting*.[41] Nichter drew on survey, interview, focus group, and participant observation data with teen girls to explore how they felt about their bodies, how they talked about body image with their moms and girlfriends, their dieting practices, and how their families influenced their ideas about body image. She found that African-American girls were more satisfied with their weight and expressed more flexible, realistic ideas about beauty and body image than white girls. Nichter also found that girls engaged in "fat talk" to express concern about their weight, solicit emotional support from friends, and call attention to their flaws before others do. *Schooled on Fat* expands on Nichter's research to include both girls and boys and examine fat teasing as well as attitudes about, and engagement in, physical activity. Whereas Nichter's book looks at ethnic differences between white and black girls, I focus on gender differences, drawing on data collected from boys and girls.

Nichter conducted her research in the mid-1990s amidst widespread concern about eating disorders and dangerous dieting behaviors among teenage girls. She challenged this crisis-oriented rhetoric, illustrating that the vast majority of girls do not have an eating disorder and, in fact, engage in healthy food-related behaviors, such as watching what they eat. I similarly frame my research on youth, gender, and body image within the current social milieu, which has now shifted to angst about overweight and obesity rates in the United States. This dominant, mainstream anti-fat narrative is the cultural and historical backdrop against which the teens in my study negotiated their beliefs about body image, judged their own bodies and those of their peers, and made decisions about food consumption and exercise. In the next chapter I set the scene with a brief description of my research site, participants, and methods.

Notes

1. Boero, 2007.
2. Carmona, 2003, 2004; "Surgeon general to cops," 2003.
3. "Pentagon Attacks Obesity," 2012.
4. Bordo, 1993; Brumberg, 1997; Huff, 2001; Sobal, 1995; Stearns, 2002.
5. Bordo, 1993:192.

6. Veit, 2013:164.
7. Veit, 2013.
8. Huff, 2001; Ritenbaugh, 1982; Schwartz, 1986.
9. Biltekoff, 2013.
10. Ibid.
11. Ibid.
12. Ibid.
13. Bordo, 1993.
14. Brumberg, 1997.
15. Brumberg, 1997; Veit, 2013.
16. Bordo, 1993, 1999; Crawford, 1984, Connell, 1995; Huff, 2001.
17. Gill, Henwood, and McLean, 2005; Grogan and Richards, 2002; Kehler, 2010; Ryan, Morrison, and Ó Beaglaoich, 2010; Taylor, 2011.
18. Sobal, 1995:69.
19. Kwan, 2009.
20. Bordo, 1993.
21. Boero, 2012; Brewis, 2011; Kwan, 2009; Kwan and Graves, 2013; Saguy, 2013; Saguy, Gruys, and Gong, 2010; Saguy and Gruys, 2010.
22. Kwan and Graves, 2013; Boero, 2012; Saguy, 2013.
23. Sobal, 1995.
24. Nichter, 2000; Parker et al., 1995.
25. Rubin, Fitts, and Becker, 2003.
26. Bordo, 2013.
27. McClure, 2013, forthcoming.
28. Brewis, 2011; Gremillion, 2005.
29. Anderson-Fye, 2004.
30. Sobo, 1994.
31. Becker, 1995.
32. Trainer, 2013, forthcoming.
33. Hrushka, forthcoming.
34. Anderson-Fye, 2011; Anderson-Fye et al., forthcoming; Becker, 2004, forthcoming; Brewis, 2011.
35. Boero, 2012.
36. Kwan and Graves, 2013.
37. Saguy, 2013.
38. Kwan and Graves, 2013.
39. Oliver, 2006.
40. Brewis, 2011.
41. Nichter, 2000.

1
ABOUT MY STUDY

In light of mainstream ideas about body image and fatness, I wondered whether adolescent girls and boys felt personally responsible for their body size and how those who were overweight felt about the increasingly widespread moral panic focused on large bodies, especially since mainstream media messages about obesity were reinforced at school. For example, teachers used news and op-ed articles that year to generate discussion about the dangers of obesity and what could be done to prevent weight gain. Such discussions always focused on the importance of individuals taking responsibility for managing their weight through diet and exercise, a message that was in lockstep with the dominant narrative.

I wondered how this media hype would influence teens' ideas about body-image ideals and norms and what it would mean for teens to be considered fat during a time in the United States when obesity was framed as a threat despite the fact that most Americans were overweight or obese. As adolescents increasingly encountered overweight and obese people in their daily lives, either out in public or within their social networks, and as they engaged in the battle of the bulge, would they be more accepting of themselves and their overweight peers? I also hoped to explore how popular media-generated discourses on obesity would influence teens' relationships with food and the ways in which they approached physical activity.

More broadly I wanted to understand how body image-related concerns and behaviors intersected for teens in their everyday lives and from their perspectives. I wondered how they thought and talked about body image and fatness, how that influenced the way they thought about and ate food and engaged in physical activity at school, and how it shaped social relations among teens at the high school.

To address these questions, I conducted interviews that included in-depth, open-ended questions and discussions with individual teens and groups of friends. I also observed how teens talked about these issues with their friends and peers at school while hanging out at lunch, in the hallway during passing periods, and during physical education (PE) classes. I obtained approval from the university institutional review board, the school district's research and evaluation department, and the high school principal prior to participant recruitment and data collection. Names of individuals included in this book are pseudonyms to protect confidentiality.

Some participants volunteered height and weight information during interviews, but this data was neither systematically collected nor solicited. For those who volunteered this information, body mass index (BMI) was calculated using the Centers for Disease Control and Prevention's online BMI calculator for children and teens.[1] Throughout this book, when participants are described as underweight, healthy weight, or overweight, these classifications are based on BMI calculations from self-reported height and weight data.

Body size classifications are included only for the purpose of providing insight about participants' self-perceptions of body size within the context of peers' perceptions of their body size and are not intended to represent accurate or objective BMI measurements. In a study examining how adolescents defined and negotiated the boundaries between normal/acceptable weight and overweight, it is informative to note, for example, that many female participants who were criticized by peers for displaying too much body fat self-reported height and weight within the healthy weight BMI range.

I found that teens had, for the most part, internalized popular media messages about body size and personal responsibility, which resulted in students feeling guilt and shame about their own bodies and teasing their overweight classmates. In fact, even students who were not noticeably overweight but simply failed to effectively hide their body fat beneath clothing were subject to critique. Teens were more focused on managing and obscuring their body fat than engaging in behaviors that would help them lose weight or tone up, like eating healthfully and exercising.

I also discovered that the way teens felt about their bodies was so enmeshed with their relationship to food, exercise, and their peers that these issues could not be understood in isolation. For example, many students I interviewed, especially girls, felt guilty about eating fattening foods. Their feelings of guilt were tied to beliefs about personal responsibility, body-image ideals, and anxiety about fat stigma and social positioning among their peer groups. Girls' guilt around junk food consumption contributed to negative feelings about the way their bodies looked, which in turn, made them feel self-conscious about exercising in front of their peers in physical education class.

The school set students up for failure by reinforcing messages about body size as a personal choice while making fattening junk foods readily available. This book explores how teens navigated a discordant school environment in which many wanted to lose weight and get in shape but felt unable to resist consuming widely available junk foods and felt too self-conscious or unmotivated to actively engage in physical education class. It also illustrates the complex ways in which body image, social status, fat stigma and teasing, food consumption behaviors, and exercise practices intersected in the daily lives of teens from their perspectives.

Teens attempted to work through their body-image concerns largely through talk. Girls, for example, alternately supported each other through conversations about body image and junk food consumption and competed with each other to look the best in form-fitting clothes through gossip and teasing. Boys made fun of their own body fat to solicit support from girls, called each other fat, and engaged in verbal dueling with each other to compete over muscle tone and strength. Boys and girls both continually critiqued their peers' bodies as a way to develop a shared understanding of the blurry line between acceptable and unacceptable body size but also to shift the focus away from their own bodies and momentarily position themselves as thinner than the object of critique.

I ultimately argue that schools, parents, and communities need to offer counter messages to mainstream fat shaming rhetoric and support youth in achieving healthy body weights. Teens must learn to critically examine public obesity discourses that simultaneously blame and stigmatize fat people while bombarding them with ads for fattening junk foods. Teens also need a reality check about what healthy bodies look like. Before they can accept or even feel good about their bodies, youth need to understand that the complete eradication of body fat is not possible. I urge schools, with the support of parents and local communities, to teach media literacy as well as continue efforts to offer more nutritious meals and find ways to actively engage all students in regular physical activity.

The high school where I conducted my study was located in a suburban farming community I call Montaña located thirty miles outside of Tucson. Montaña had a population of approximately 13,500 at the time of the study but was in the midst of rapid expansion. The town experienced a 150 percent rate of population growth between 2000 and 2010. When Montaña was incorporated in the late 1970s it was a small agricultural community. At the time of my study, some families in the community still ranched or farmed for a living; however, most residents either commuted to Tucson and other nearby towns to work or were employed locally by one of the major defense or mining companies, the city government, school district, local community health center, or one of the major retailers in town.

The two high schools that served the town of Montaña, Desert Vista and Arroyo Viejo, reflected the rural/suburban dichotomy within the community. Desert Vista students tended to come from middle-class socioeconomic backgrounds and suburban neighborhoods (approximately 15 percent of students were eligible for the school's free lunch program at the time of the study), while Arroyo Viejo students came from lower socioeconomic backgrounds and more rural neighborhoods (approximately 40 percent of students were eligible for the school's free lunch program at the time of the study). In terms of geographic location, Desert Vista was situated within the newer suburban part of the community, just off of the major freeway that connects Tucson to Phoenix. In contrast, Arroyo Viejo was located in the older, more rural part of the community well off the beaten path.

Southern Arizona is home to a relatively large population of Latinos, a minority group that has not been studied extensively within the body image and obesity literature. The student population reflected this ethnic diversity; both high schools served approximately 2,000 total students with 30–35 percent identifying as Hispanic or Latino and 60–65 percent identifying as white. I chose Desert Vista as my research site for its ethnic diversity but also because of its predominantly middle-class socioeconomic status and suburban location. If my study was to explore relationships among food consumption, personal style, and body image, students needed to have some degree of purchasing power to make choices about food and clothing.

I found it difficult to gather reliable socioeconomic status data from my participants because most could not clearly articulate what their parents or guardians did for a living. Indirect information on the topic emerged during interview discussions about how much lunch money and allowance students received from their parents. Additionally, during discussions about constructing personal style through clothing, makeup, and other consumer goods, I gleaned information about participants' socioeconomic status as I listened to them talk about where they shopped, what clothing brands were their favorite, and whether or not they could afford to buy the things they wanted.

Based on the information I was able to gather, I would classify the majority of my sample as middle class and a handful of participants as lower middle class or working class. Most participants received various amounts of allowance and lunch money each week that they used to buy food, clothes, and entertainment related items such as movie tickets and music. Most said they had to budget their money in order to buy things they wanted, indicating that they had access to a modest disposable income. Six of the fifty participants in my study told me they did not receive any allowance because their parents could not afford it and two of those said they participated in the free lunch program at school.

In terms of home life, half of the participants had parents who were married and half had parents who were divorced or separated. Of the twenty-five whose parents were no longer together, ten lived in single-parent households, primarily with their mothers, and the remainder lived with one parent and either a step-parent or the parent's live-in partner. Seven of the forty participants who lived in two-adult households had one parent or guardian who stayed at home, while the remainder lived in homes where both adults worked. Two participants with a stay-at-home parent or guardian said they stayed home by choice and the other five had a parent or guardian who could not find work or was disabled.

Most participants spent time at home alone or with siblings at the end of the school day because their parents were at work until 6 or 7pm. They generally watched television or played around on the computer until dinnertime. In any given week, most participants' dinnertime routines varied in a pretty consistent way. Some nights they ate together as a family, either take-out or a home cooked meal and some nights they were responsible for providing their own dinner, which was generally pre-packaged and easy to prepare, like ramen noodles, frozen pizza, or cereal.

The most strikingly consistent food related trend that transcended home and school was a tendency to constantly snack on "junk foods" between meals. Teens reported grazing on vending machine fare (e.g., chips, cakes, candies) all day during school and then going home and snacking on similar types of foods all evening. While my study focuses on teens' experiences with body image, food, exercise, and fat teasing within the school context, it is important to remember that teens operate within multiple environments, including school, home, and community. Their experiences across these environments influence their beliefs, behaviors, and relationships in complex ways. I've offered a bit of context about my participants' home lives, family dynamics, and community history to give the reader a better sense of who they are and where they come from before honing in on their experiences at school.

When a student enrolled in my study by submitting signed assent and consent forms, I would ask them to complete a one-page screener designed to gather basic demographic and background information. The screener asked for their name, gender, ethnicity, level of body satisfaction on a scale of one to five, self-perception of body size on a scale ranging from smaller than average to obese, whether or not they had ever been teased about their weight and, if so, by whom. I recruited thirty girls and twenty boys, all of whom were fourteen- or fifteen-year-old freshmen.

Of the fifty total participants, half identified as Latino or Hispanic and half identified as white. I was thrilled at the sample's ethnic composition because my initial research plan focused on examining gender and ethnic differences as key variables in adolescent discourses about body image, food, exercise, and fat teasing practices. What I failed to anticipate was the dissonance in how youth identified ethnically outside the high school setting in their homes and communities and their lived ethnic identities day-to-day within the social context of the high school.

Over the school year, I became increasingly skeptical of the social meaning of ethnicity among adolescents as I observed student behavior. For one thing, during interviews I learned that some participants who had initially identified as white on the screener and in the high school social context identified as Latino or Hispanic outside the school context. For example, one girl who had identified as white on the screener later told me during an interview that if she could change one thing about the way she looked, she would make her skin lighter because she did not like looking Hispanic. When I asked the girl why she thought she looked Hispanic, she blushed, looked down at the table, and sheepishly told me she was Hispanic.

Similarly, I learned through an interview with a boy who had identified as white on the screener that he really considered himself Latino. His friends on campus were white, and so he identified as white at school, presumably to fit in. However, the boy's maternal grandparents had emigrated from Mexico and his mother was Mexican, though his father was white. At home, his family celebrated *quinceañeras*, ate traditional Mexican food cooked by his mother, and attended a Catholic church with mostly Latino parishioners.

Gradually, it became clear to me that at Desert Vista students defined ethnicity through social practice and that it varied depending on context. The lines between socially enacted ethnic identities across family, community, and school contexts were sufficiently blurred that the concept of ethnicity among these teens raised more questions than my study on body image and obesity could sufficiently address or incorporate. Consequently, I realized that if I were to analyze my data according to ethnicity I would have to impose my own categorization onto teens because their perceptions about what it meant to be "Hispanic," "Latino," or "white" were neither consistent nor apparent.

As an anthropologist who is committed to foregrounding the voices of the individuals I work with, I felt it would be unethical to impose ethnic labels on these adolescents, many of whom felt conflicted about this aspect of themselves and enacted different ethnic identities depending on the context. I also chose not to analyze data according to ethnicity because it did not emerge as a salient category for teens during interviews. Instead, gender and, to a lesser degree, social group affiliations were the most meaningful categories to teens at Desert Vista.

With regard to social cliques, the vast majority of teens at the high school were part of small, fluid groups with few defining features, membership of which shifted and overlapped in a complex network of social relations. However, a few high-profile social cliques that were readily identifiable in terms of personal style were referenced and discussed at length in interview discussions by both members and outsiders. These few high-profile social cliques – the Goths/Punks, Jocks/Preps, and Mexicans – represented a small percentage of the overall high school population and yet their influence on the school's social scene was impactful, extending much further than the "boundaries" of their group identities. They essentially served as reference points for teens negotiating their own ideas about body image and personal style and are therefore worth describing briefly. Of my fifty study participants, eight were members of the Goths/Punks, six were members of the Jocks/Preps, and five were members of the Mexicans.

The Goths/Punks were a relatively large social clique consisting of approximately forty to fifty teens. Goths/Punks prided themselves on "being different," an image that resulted in members getting teased for the way they looked. Members of this group made fun of normative body-image ideals, like "six-pack abs" (clearly defined rectus abdominal musculature), wore all black clothing, and projected a lack of concern for anything considered popular or mainstream. Despite their cultivated image, the Goths/Punks I interviewed worried about the way their bodies looked and wanted to achieve status through normative pathways, such as slenderness for girls and muscle tone and athletic skill for boys. The Goths/Punks may have worn all black to make a statement against normative fashion, but many of the girls wore form-fitting black outfits in line with the popular feminine style. They may have joked derisively among friends about dominant body-image ideals, but with me most expressed a desire to achieve those ideals.

The Jocks/Preps was another prominent social clique on campus. This group primarily included male athletes, such as basketball, baseball, and football players, and thin girls, some of whom were members of the dance team and cheerleader squad, but most of whom did not participate in team sports at all. Female athletes were not part of this group, probably due to the relatively widespread perception among boys that female athletes were "masculine," "butch," and therefore unattractive, a topic discussed at length in later chapters. For girls, group membership in the Jocks/Preps required not only that they wear tight-fitting clothing but also that they have the thin, toned bodies to look good in it. Jocks/Preps were the proverbial "popular crowd" and its members were generally perceived to be the best-looking and the most socially powerful group on campus.

A group calling themselves "the Mexicans" was relatively small, with a membership of only about twenty students, but had a large presence on campus. The Mexican guys typically dressed in baggy pants and oversized T-shirts with loosely tied white leather tennis shoes, and the girls often wore tight-fitting jeans or very short miniskirts, fitted tank tops, and high-heeled shoes. Boys and girls in this group had gold or silver medallions of various sizes around their necks and most of the girls wore multiple gold bracelets and large gold hoop earrings. All the Mexicans appeared to be Latino and socially aligned with what was perceived by most students to be a stereotypical "gangster" identity. In terms of body-image ideology, male and female members of this group aligned with mainstream ideas. Mexican boys wore their clothes slightly baggier than the popular style at the time, but like other boys I interviewed they were concerned with what their bodies looked like underneath. Most wanted to achieve lean muscle tone and six-pack abs. The girls in the group, like all the other girls I interviewed, aspired to be thinner than they were.

Throughout the book, teens are described in terms of their social group affiliation as a way to provide contextual information about participants but also to illustrate differences in the carefully crafted image teens projected for their peers and what they said in interviews with me. I also explore how social group affiliation influenced the degree to which teens were targets of fat teasing. That said, the biggest differences in body-image ideals, food consumption, fat teasing, and exercise practices were between boys and girls. For this reason, gender is the most prominent and consistent analytic thread discussed.

In addition to interview and observational data that appear throughout the book, artistic interpretations of body image by high school students are featured on the companion website*. The idea for an arts-inspired inquiry emerged in dialogue with Innovative Ethnographies Series editor, Phillip Vannini, who encouraged me to explore the topic in a more dynamic, multimodal way. Teens who contributed creative expressions in the form of drawings, photographs, poetry, music, and essays, live in a different community from where I conducted research and are a decade younger than teens I worked with at Desert Vista. Their artistic representations of body image illustrate the continued timeliness of the topic and its resonance across a broader youth community.

Throughout the process of developing this manuscript, I piloted tested chapter drafts with high school teachers and students in communities where my family lived and worked to assess the extent to which my findings and writing style resonated with them. My husband, who is a high school English

---

•   www.innovativeethnographies.net/schooledonfat

teacher, facilitated this feedback. Teachers and students from several communities in three states responded that the themes and stories in my book could have come from their school, their students, and their friends. As a result of this feedback and encouragement from the series editor, I pursued gathering creative expressions of body image from students of a different generation and community to broaden and deepen teen perspectives.

I approached a couple of high school teachers who were familiar with my work to ask if they would solicit artistic interpretations from students and they readily agreed. These teachers had already used vignettes from my manuscript to elicit discussion about body image and teasing in their classes, so it was a natural segue. I asked them to distribute a prompt that included a brief description of my research and a couple of opening vignettes from the chapters. The prompt instructed students to provide non-narrative expressions of body image for the book's companion website that either focused on their own feelings and experiences or expressed their beliefs about society's expectations and the media. Students submitted work to their teachers, who asked them to sign a permissions form.

Over the course of a school year, I received an inspiring and thought-provoking collection of artwork, poetry, photography, music, and essays. I found myself once again humbled by the willingness of youth to openly express their emotions and share their experiences. Artistic expressions on the website are meant to supplement narrative and analytic expressions in the book to stimulate the intellect and senses of the reader and provide a more comprehensive, three-dimensional representation of how teens experience body image.

Before diving into the experiences of teens, it is important to understand how ideas about gender, body size, and attractiveness become the unquestioned norm and how youth engage with these beliefs in a social context. Language was the primary medium through which the teens in my study negotiated their beliefs about body image, positioned themselves and each other within the social hierarchy, and worked through their food and exercise-related struggles. In the next section, I discuss why fat is fundamentally a linguistic issue and how the study of everyday conversation can provide new insights into research on body image and obesity.

The Weight of Words

At Desert Vista, language played a key role in shaping teens' ideas about how boys' and girls' bodies should look, their attitudes toward body fat, how they felt about their own bodies, and how they treated those who were considered too fat. Broadly speaking, everyday conversations about workplace politics, relationships with romantic partners, or community gossip, topics that appear innocuous or even meaningless, have the power to shape people's perceptions and ideologies about weightier subjects, such as gender roles, racial and ethnic stereotypes, and body image. Through these sorts of discourse interactions, people make sense of the world around them; negotiate meanings, opinions, and beliefs; and construct their identities in relation to shared or contested ideologies. That is, through everyday conversation individuals experiment with who they are, who they want to be, how they wish to be perceived, how they relate to others, and their belief systems.

For example, every day during lunch, groups of friends at Desert Vista engaged in back and forth commentary and critique of how their peers looked in clothing. It would often begin with someone making an evaluative statement about a nearby student, such as, "What was she thinking this morning when she got dressed?"; "She should not be wearing that tight shirt!"; or "Look at that back fat. Gross!" Then others in the group would weigh in, either agreeing or disagreeing (e.g., "Yeah, she looks huge in those pants;""At least her shirt covers her belly rolls"; or "She's not really that fat.")

These teens were doing more than engaging in seemingly meaningless banter about other students. They were negotiating their beliefs about gender and body image, comparing and contrasting themselves and each other to ideas about how people should look, socializing each other into appearance norms, and developing (or contesting) a shared worldview that provided a lens for interpreting what they experienced going forward. This kind of banter can, over time, influence how these adolescents feel about themselves, their relationship to food and exercise, the type of people they find attractive, and how they interact with those whom they perceive as thin or fat.

Through this type of everyday conversation, teens at Desert Vista co-constructed a shared worldview of attractiveness that included ideas about how much body fat was acceptable and how the rules differed for boys and girls. Linguists Sally Jacoby and Elinor Ochs define co-construction as "the joint creation of a form, interpretation, stance, action, activity, identity, institution, skill, ideology, emotion, or other culturally meaningful reality."[2] This definition emphasizes collaborative creation of shared meaning; however, it may also include processes that are non-cooperative, such as disagreements. The basic premise is that individuals develop a mutual understanding of reality through communication with other people.

A little background information on foundational theories of subjectivity and meaning-making is necessary for understanding how co-construction works. Symbolic interactionists, such as George H. Mead,[3] believed that reality is socially constituted through our interactions with others rather than individual mental processes. That is, people develop an understanding of their social and physical surroundings by communicating with other people rather than thinking about things in isolation. For example, widely shared beliefs about body image and fatness among students at Desert Vista emerged socially through gossip, teasing, and the constant critique of others' bodies. This is one way in which teens negotiated popular media-generated ideas about body image and fatness.

Mead assumed a fundamental "intersubjectivity," or shared experience of the world, among groups of people as a starting point for co-construction of culturally meaningful realities through social interaction. Intersubjectivity is both strengthened through social interaction and precedes it. That is, people must come to the conversation with some degree of shared experience or knowledge to make sense of what is being said. At the same time, shared experience or knowledge is strengthened through social interaction because the process of co-constructing culturally meaningful realities can reinforce strong beliefs shared by a group. For teens at Desert Vista to engage in, or make sense of, the constant banter-style critique of their peers' bodies they had to have a basic understanding of dominant body-image ideals in the United States that favor slenderness over fatness.

For example, the concept of "muffin top" started to emerge in everyday conversation among teens at Desert Vista during the year I conducted fieldwork, referring to body fat that flows over the waistband of a person's pants or skirt. The popularization of this concept at the high school involved teens negotiating its meaning and, in the process, codifying its negative valuation through constant critique of girls' bodies. Teens drew on their common knowledge about the concept of "muffin top," introducing the phrase to those who were not yet familiar with it and arguing the fine points of fat rolls as they worked toward a shared understanding.

A typical "muffin top"-focused interaction included someone pointing to a girl nearby and declaring "muffin top," followed either by unanimous agreement or a dialogue among group members about how much fat was required to constitute a muffin top, whether or not the girl in question truly qualified for the label, and so on. In this way, groups of teens drew on common cultural knowledge (e.g., the concept of "muffin top") to co-construct a shared worldview related to gendered body-image ideology (e.g., ideas about how girls should dress and how their bodies should look). During these conversations, even those who had not yet heard the phrase "muffin top" understood that allowing fat to flow over their waistband was socially unacceptable or "gross" in teen-speak.

Philosopher and literary critic Mikhail M. Bakhtin thought of human communication as heteroglossic in nature. That is, utterances and ideas are the products of previous, current, and hypothetical future dialogues with other people. He wrote, "Of all words uttered in everyday life, no less than half belong to someone else."[4] Simply stated, our ideas develop and change as a result of ongoing (real or imagined) conversations with other people. Such social interactions not only shape how we think about things but also influence how we articulate ideas in future conversations. In contrast to the notion of a "self" (versus an other), Bakhtin conceived of a "dialogic self" that is socially constituted through past interactions with other people as well as internal interactions between and among hypothetical subject positions.

Sociolinguist Judith Irvine expanded Bakhtin's concept of multivocality from the self to the speech interaction. She writes,

> Rather than multi-vocal, we might consider a speech situation to be multiply dialogical: it is not just the speaker who is doubled (or multiplied) by other voices, but a set of dialogic relations that are crucially informed by other sets—shadow conversations that surround the conversation at hand."[5]

In the same way that hyperlinked text on Wikipedia, for example, is multiplied and informed by the various other texts to which it refers, conversations in the present are similarly linked to, and informed by, previous conversations we have had with other people. This is how ideas develop, circulate, and become codified.

The following example from my research illustrates how multi-vocality works. During a mixed-gender focus-group discussion about girls who transgress the boundaries of appropriate body presentation, a boy pointed to a girl chatting with her friends nearby and stated that she was an example of a girl who wore clothing that was too tight. The group proceeded to talk about the way her body looked in the outfit she was wearing:

Eddie: Pink skirt [pointing to a girl standing nearby].
Kira: She's really nice.
Eddie: I'm just saying.
Kira: And she's wearing bigger sizes. It's not like she's trying to wear—
Tyler: —She's wearing big sizes because she is big.
Laura: She's not showing pudge. It's not hanging out everywhere … She's not fat. She's not—
Kira: —She's a little chunky.

Such conversations occurred among groups of friends continually at school. One teen referred to the everyday evaluation of how their peers' bodies looked in clothing as "constant nagging."

The influence of these types of everyday conversations about body image in which adolescents engaged extended beyond the scope of the present interaction, simultaneously drawing on past conversations that had shaped their current opinions and informing future conversations they would have on the topic. Through these ongoing discursive processes, adolescents negotiated beliefs about gendered body-image norms, socialized each other into those norms, evaluated themselves and each other accordingly, and learned that the consequences of "breaking the rules" included being gossiped about and teased by their peers.

The concept of co-construction provides a useful framework for understanding identity formation as well. I draw on Mary Bucholtz and Kira Hall's definition of identity as "the social positioning of self and other,"[6] a view that captures the dynamic nature of identity construction as emergent through discourse interaction, context-sensitive, relational to co-constructed identities of others, perceived identity categories, and ideological stances, as well as both malleable and enduring. That is, people negotiate or, "try on," identities in specific social contexts and in relation to their perceptions of individuals with whom they are interacting. Identities that people negotiate are changeable in the sense that they experiment with various ways of being but also enduring in that there are aspects of identities that may feel essential to how they perceive themselves to be in an ongoing way.

In this book I examine how body image-related conversation, fat teasing, social group affiliation, body presentation through clothing and stance, level of engagement in physical activity, and food consumption combined in different ways to contribute to the co-construction of gendered identities among teens and the subsequent positioning of youth within the high school's social hierarchy. Other scholars of youth culture have similarly explored processes of identity co-construction through symbolic creativity.[7] Drawing on the notion of *bricolage*,[8] these scholars examine how teens appropriate and recombine existing objects of the dominant culture, including makeup, clothing, stance, and language, in new ways to create distinctive styles.[9]

For example, sociolinguist Penelope Eckert examines how preadolescent girls experiment with use of "valley girl" speech, makeup, hairstyles, and even ways of walking to align with popular feminine beauty norms and thereby increase their status in the heterosexual marketplace.[10] Cultural anthropologist and linguist Norma Mendoza-Denton examines the complex and nuanced ways in which Latina gang girls embody an alternative feminine and ethnic identity through language use and cultural practices, such as "talking shit"; engaging in secret word games; circulating anonymous poetry notebooks, drawings, and photographs; using and pronouncing words in unique, patterned ways; and creatively combining eyeliner, lipstick, and hairspray in ways that are nontraditional.[11]

Schooled on Fat also explores how teens positioned themselves and others using the lens of "disciplinary power,"[12] a process involving the differentiation of individuals, hierarchical observation, and normalizing judgment. Social philosopher Michel Foucault conceives of disciplinary power as a network of relations among individuals. He writes, "Discipline is an art of rank, a technique for the transformation of arrangements. It individualizes bodies by a location that does not give them a fixed position, but distributes them and circulates them in a network of relations."[13] This network of relations is both asymmetrical and unstable as individuals negotiate their own and others' positions in a continuous vie for power.

According to Foucault, discipline in modern society occurs partially through the institutionalized establishment of norms so that individuals are measured and judged by their ability to adhere to those norms. It occurs specifically at the site of the body as individuals internalize social norms, self-regulate their behavior and appearance, monitor the behavior and appearance of others, and constantly compare themselves and others against perceived norms. Through these internalized, dual processes of hierarchical observation and normalizing judgment, individuals become both the object and enforcer.[14]

Identity co-construction and disciplinary power are primarily achieved through communication.[15] For example, the teens I worked with negotiated and internalized perceptions about their own and others' bodies by engaging in everyday conversation about body image, gossiping about their classmates' appearance, and teasing each other for transgressing mutually agreed-upon norms. Through constant comparison of themselves and their peers against discursively negotiated body-image norms, teens circulated themselves and each other in a network of hierarchical social relations largely based on how they "stacked up" against their peers in terms of physical appearance, which was closely tied to popularity.

The boundary between thin and fat among these adolescents was both discursively constructed and relative. Regardless of their actual weight or body size, youth positioned themselves as thinner than their peers through continuous critical discourse about their peers' bodies. Adolescents distanced themselves from the reality of everyday fatness and diverted attention away from their own bodies by calling attention to their peers' fat.[16] This type of day-to-day discursive negotiation of what constitutes unacceptable displays of body fat also functioned as a tool of disciplinary power within the high school setting in which teens were both the object of constant scrutiny and critique and participants in that process.

In this way, language shapes bodies because it shapes people's perceptions of what looks good, how they categorize their peers in terms of body size and attractiveness, how they feel about the way their own bodies look, and how they relate to other people based on perceptions of their body size. Further, how people feel about their own bodies impacts their relationship with food, the way they talk about food with friends, and what they choose to eat. It also influences people's attitudes about exercise and the extent to which they engage in physical activity.

What are the social and health implications of the ways in which body-image related beliefs and perceptions, which largely emerge from language interaction, influence food consumption, participation in exercise, and how people treat others based on their physical appearance? For example, are teen boys and girls ashamed of how their bodies look in exercise clothing, worried their body fat will noticeably jiggle as they run, or do they have the confidence to play sports fully and unselfconsciously? To what extent are their food consumption behaviors and attitudes related to body-image concerns, ideas about fat stigma, and experiences with fat teasing? These are the kinds of questions I explore, primarily through a theoretical lens of language and identity and within the context of US culture around body-image norms and the social milieu of the high school campus where I conducted research.

Chapter 2 explores how teens managed and obscured their body fat through clothing and language. I discuss rules among teens regulating who was allowed to wear particular clothing styles, social consequences for breaking the rules, what teens had to say about their body-image goals, and how that differed by gender and, to a lesser degree, social group affiliation. I also describe how teens talked with each other about their body-image concerns, including the social functions of body-image talk and rules governing who was allowed to engage in this type of discourse and with whom.

Chapter 3 explores the relationship between fat stigma and ideas about personal responsibility, including how teens negotiated boundaries between thin and fat through gossip and teasing. I discuss differences in how boys and girls teased their peers and responded to being teased, including the pressure felt by many teens, especially boys, to "play it cool." A section on boys' locker room talk, based on interview data, provides rare insight into the ways boys teased each other in this all-male space, both verbally and physically, for how their bodies looked. The chapter concludes with a discussion of teasing versus "just joking" and the social functions of both types of discourse.

Chapter 4 explores how teens constructed gendered identities at the site of the body through their relationship to exercise, why boys and girls participated differently in PE class, and the broader implications of this. I discuss how teens' ideas about athleticism and gender roles, and their concerns about body size and physical appearance influenced the degree to which they actively engaged in exercise. Some girls' resistance against traditional gender roles through participation in traditionally male sports (e.g., wrestling, football) is discussed, as well as what boys had to say about it.

Chapter 5 focuses on how teens negotiated the school food environment and reconciled consumption of fattening "junk foods" with their body image ideals, sense of self, and personal beliefs about weight as a matter of personal responsibility. I discuss factors that influenced what teens ate at school, including peer influence, taste preference, personal body-image goals, and the overall food environment. I also explore the relationship between food and body fat in popular media, the school curriculum, and the everyday discourses of teens.

Chapter 6 summarizes the patterns of intersection among topics discussed in preceding chapters and explores policy implications of my research. In particular, I share evaluation findings that provide insights about where we are as a nation in addressing student wellness through the improvement of school environments. I also examine the complex nature of policy as it relates to school-based obesity-prevention efforts, suggest how my research findings might inform existing school-based policy recommendations, and offer practical strategies schools and parents can use to promote teen wellness.

Throughout this book, the voices and experiences of adolescents are central. I include direct quotes as much as possible in an effort to provide a space for teens to tell their own stories. The chapters themselves are organized topically, presenting thematic analysis across all data sources and therefore incorporating relevant examples from the entire sample. Each chapter begins with a vignette that tells the story of an individual participant to emphasize the visceral nature of the teens' experiences as recounted in their own words and to illustrate how the book's themes are interconnected in the everyday lives of adolescents.

Because body-image concerns were so entangled with teens' relationships to food and exercise, their ideas about fatness and personal responsibility, how they related to each other socially, their sense of identity, and their place in the adolescent social hierarchy, it was difficult to do these themes justice without exploring their relationships to each other; the introductory vignettes highlight these relationships in concrete ways. The chapters also build on and integrate earlier themes to further explore the complexity of social issues related to body image and fatness.

Notes

1. Centers for Disease Control and Prevention, n.d.
2. Jacoby and Ochs, 1995:171.
3. Mead, 1934.
4. Bakhtin, 1935:339.

5. Irvine, 1996:151–152.
6. Bucholtz and Hall, 2005:586.
7. Willis *et al.*, 1990.
8. Hebdige, 1979; originally discussed by Lévi-Strauss, 1966.
9. Bucholtz, 1996, 1999, 2002, 2011; Cheshire, 2000; Coates, 1999; Eckert, 1989, 1996; Eckert and McConnell-Ginet, 1995; Eder, 1993; Eder, Evans, and Parker, 1995; Mendoza-Denton, 1996, 2008; Nichter, 2000.
10. Eckert, 1996.
11. Mendoza-Denton, 2008.
12. Foucault, 1975/1977.
13. Foucault, 1975/1977:146.
14. Foucault, 1975/1977.
15. Bucholtz and Hall, 2005; Foucault, 1980.
16. Taylor, 2011.

2

"You Can't Have Your Fat Showing"

Allie, a fourteen-year-old freshman at Desert Vista wanted to change virtually everything about the way she looked. She was a noticeably large Latina with long, dark, wavy hair that she wore in a ponytail most days. Her complexion was light olive; she had light brown eyes, wore minimal makeup, and typically dressed in slightly baggy jeans, T-shirts, or button-down shirts with tennis shoes or sandals. Allie told me that she was five feet three and weighed 174 pounds, which is considered obese for a girl her age by the Centers for Disease Control and Prevention. Allie wanted to be tall and thin, about five feet eight and 116 pounds, have a lighter complexion, green eyes, thin legs, and a "perfect hourglass figure."

When I asked Allie to rate how satisfied she was with the way her body looked on a scale of one to five with five being the most satisfied, she responded, "Two," explaining:

> Um, basically in today's society the skinny person is, like, more involved in everything. And, like, I can still be involved, but they're more accepted. And, I don't know. It would just be more comfortable to be me. I'd feel more satisfied with myself. I know that I'd be able to fit into certain clothes, and I'd be able to eat without gaining as much weight. I wouldn't have to worry so much.

Initially, she had indicated "three" as her level of body satisfaction on the screener, so I asked her why it had changed to "two." She said the way she felt about her body fluctuated depending on her mood, how her clothes fit, and what other people said about her weight:

It varies. Like, when you go to a store and you try on clothes and stuff, and if they don't fit it makes you feel less confident in yourself and less satisfied with who you are. And then when I'm around friends and family who, like, help me fit in I feel a lot better about myself. Sometimes when I hear mean comments about my size it hurts my feelings and makes me feel bad about myself. So it all depends on what's happening and who's around me.

Earlier that week Allie had heard a boy on campus call her a "heifer" as she walked by and was still upset about it.

Allie felt fortunate to have a small group of loyal, supportive girlfriends at school. She and her friends had created a safe space where they complimented themselves and each other for how they looked. For example, Allie said one of her friends might compliment Allie's smile and Allie might respond by saying, "Well, your smile is nice, too." Another friend had recently admitted to the group that she liked having large breasts, and that had helped Allie feel better about her own large breasts, which she normally downplayed by slouching. Some of her thinner friends had also initiated the fat talk ritual, calling themselves fat to solicit statements of disagreement, such as, "No you're not! You're really thin."

Allie talked a lot about fat teens being teased on campus. At the beginning of the year, she had had a friend named Helena who was also obese. Helena had been regularly called names, pushed around, and once a boy even spat in her hair. Allie said that Helena would respond angrily and "go off on people," which had drawn attention to Allie and made her feel embarrassed. Allie had also felt unsure about how to respond—she had not wanted to stand up for Helena and risk becoming the object of teasing, but she had felt badly just watching silently while her friend was abused on a regular basis. "You don't want to stand up for someone. You don't want to put yourself in that position because if you do you're considered odd, strange. Like, if you stand up for someone you'll automatically get categorized with that person, and you'll get teased, too," Allie said. Consequently, Allie had stopped hanging out with Helena because she had grown tired of her friend's angry responses to getting teased and wanted friends who were more positive.

Allie had been dissatisfied with her appearance for some time. She told me she had been about twenty pounds heavier in eighth grade. She had tried Weight Watchers for nine months and lost some weight, but when she had started ninth grade at Desert Vista, she found it impossible to stay on the diet. Allie readily admitted her eating habits were terrible but didn't know what to do about it. She said that most days she didn't eat anything until dinner, as mornings were too hectic.

Every weekday Allie woke up at 3:30 a.m. to get ready for a 6:00 a.m. "zero period" class, and she stayed after school until 6:00 p.m. to be water girl for the school's football team and then usually overate because she was so hungry. She knew breakfast was the most important meal of the day and wanted to eat something healthy, but she often forgot in her rush to get out the door. When she did eat breakfast, it was usually a pop tart or bagel hastily shoved in her mouth on the way to school. She didn't like to eat at school because she had been teased in the lunch line by teens saying things like, "You don't need to eat!" or "Aren't you fat enough?"

Though Allie's busy schedule left little time to exercise she found a way to squeeze in regular workouts. The first time I interviewed Allie in the fall, she said she went to the gym, where her parents had a family membership, once or twice a week to walk on the treadmill for half an hour. When I interviewed her again in the spring, she had begun taking boxing lessons after school and was really enjoying it. The classes were vigorous and included sprints, jumping rope, push-ups, sit-ups, and boxing drills. In addition, she went to the gym once or twice on weekends to walk on the treadmill.

When I asked her what had prompted the dramatic change in her exercise habits, she said she had been diagnosed with high blood pressure, and her doctor had told her that if she couldn't lower it through diet and exercise she would have to take medication. Allie said that diabetes runs in her family on both sides and that the doctor's visit had been a "wake up call," motivating her to start exercising regularly. By the time of the second interview, she still wasn't eating breakfast or lunch daily but was trying to limit the amount she ate at dinner in an effort to lose weight and lower her blood pressure.

During the second interview, it occurred to me to ask why she did not have time to eat breakfast since she woke up at 3:30 a.m. and didn't have to be at school, less than ten miles away, until 6:00 a.m. In other words, what did she do for two and a half hours in the morning instead of eating breakfast? Allie said her first priority in the morning was to straighten her hair, which took over an hour because it was so long, curly, and thick. She also spent a lot of time each morning putting on makeup and choosing just the right outfit.

* * *

Allie's relationship with food and exercise was influenced by her body-image goals, her desire to avoid ridicule from peers, and her weight-related health concerns and was negatively impacted by her lengthy morning beauty regimen, which interfered with her ability to eat healthfully. Allie's feelings about her body fluctuated depending on her mood, how her clothes fit, and what others had to say about her appearance, which was true of many teens I interviewed. As they did for Allie, clothing fit and talk about body image also influenced other teens' ideas about broader issues, such as acceptable body-size norms for girls and boys in general, as well as the "rules" for how boys and girls dressed and talked about body image with their peers.

Through everyday clothing choices and conversations about body image, teens at Desert Vista negotiated what it means to be a socially acceptable and sexually desirable male or female. In this chapter I explore how teens managed their body fat as well as their gendered identities and relationships with each other through clothing and language. Displaying heteronormativity, a belief in traditional, complementary gender roles and heterosexuality as the norm, was a daily identity project for most teens at Desert Vista. For boys and girls, the construction of heteronormative identities relied on daily practices of bodily management that upheld masculinity as strong and powerful and femininity as weak and inferior.

Body management practices among boys included wearing baggy clothing that hid their fat, competing with each other over strength and muscle tone, and engaging in constant critique of girls' bodies. Girls practiced body management by displaying their curves through fitted clothing, internalizing anxieties about body fat, and gossiping about other girls' bodies. In her research on masculinity and sexuality among teen boys in high school, sociologist C. J. Pascoe dubs these kinds of day-to-day ritualistic interactions that "continually affirm masculinity as mastery and dominance" compulsive heterosexuality.[1] The concept of compulsive heterosexuality is a useful lens for understanding the intersection of gender, body image, and social status among teen boys and girls at Desert Vista.

Fit and Brand

Clothing played an important role in socially positioning teens, revealing or hiding body fat, and shaping bodies as well as perceptions and daily narratives about acceptable body presentation. For girls, wearing tight clothes as fitted as possible without showing any body fat was central to displaying a normative feminine identity, which was stressful for girls who wanted to be seen as feminine but felt self-conscious about showing off their bodies.

Girls across social groups consistently said that tight and revealing clothes were the most stylish. For example, Allie said, "Um, right now for, um, for our age, probably like mid-section showing and like a lot of cleavage and like shorter things and stuff like that." A soft-spoken, overweight Goth/Punk girl named Jamie who sat hunched over and cast her gaze downward as she spoke said, "Just tight jeans and tight shirts that are prob-ably low cut in the front." And Jackie, a slender but shapely girl who hung out with the Mexicans said, "Just like tight clothes or a tight shirt with some tight jeans."

Girls explicitly equated tight clothing with normative femininity. For example, Demi, a tall, stocky, and confident girl with a dark maroon bob referred to tight-fitting clothing as "girly" and said that people call her a tomboy for wearing baggy clothes. She explained, "I don't like to wear girly clothes … because they're uncomfortable. You're always pulling down your shirt or, you know, stuff like that. I have like this girlier shirt under this, and I put my sweatshirt over it cause I was just like tired of it." I asked to see the "girlier shirt," and she unzipped her sweatshirt to reveal a tight-fitting T-shirt. Jamie, the Goth/Punk girl introduced above, similarly equated baggy clothing with boys and tight clothing with girls when she said during an interview, "I used to wear a lot of baggy clothes. I used to kind of dress like a guy. And now lately I've just been wearing only tight jeans and stuff."

Boys, on the other hand, were more concerned with style and brand name of clothing as markers of social group affiliation and indices of "coolness." Wearing loose-fitting clothing reflected normative masculinity, which allowed boys to hide their body fat but still feel manly. Loose-fitting cloth-ing had the added advantage of keeping people guessing about how big and strong a boy might be—whether the bulk beneath a boy's shirt was muscle or fat or whether a guy was as scrawny as he appeared or really had lean muscle tone underneath his baggy clothes.

Boys across social groups consistently reported that the "right" fit for guys' clothes was a little baggy. Reggie, a boy who hung out with the Mexicans, said boys should wear their clothes "not too baggy but not like all tight on you." When I asked what constitutes "too baggy," Reggie said, "Like so that your pants are hanging all low and your shirt's all hanging down to your knees or whatever." Kirk, a tall, blond, healthy-weight Jock/Prep and quarterback of the school's freshman football team, responded similarly, saying, "I don't like really baggy, just maybe a little bit."

Although boys commented on clothing fit during interviews, they prima-rily referenced clothing brand when asked to describe the kinds of clothes currently in style for guys. Boys associated specific brand names and specialty clothing stores with social cliques. Boys who identified with the high-profile social cliques on campus, such as the Jocks/Preps, Mexicans, and Goths/Punks, all wore different clothing brands and shopped at vari-ous stores according to their group's style of dress. Knowing the "correct" clothing brands and displaying those brand-name labels was an important part of group membership for boys.

Clothing was an important strategy teens used to socially position them-selves and others, but it also had important implications for body image, the management of body fat, and constructing gendered identities. In order for girls to be considered stylish and trendy, they had to wear fitted cloth-ing, which made it very difficult to hide body fat. The consequence for girls showing body fat was being gossiped about and teased, which is described below and discussed at length in Chapter 3. Boys, on the other hand, were able to hide their body fat underneath loose clothing and still be considered stylish. Despite the fact that their body fat was not on display for all to critique, boys were concerned with how their bodies looked, a topic that is explored later in this chapter. The ability to "pull off" fashionable styles was important for all teens but the rules and consequences for fail-ing to do so were quite different for boys and girls.

Pulling it Off

I learned during interviews about gender differences in de facto rules dictat-ing who was allowed to wear particular clothing styles and brands. Boys and girls talked about these clothing rules in terms of who could and could not "pull off" fashionable styles. Social group affiliation and stance, but not body size, determined what styles could be worn by boys. For example, boys would often point out that they were "small" or "scrawny" but could still look cool in the clothes they considered stylish and that were appro-priate to their social group affiliation. One boy I interviewed who was not a member of any well-known social group explained, "You've gotta act all big and tough to wear gangster-style clothes because people will pick fights with you."

Ricky, a gregarious, overweight boy who hung out with the Mexicans, said, "You can't wear, like, real cool clothes and hang with the nerdy group." Kirk, the freshman quarterback, said,

> There's kids who, like, when they were in middle school and stuff they just kind of annoyed people a lot. They tried too hard to fit in but didn't. So when they do [wear clothing brands that Jocks/Preps wear] people are gonna say something to them.

Another boy who did not belong to an identifiable social clique similarly explained that "small" popular guys can wear preppy clothing, but a guy who is not popular, regardless of his body size, will get made fun of for wearing such clothing.

Jesse, a tall, thin boy who hung out with the Mexicans, confirmed that stance was important for "pulling off" his style of clothing, which he described as "gangster": "It's about attitude, the way you walk, the way you talk." When I asked Jesse to describe the way members of his group walked and talked, he replied, "They talk slang and, like, most of the people always cuss a lot and you can just tell in how they walk." When I further asked Jesse whether or not body size affected ability to successfully wear gangster-style clothing he said "no" and pointed out that he was "really skinny."

Though only boys talked about the rules of guys' clothing brands and styles, both boys and girls talked about girls' clothing in terms of who could "pull off" the tight, revealing clothes considered stylish for girls at the time. Such commentary was often unsolicited and in-depth, much more so than talk about guys' ability to "pull off" clothing styles.

At Desert Vista, having a thin, toned body was a requirement for wearing tight-fitting, revealing clothes considered fashionable for girls. Although body-image ideals for women in the United States have shifted throughout history, the importance of appropriate body presentation has remained constant.[2] Throughout the twentieth and early twenty-first centuries girls have focused on controlling and containing their bodies. While women in the 1950s used girdles to contain their flesh, as clothing styles increasingly became more revealing in the latter half of the twentieth century slenderness became imperative.[3]

For example, Allie, introduced in this chapter's opening vignette, said that to wear tight-fitting clothes "you *definitely* have to have like a certain type of body." She explained:

[Sigh] You have to be skinny and you have to look good in it. You can't just have everything hanging out … Like, you can't have your stomach hanging out, cause that just looks bad anyways [laughs]. And, um, you can't have your fat showing. It's just not right.

Similarly, Jill, a plainspoken, overweight Latina with thick, kinky hair, and a shy smile who did not belong to an identifiable social clique, said during an interview that she did not like to wear tight clothes because she did not think she looked good in them: "I don't think I have the body for it, so I don't really dress like that. I just wear the loose stuff. I don't wear tight, tight clothes." She typically dressed in an oversized T-shirt or sweatshirt with jeans and loosely tied white sneakers.

Showing off one's flat stomach and thin thighs by wearing low-rise jeans, halter tops, and mini-skirts symbolized more than access to fashionable clothing through adherence to heteronormative feminine body-image ideology. The presentation of taut flesh provided access to a higher status within the school's adolescent social hierarchy. Girls who could "pull off" wearing tight, revealing clothing resided at the top of the adolescent social hierarchy. Not only were these girls envied by their female peers, they were also pursued by the most popular, handsome boys.

The meaning of clothing for boys was more multifaceted—it was about displaying the right brand names, carrying themselves in a way that aligned with the image of the clothing brands they were wearing, and hanging out with the right crowd. In some ways, the multiple elements of crafting an image through clothing gave boys more leeway in projecting normative masculine identities; if they cultivated the correct stance and were members of the right social clique, they could get away with generic-brand clothing that looked similar to the high-status labels. For girls, on the other hand, the only pathway to high status in terms of body presentation was to wear tight, revealing clothing without showing any body fat. For girls, there was no way to way to "fake it," so to speak, by highlighting other aspects of their identity.

Failure to Pull it Off

Though all teens who failed to "pull off" the proper image through clothing risked becoming objects of ridicule among their peers, the consequences were more severe for girls. Because girls who tried to "pull it off" risked revealing all of the lines of their bodies underneath form-fitting outfits, they left themselves open to evaluation and critique. Boys and girls emphasized the importance of girls wearing their proper clothing size and often went into great detail to describe the appearance of girls who wore clothing that was too small or too tight. In the context of talking about girls' clothing during an all-boy focus group, Ricky said, "Some fat girls don't know they're fat because they wear clothes that are too tight." The other focus-group participants responded with comments like, "It's nasty," "Once they have a roll it's bad. It squishes out, pops out," "It's like cottage cheese."

During an all-girl focus-group, participants talked about girls spreading rumors about each other when the discussion turned to wearing clothing that was too small. A transcribed segment of this discussion between two participants who were close friends, Mia and Jen, follows. Mia was a soft-spoken, healthy-weight Latina with long dyed blonde hair. Despite her curvy, slim physique, Mia had low self-esteem and was the victim of cruel teasing. Her friend, Jen, was a slender, blue-eyed cheerleader:

Mia: Like you'll see a girl and say, "What was she thinking when she got up this morning? Why would she wear that?" I hate it when big girls wear little clothes.

Jen: And then it squeezes here and squeezes here, and then there's this chunk just hanging out here.

Mia: They look better if they wear, like, their size clothes.

Similarly, during a mixed gender focus-group, participants were talking about shopping and girls' clothing sizes when a tall, thin Goth/Punk boy said, "The thing I hate most when it comes to girls' fashion is the fact of let's say they're supposed to wear a size 7 or 8 and then they wear a size 3 … And then right here they have all this fat hanging out." Other participants, including girls and boys, responded with the following comments: "Yes, ugh ugh," "It's so gross," "They have, like, big old fat rolls."

This kind of running critique among friends is one way in which teens at Desert Vista negotiated or co-constructed gendered body-image norms. It also socialized them into the boundaries of acceptable body presentation for girls and boys. In the example above, they came to a shared understanding about the rules of publicly displaying body fat. The socialization of body-image norms occurs on many levels, including mass-media messages, everyday conversation among friends and family, and the influence of local community and cultural values.

While this book focuses on socialization of body-image norms through everyday conversation among friends at school, it is important to remember that the ideas and attitudes about body fat that teens brought to the conversations with each other were shaped by media messages and interactions with other people in their family and community outside the school context. Feminist scholars have illustrated how the advertising of diet products, exercise equipment, and plastic surgery procedures reinforces the thin, toned body as normative for women.[4] It is through everyday conversation that people negotiate their beliefs in relation to ideals presented in the media. For example, focus-group participants in the examples above defined appropriate body presentation norms for girls through mutually agreed upon descriptions of what was not acceptable.

Just as girls' clothing choices were talked about more frequently than boys' clothing choices and evaluated by all teens, girls who failed to follow the rules for how clothing should fit were gossiped about more frequently than boys who broke the rules because they were subject to criticism by all their peers. For example, during an all-boy focus-group interview, an overweight boy who hung out with the Mexicans said, "Some fat girls act like they're skinny. They wear them short little skirts." I asked whether or not people tease these girls, and a short, skinny member of the Mexican clique responded that people "talk trash" behind their backs.

Gossip, which was pervasive at Desert Vista, was one way in which teens not only negotiated their ideas about what looked good, but also positioned each other socially. Examples provided above illustrate how boys and girls at Desert Vista defined appropriate body presentation for girls and taught those presentation norms to others through gossip. Gender and language scholar Jennifer Coates asserts, "One of the chief things that is being done in the talk of teenage girls is the construction of gendered subjectivity: in the girls' case, the construction of femininity."[5] In contrast to previous assertions that gossip is "women's talk,"[6] more recent gender and language research has shown that boys and men engage in gossip as well,[7] which was true of teens at Desert Vista.

Although boys and girls participated in body-image-related gossip, girls were the main target, which meant that girls were both the enforcers of rules and the objects of critique. Sociolinguist Penelope Eckert argues that by gossiping, girls "increase their stake in the norms, simultaneously tying together the community and tying themselves to it."[8] In this way, girls participate in their own subjugation, unwittingly presenting themselves for scrutiny by both their male and female peers. While gossiping about other girls' bodies may momentarily take the spotlight off of those engaging in the critique, the normalization of this kind of scrutiny ultimately makes girls vulnerable to the same kind of harsh treatment.

Looking Cute or Scrubbin It

Because girls at Desert Vista were the most frequent objects of scrutiny and critique of their male and female peers, girls felt a greater sense of pressure than boys to attend to the details of their appearance and look "put together." Boys did not escape scrutiny or critique, but it tended to be limited to particular settings where their bodies were more visible, like the gym locker room and PE class, while elsewhere, boys' bodies were hidden underneath loose-fitting clothes. This difference between boys and girls is illustrated in the following interview excerpt:

Jen: Girls are insecure about the way they look.
Nicole: So do you think girls are more insecure overall than guys?
Jen: Yeah.
Nicole: Why?
Mia: Just cause guys don't have to do—like girls have to have the cute hairstyle, they have to have, you know, the new "in" makeup, they have to have the push-up bras, the cute underwear, you know, the cute skirt, the cute shirt.
Jen: Guys, I guess, just don't really—I mean they care about their looks, but it's not that hard to wear baggy pants and a baggy shirt. I mean, if girls did that I'm sure they would be less insecure, you know, because that wouldn't show their body as much. But, like, girls, you know, they think they have to look cute constantly, so they have to wear the tight clothes and everything. They'll put on jeans and think, "Oh those are too tight so I guess I'm fat cause

	they don't fit me right, and this girl wears this size so she's skinnier than me, and I don't look as good and na na na."
Mia:	I do that.
Jen:	And they [girls] think, "You look better in that shirt than I do" or "Those pants fit you better than they fit me" and just stuff like that. When my friends borrow my clothes, the pants will look looser on them than on me, and I'm like, "Oh I guess I'm fatter than you cause they fit me better than they fit you na na na." Just stuff like that.
Nicole:	You don't hear guys talking like this?
Jen:	No I don't.

Many girls talked about the pressure to "look cute constantly" and expressed concern about choosing clothes to wear to school, the clothing size they wore compared to the sizes their friends wore, and the difficulty of finding clothing to buy that fit just right, which meant as tight as possible without allowing any fat to show.

In contrast, boys talked about clothing choice as being virtually effortless. When I asked boys how they picked out clothing to wear, many said they just chose something clean and "threw it on." One boy said, "I mean, like, when I dress up in the morning I just put on something comfortable, you know. I don't really care." Another boy explained, "I wake up at six-thirty and put my clothes on and brush my teeth and I'm gone." Many boys said girls felt pressure to look more "put together" than guys because girls were more harshly evaluated by their peers for how they looked. During an all-boy focus group, a boy who hung out with the Mexicans explained that girls who don't "look good in a nice way" were thought to be "scrubbin it," [slang for lack of concern with appearance]. The focus-group participants emphasized how important it was for girls to "look nice" to avoid being criticized by their peers.

Looking nice entailed much more than clothing fit for girls. The conversation excerpt earlier between Jen and Mia illustrates the numerous elements of personal style girls felt pressured to maintain, including clothing fit, hairstyle, makeup, and even undergarments. Girls were socialized into appearance norms through gossip, teasing, and explicit talk about the way clothing should fit, makeup should be worn and hair should be styled. The fact that this socializing discourse occurred among both boys and girls served to doubly reinforce appearance norms for girls.

French philosopher Michel Foucault asserts that norms for behavior, which are initially imposed from external sources, eventually become internalized so that individuals begin to police themselves.[9] Norms for appearance operate in much the same way, as they are established through the media and reproduced through discourses of everyday life. Ongoing dialogue among teens about the way girls looked codified appearance standards for girls, which eventually became internalized by girls at the high school so that the constant worry about appearance became part of constructing feminine identity.

Matching Up

In light of the pressure girls felt to "look cute all of the time," it is not surprising that when I asked girls to describe what they would most like to change about their bodies, the majority, regardless of social group affiliation, said they wanted to lose weight, have a flat stomach, and have thinner thighs. The ability to "pull off" tight, revealing clothing affected their self-image and their place in the social hierarchy, the way they were perceived and treated by their classmates, and their ability to confidently wear many different types of outfits. Girls wanted to look as good as or, ideally, better than their friends in clothes. Girls bonded with each other through clothes sharing while competing with each other to look the best in each other's outfits.

For example, Jackie explained why she wanted a flat stomach: "When you have that, like, you could wear little tops. You could wear bathing suits and do mostly anything." Jackie's use of the verb *could*, an expression of conditional possibility, illustrates her knowledge of the rules governing which girls can "pull off" wearing the most fashionable clothing and, by extension, have a higher degree of social mobility. Similarly, Allie said she wanted a flat stomach "cause like pants and everything—it's all focused around your stomach." Another girl said that she wanted to be thinner "because there are a lot of cute clothes for skinny people."

For most girls, being able to fit into certain clothes was directly tied to self-esteem. Allie explained during one of her interviews, "Like when you go to a store and you try on clothes and stuff, if they don't fit that makes you feel less confident with yourself and less satisfied with who you are." Leslie, a slightly overweight girl who identified herself as a "non" (for non-popular), explained: "Well, I don't think I'm fat, but, you know, when you go and try on clothes and you see the shirt on the little mannequin and you're like, 'God it's the sexiest most awesome thing.' And then you try it on and you're, like, 'No' and my friends are, like, 'Do not wear that.'" In addition to the anxiety associated with being able to fit into clothing at stores, girls also felt pressure to fit into each other's clothing.

Girls frequently shared and traded clothing and, for a girl who wore larger sizes than her friends, this could be an embarrassing and exclusionary social practice. Jamie, the Goth/Punk girl introduced above, explained:

> My friends, they wanna either borrow my clothes or I let them borrow shirts and stuff. But when they wanna borrow pants I don't let them because none of my pants fit them cause they're too big. And when they wanna let me borrow their pants none of them fit me. It brings me down a lot.

Just as wearing similar clothing styles and displaying the same brand-name labels identified group membership for boys, sharing clothing was a marker of group membership among teenage girls. Not being able to participate in clothes sharing with friends made girls feel like outsiders.

Many girls said they felt pressure to look as good as their friends in clothes. During interviews, I asked which girls on campus received the most positive attention from guys, and most said it was the thin girls who "wear little bitty clothes." Jen, the cheerleader, explained:

> Angie is the girl who all the guys like. So, like, when I go running with her she wears little tiny wife beaters [form-fitting white-ribbed men's tank tops] and these shorts where her butt hangs out, and I feel very uncomfortable running with her. Like, I'd rather run by myself and not be compared to her, you know [laughs nervously].

Mia said that even in PE class girls competed to look the best in their exercise clothes.

> Like, in my PE class, Jen wears shorts and her butt's hanging out, and you can see her cooch and she likes to stretch in front of guys. Like, she likes to show off. And then, you know, she always lifts up her shirt and plays with her belly button ring, and she has, like, the tiny waist. And then all the girls feel like they have to match up, so more girls start wearing short shorts. And, you know, I like to wear pants during PE cause I don't like to shave my legs every day [laughs and blushes].

In the examples above, Mia and Jen both expressed how they felt compelled to wear tight, revealing outfits and look as good as other girls in them, the pressure so intense for Jen that she didn't even want to exercise with her best friend because she thought others would compare their bodies.

Although some girls attempted not to succumb to the pressure to compete with friends over appearance, they often gave in as the school year progressed. For example, Leslie, the self-identified "non," vehemently rejected feminine norms the first time I interviewed her but had changed her perspective six months later when I interviewed her again. During the first interview, Leslie repeatedly denied feeling pressure to be thin or wear tight clothes. She talked at length about eating large amounts of food without feeling guilt, proudly contrasting herself to girlfriends who worried about eating too much for fear of gaining weight. Leslie dressed in long, baggy basketball shorts, baggy T-shirts, and tennis shoes. She wore no makeup and her hair was typically pulled back in a ponytail.

However, as the school year progressed, I noticed that Leslie had replaced her baggy clothing with fitted clothing and that she had begun to wear makeup. When I interviewed her again in the spring, instead of rejecting feminine norms she expressed a desire to shed her "tomboy" identity in favor of a more feminine look:

> I've always been, like, a tomboy but I wanna get out of it. When I go out with my friends, I don't look, you know, nice. But I should. I should get more ready than I do. This is the biggest pressure I feel. Like, my three best friends are really pretty. I'm the ugly duckling of the group, and, I mean, I'm okay with that, but they're getting boyfriends every day, and I'm feeling like maybe I should be doing something more. They flirt with guys at the mall all the time, and I'm just sitting there. I want to get up with my friends a little bit. They all have skirts on, and I don't want to be, like, in basketball shorts and tennis shoes.

With her desire to look as good as her friends and attract more positive attention from boys, Leslie began to express concern about the appearance of her body. During the second interview, Leslie told me that she wanted a flat stomach so that she could wear fitted shirts without her "love handles" showing.

Boys also talked about girls competing to look better than each other in tight clothes. During an all-boy focus-group interview, participants said that girls wore tight clothes "to impress guys" and that girls were more concerned than guys with their appearance in general. When I asked the group to elaborate, they explained:

Ricky: I mean, guys don't really compete with each other, like, with what you're wearing. Girls do.

Nicole: So girls are more competitive with each other about that kind of thing?

Robbie: Yeah.

Nicole: What are guys competitive about?

Reggie: Like, sports and stuff.

Ricky: Not really anything except that. Sometimes it could be clothes and stuff ... Like, I could be wearing Wal-Mart brand and they could be wearing Tucson Mall clothes.

Two important points are made in this example. First, the boys distinguished between the ways in which girls and boys were competitive about clothing, stating that girls were competitive about looking good in clothes to impress guys and look better than other girls, whereas boys competed over clothing brand. Second, Reggie and Ricky explained that while girls competed over appearance boys tended to compete over "sports and stuff," a topic that is elaborated on later in this chapter as well as in Chapter 4.

Researchers who study youth have documented the competitive nature of adolescent girls' relationships.[10] My data supports the "cooperative competition" among girls that Eckert writes about.[11] Her research suggests that while girls compete to establish status among their peers, they attempt to frame their competition as cooperation because dominant gender norms associate competition with masculinity and cooperation with femininity. The girls at Desert Vista cooperated through the sharing of clothing and shopping for clothes together while they competed to look better than each other in the clothing. In a broader sense, as Ricky and Leslie stated in the previous interview excerpts, girls were competing for the attention of boys and a higher status in the school's social hierarchy.

Muscle, Strength, and Six-Pack Abs

Most boys in my study were just as invested as girls in vying for a top position in the social hierarchy and attracting the attention of the opposite sex. Virtually all the boys I interviewed, regardless of social group affiliation, said they wanted to be lean, muscular, and have six-pack abs (clearly defined rectus abdominal musculature). In contrast to girls, who masked their body-image-related competition in bonding behaviors, such as clothes sharing, boys openly competed with each other over muscle tone, strength, and athletic performance.

Boys gave several reasons for wanting more muscle tone, including improved athletic performance and self-confidence, aesthetics, and a desire to be attractive to girls. Muscle tone was a marker of strength and power, both of which were important aspects of heteronormative masculinity. My findings are consistent with extant research suggesting that boys are, in fact, concerned with how their bodies look and that the heteronormative male body-image ideal is toned, lean, and muscular.[12]

In contrast to early research on boys' body-image ideals suggesting that boys want to develop such large muscles that their bodies would not realistically be able to support the weight of their musculature,[13] the boys at Desert Vista said there was a limit to how muscular they wanted to be. Several boys from a variety of social cliques cited Arnold Schwarzenegger as an example of someone who was too muscular, with his huge, bulging muscles and veins "popping out." Also both boys and girls said individuals featured in bodybuilding magazines were too muscular.

Boys competed with each other directly and in the presence of their peers. While some boys claimed to be competitive about athletic ability and clothing brands but not body image, my interview and observation data suggest that boys were just as competitive as girls about body image. When I asked Kirk to describe how he and his friends talked about body image, he replied, "Like, 'My six-pack's better than yours' and stuff. It's like a competition." In response to this same question, a healthy-weight Goth/Punk boy replied, "It's like, 'I'm bigger than you. I'm tougher than you.' That sort of thing."

Jerry, a short, thin, nervous boy who constantly fidgeted during interviews and did not affiliate with an identifiable social clique on campus, described a recent conversation he had had with another boy who had claimed to have lifted fifty pounds at the gym the previous day. Jerry responded to the boy by saying, "Yeah, me, too," which he admitted to me was a lie. One girl I interviewed said she had heard guys say to each other, "I can bench press two hundred pounds" or "I have a six-pack." Sociologist Donna Eder and her colleagues argue that verbal dueling is a way for adolescent boys to establish a hierarchy among male peers, and they illustrate how physical strength is linked with dominance among boys.[14] As the examples above suggest, boys at Desert Vista incorporated assertions of physical strength into verbal dueling matches to negotiate social rank among male peers.

When asked about body-image goals, boys who participated in sports explicitly linked their goal for increased muscle tone with a desire to improve their athletic performance. For example, Kirk, the quarterback for the freshman football team, who also played basketball and ran track, told me that he wanted "bigger legs" so he could jump higher and "bigger arms" so he could throw further. Jerry, the nervous, fidgety boy introduced earlier, aspired to be on the school's basketball team. He told me that he wished he were taller, had "bigger calves" and "bigger biceps" to help him perform better in basketball tryouts. These were typical responses among boys who participated in sports. Most of these boys admitted that their body-image-goals were appearance-related as well.

Boys across social groups reported wanting more muscle tone to improve their appearance and self-esteem. For example, one Goth/Punk boy told me he wanted to start lifting weights "for big arms and everything." When I asked why he wanted big arms, he laughed and said, "Isn't that self-explanatory? It's attractive. It is to me anyway." Some boys said that having more muscle tone would improve their confidence. For example, a boy who did not identify with any of the well-known social cliques said he wanted "stronger biceps" because "it's just kind of like a guy thing. I just want stronger arms. It just makes you feel more confident."

Boys also said that girls were attracted to muscular guys, sometimes citing this as their main reason for wanting to increase their muscle size and tone. Ricky said during an interview that if he were more muscular he would "get more girls." He explained, "I'd have more friends, too, cause people would be like, 'Aw if I chill with that guy I'll get more girls [laughs].'" Just as girls wanted to look good in tight-fitting clothing to attract boys, boys at Desert Vista wanted well defined, lean muscle tone in order to attract girls. Boys were correct in their belief that girls found lean muscle tone attractive on boys. With the exception of one Goth/Punk girl, who said that muscles "don't look good on guys or girls," all of the girls I interviewed said they were attracted to guys with some muscle tone and six-pack abs.

Displaying muscle tone was an important part of constructing heteronormative masculine identity because it demonstrated strength and power. A girl who hung out with the Mexicans explained that guys with muscles are attractive "because a guy is supposed to look like he's capable of doing everything." A boy who did not affiliate with any of the identifiable social cliques explained that for guys "the goal is muscle because muscle is strength and strength is power." Boys and girls consistently said during interviews that they associated muscles with boys and that muscles did not "look right" on girls, reflecting widely held gender stereotypes.

All the boys, with the exception of one Goth/Punk, said they would like to have six-pack abs. When I asked boys why, I heard a variety of responses. Most said they liked the way it looked and they thought girls found it attractive: "It [six-pack abs] turns girls on;" "Uh, it just kind of shows, like, a better body, and girls tend to go for better bodies most of the time." Many boys associated six-pack abs with strength: "Girls like boys with six-packs because it shows that they are strong;" "It looks very strong and manly." One boy explained that girls are attracted to guys with six-pack abs because "it just looks good, and girls like to have strong, strong boyfriends. Like, tough usually." The desire for tough, strong boyfriends was widespread among girls I interviewed.

Six-pack abs were a powerful form of "symbolic capital"[15] at Desert Vista because they reflected strength and power. However, symbolic capital functions differently for adolescent boys and girls within the "heterosexual marketplace" of a high school campus.[16] While boys gained status through the display of their own six-pack abs, girls gained status through their relationships with boys who had six-pack abs. Due to female body-image norms disallowing girls to display muscle (or power), most girls did not want to obtain six-pack abs themselves but instead wanted a boyfriend who had six-pack abs.

As I listened to teens discuss in detail boys' abdominal muscles, it became clear to me that the adolescents I talked with knew which guys had six-pack abs. I wondered how this form of symbolic capital had become public knowledge when baggy clothing typically covered the stomach. I asked about this during interviews and teens told me that boys who have six-pack abs announced it and lifted their shirts to display their stomachs to their male and female classmates.

Tim, a healthy-weight boy, explained, "If someone has a six-pack, they gotta tell everybody. A lot of times, like, after school, as soon as they get outside the gates out here to the parking lot, they'll take their shirt off and walk around." In this case, the display of symbolic capital in the heterosexual marketplace was more than just a metaphor. Boys were literally advertising their six-pack abs for the visual consumption of their peers.

One girl told me during an interview that guys compare their six-pack abs by lifting up their shirts and saying, "My six-pack is better than yours" while girls watch. Kenny, a slender, outspoken Goth/Punk boy with red hair and a freckled face, explained how guys with six-packs show them off:

Nicole: How do people know who has a six-pack?
Kenny: When people have a six-pack, they let everybody know.
Nicole: How do they let people know?
Kenny: They'll just lift up their shirt, and they'll be like, "Yeahhh" [spoken in creaky voice].
Nicole: Really?
Kenny: Yeah. Or if he's talking to some girl, and then after a while if he wants to impress her or something he'll just show her his six-pack, and she'll be like, "It's so pretty" [spoken in exaggerated high pitch].

Boys displayed their six-pack abs to each other as a means of competing with male peers for status, and they displayed them to girls to attract and impress them.

Teens said girls who have felt six-pack abs also spread knowledge about which guys have them. Jamie explained, "Um, usually their girlfriends or girls they've been with spread rumors about the guy having a six-pack. And then people want to see it, and usually guys don't mind showing it off." Girls who spread rumors that guys they have been with sexually have six-pack abs increased the social capital of the guys by attracting attention to their abdominal muscles, which were a highly valued commodity among teens and, by virtue of their relationships with such guys, these girls simultaneously increased their own value within the adolescent social hierarchy.

Girls and boys explained during interviews that girls' discourse about boys often centered on speculation about, and admiration of, boys' abdominal muscles. Kenny said he had heard girls say things like, "My guy has a six-pack. Yours doesn't" or "My guy's hotter than yours." When I asked one girl to describe a typical conversation she and her friends have had about six-pack abs, she shyly answered: "Um [laughs] how nice their stomach is and, like, even if the skin color looks good with their six-packs. Just stuff like that."

Girls played an important role in helping boys construct heteronormative masculine identities through their admiration of boys' muscle tone and spreading positive rumors about boys' strong, toned bodies. The body-image ideal girls worked toward also served to reinforce and strengthen boys' masculine identities. For boys' images as strong, powerful males depended not only on how they stacked up against other boys but also on the presence of girls who were smaller, weaker, and less athletically adept than them, a topic that is discussed in the next section and at greater length in Chapter 4.

Petite or Butch

Boys did not consider girls who displayed muscle tone, strength, or even athletic ability attractive. For boys I interviewed at Desert Vista, the most desirable romantic partners were girls who appeared physically weak and, by extension, incapable of physically dominating a boy. In fact, boys vehemently said during interviews they would not consider dating a girl who was physically strong or had visible muscle tone. Girls understood and internalized boys' beliefs about what girls' bodies should look like, and those who participated in sports worried about developing visible muscle tone. Boys and girls both attributed these traditional, narrow, gendered body-image ideals to mass-media messages and articulated the power of media in shaping their beliefs.

Data linking muscle tone with masculinity primarily emerged in response to interview questions about the degree to which muscle tone looked attractive on girls. Most of the teens I interviewed expressed strong, negative opinions about girls showing muscle tone. Boys and girls used the following adjectives to describe how muscles look on girls: *guyish, manly, weird, gross, like ew, ugly, creepy, scary, nasty, butch, odd, inhuman, unnatural,* and *intimidating*. For example, one girl said, "Like, on a girl … if you look really, um, muscular then you kind of look like a guy."

The image of a hypothetical muscular girl beating up her boyfriend pervaded teens' discourse about girls and muscle tone and was the primary reason given for why boys felt intimidated by girls who displayed muscle tone. Eddie, a Goth/Punk boy who wore black clothing and styled his chin-length dark hair with a flat iron, explained:

Nicole: What about girls with muscle tone? Does that look good?
Eddie: Uh, not really cause with girls it's usually not about them trying to look strong or anything. It's more about them just being fit and in shape and skinny.
Nicole: Okay. Would you date a girl who was muscular?
Eddie: Probably not.
Nicole: How come? Like, what does that mean to you?
Eddie: It's almost kind of creepy. If they're, like, really big and muscular and everything then they'll probably beat you up [laughs] and, uh, that wouldn't be too attractive for me.

Kenny responded similarly when I asked him whether or not muscular girls were attractive:

> If a girl's, like, really, really buff they're usually really, really butch. I've gone out with a butch girl, and it was too much like dating a guy and it was scary. It's kind of scary to go out with a girl that can beat you up, cause, you know, if you forget an anniversary or something you're screwed.

Sociolinguists Penelope Eckert and Sally McConnell-Ginet assert, "Hegemonic masculinity emphasizes the possibility of physical force. It has been a central symbolic component in constructing heterosexual men as different from both women and gay men—in principle able to beat up either."[17] Boys I interviewed said it was important to be stronger and more muscular than their girlfriends to avoid being teased by their male peers. As explained by one boy, "You'd get made fun of cause your girlfriend sticks up for you rather than you sticking up for your girlfriend."

A girl I interviewed expressed skepticism when I asked her whether or not she thought guys would be attracted to a girl with muscle tone:

> They might think about how, like, if they ever get into a fight then his girlfriend would have to protect him, and then he would feel really down. He would probably start yelling at her because he'd feel like he's not powerful enough to defend himself, and he'd feel pretty weak. So he'd have to think of something to bring himself back up.

She was clearly aware of boys' desire to feel more powerful than girls.

In fact, most girls were aware of boys' opinions about girls who displayed muscle tone. The following interview excerpt from an interview with Cory, a thin Goth/Punk with long dark hair, green eyes, and a freckled face, is typical of what most girls had to say about the topic:

Nicole: What about girls who are muscular? Do you think guys find
           that attractive, or do you think that's attractive?
Cory: No. I think it's intimidating for a guy.
Nicole: Oh. Tell me about that.
Cory: Well, if a girl is bigger than you and stronger than you, and you're
           a guy it's just kind of scary ... and they've said that, you know.
           They've said like, "Well, if a girl was stronger than me or if she's
           bigger than me, you know, that's kind of intimidating, and I
           wouldn't really go out with her or whatever."
Nicole: So guys have actually commented on how that would be intim-
           idating?
Cory: Yeah, how that would be weird almost if the girl's bigger than
           the guy. Cause generally the girl's supposed to be small and petite
           or whatever.

Cory not only echoed the opinions of boys at her school regarding muscular women, but she gave primacy to their opinions over her own. In my
question, I asked her to comment on either boys' opinions of muscular
girls or her own, and she chose to discuss what boys think of muscular
girls instead of what she thinks.

Several girls who had muscle tone as a result of sports participation
said they wanted to "get rid of" their muscle tone because it made them
look masculine. One girl who had participated competitively in gymnas-
tics for ten years said that boys often expressed a desire to have muscles
like hers. She also said she thought muscles look "ugly" on girls and
that guys do not find it attractive. Jen similarly told me that cheerleading had made her legs muscular and that guys had often commented that
her legs were bigger than theirs. Jen thought guys should be more muscular than girls and said that guys were not attracted to muscular girls
because "girls are supposed to be petite and just sit there looking cute."
The cheerleader and former gymnast were clearly aware of boys' negative attitudes about muscular girls and both had internalized those
attitudes.

These examples support the findings of education scholar Lyn Mikel
Brown in her research on adolescent girls' social and psychological devel-
opment. Drawing upon Mikhail M. Bakhtin's concept of multivocality,
Brown writes:

Women and girls who speak through patriarchal voices do so in part
to appropriate the power these voices have in the world, and yet the
voices they speak carry with them the attenuation of female power,
both personal and political. Such ventriloquation of conventionally

feminine voices thus unwittingly reflects and contributes to a larger cultural silencing of women.[18]

Many of the girls I talked to at Desert Vista voiced dominant gender ideologies regarding body-image norms that they had internalized.

Just as most teens said muscular girls were not attractive, the majority of boys and girls I interviewed believed girls should have "flat, toned stomachs" rather than six-pack abs: "I definitely wouldn't see a girl with a six-pack looking that good cause, like, that's kinda muscular. But if you have a flat stomach that's nice," said Demi, the girl with a maroon bob. Boys and girls primarily used the adjectives *gross*, *intimidating*, and *weird* when I asked whether or not six-pack abs looked attractive on girls. Teens also said girls with six-pack abs were "too buff," "too muscular," and "manly."

When asked where their perceptions about body image came from, most teens said "the media" or "society." The strong influence of popular media on body-image ideals has been well documented.[19] It is estimated that the average American watches three to four hours of television per day.[20] Factoring in other forms of media consumed by Americans, such as fashion and lifestyle magazines, movies, and music, it becomes clear why media images have such a significant impact on our ideas about body image.

Kirk explained how he thought media influence worked:

Kirk: I guess it's the way society's supposed to be. Like, the image of a girl and a guy, it's what you see on TV and stuff.
Nicole: So what is the image of a girl that you see on TV?
Kirk: Like, not short but not tall and skinny, pretty and stuff.
Nicole: And what about the image of a guy that you see on TV?
Kirk: Like, tall, muscular, and athletic.

When I asked teens how six-pack abs became so popular for guys, several referred to infomercials that advertise "ab machines." For example, Sammy, an affable, easygoing Latino who was new to the high school, said he wanted six-pack abs after seeing "those infomercials for ab machines where the guys have six-packs." Some girls also said music had influenced their body-image ideology. For example, Mia explained during an interview that her low self-esteem was partially the result of comparing herself to her friend who had the perfect hourglass figure described in songs about beautiful women. Another girl similarly said, "The songs say that guys like big butts and big boobs."

Only a few teens claimed the media did not influence their ideas about body image. For example, Leslie, the self-proclaimed "non" (for non-popular) who started the year wearing baggy clothes and no makeup and ended the year wearing tight clothes and makeup to "keep up" with her friends, attributed the pressure girls felt to be thin and beautiful to the media but denied feeling that pressure herself:

> It's all the media. We all have a self-conscious thing in the back of our mind telling us, "I could be a little skinnier. I could be a little skinnier." If we didn't have the media and if we didn't have those underwear models with the beautiful stomachs and the beautiful everything then we wouldn't base our opinion on that. We have to look like them, and if we don't look like them then we're bad. I don't think that. This is the way I look, and I'm not gonna get, like, the makeup and magazines and say, "Oh this girl looks pretty, and so I'm gonna put this on."

These examples illustrate how some of the teens at Desert Vista attempted to negotiate their awareness of the media's power to influence public perceptions with their desire to view themselves as individuals capable of resistance.

Overall, teens' level of awareness about the power of media messages in shaping their ideas about sex roles and gendered body-image ideals was impressive. Teachers and parents could build on such insights by guiding teens to critically examine media-generated gender- and body-image norms and collaboratively strategizing ways to resist and challenge these harmful messages.

"I'm so Fat!"

An earlier section described how girls engaged in "cooperative competition"[21] with regard to clothing and personal style. This section explores how cooperative competition extended to girls' discourse about body-image ideology. Girls competed with each other to achieve the ideal thin, toned, fat-free look. Yet, at the same time, girls supported each other through a conversational genre that anthropologist Mimi Nichter refers to as "fat talk," a social ritual among friends that elicits compliments and allows girls to show concern for how their body looks.[22] My research supports Nichter's findings that fat talk serves multiple social functions among adolescent girls, including building rapport, soliciting peer support, calling attention to perceived flaws before others do, and aligning with peers' ideas about feminine norms.

Girls said during interviews that it was common for girls to engage in fat talk while "pigging out" on junk food. For example, Allie explained, "It's like sometimes we're over at a friend's house and we'll be eating and we'll be just like, 'I'm so fat' because we'll just be eating everything and that's, like, slumber party talk." Fat talk, or as Allie called it, "slumber party talk," functioned to build rapport among girls. In this instance, the girls used fat talk to create a safe space within which to gorge on fattening foods without critique.

One day during lunch a group of girls walked over to the table where I was sitting and proceeded to say things like, "I shouldn't eat today because I feel fat" and "I need to diet, but I'm hungry" before leaving to buy lunch. When the girls came back, one was eating a large iced brownie, and another was drinking a soda and eating a candy bar. As Nichter notes, engaging in fat talk before consuming fattening foods serves as a "public presentation of responsibility and concern for appearance" among girls.[23] It is also a way for girls to solicit permission from friends to consume fattening foods or obtain reassurance that they can eat what they want because they are not fat.

Nichter asserts, "Girls are socialized to rely heavily on external acceptance and feedback to inform their identity."[24] In the case of fat talk, positive feedback is delivered in the form of reassurances from friends that a girl is not fat. Girls said during interviews that, in addition to engaging in fat talk prior to eating large amounts of food, sometimes girls call themselves fat after eating a lot of food. Kerri, a petite Latina with a boyish figure and long, curly black hair who had an officious, pragmatic way about her, explained that if she was with friends and ate "too much" she would sometimes say, "I feel fat now." In response, her friends would insist that she was not fat. In this case, Kerri solicited support from her friends through fat talk and was rewarded by assurances that she looked good. This was also a way of alleviating the guilt most girls felt when they ate fattening foods, a topic explored at length in Chapter 5.

Mia explained that she and her friends often engaged in fat talk while they were trying on clothes:

> We'll just be looking in the mirror. Like, we'll try on jeans, you know, and they'll be really big [in terms of clothing size] and we're like, "Oh my God, I'm so fat" or, you know, you'll just be like, "Oh my God, I feel so bloated. I'm so fat" [laughs shyly], you know.

In this instance, fat talk functioned as "rapport talk,"[25] communicating alignment with feminine norms that dictate how girls' bodies should look in clothing and allowing girls to call attention to perceived flaws in themselves before others do.

I witnessed another example of fat talk as rapport talk one day while standing in the girls' bathroom on campus. Two relatively thin-looking girls stood in front of the mirror fixing their hair, tugging at their clothes, and applying lip gloss. One said, "This shirt makes me look fat, like I'm trying to hide something." The other replied, "Speaking of trying to hide something, I need to hide this gut." At that point, they both turned and walked out of the bathroom. Through mutual self-criticism these two girls offered support to each other.

When asked why girls call themselves fat, a majority of girls and boys said they are "fishing for compliments." Jen, the cheerleader, explained, "I think they just want to hear, 'No you're not. You're skinny. You're pretty.'" Similar to Nichter's findings on fat talk,[26] teens I interviewed said the most common replies to a thin or healthy-weight girl calling herself fat are, "No you're not" and "Shut up." However, in contrast to Nichter's research, teens in my study stated that fat girls do, in fact, engage in fat talk. Teens I interviewed said that when fat girls call themselves fat, a prolonged and uncomfortable silence is the most typical response.

Nicky, an overweight Latina with acne and a double chin that made her feel self-conscious, explained that she had a very overweight friend who sometimes called herself fat. When she did this, it essentially shut down the conversation, resulting in an awkward silence, which was then broken by someone in the group changing the subject. Similarly, a boy described the fat talk ritual among thin girls during an interview, adding, "Sometimes fat girls say that." When I asked him how people respond when a fat girl calls herself fat, he mimicked being uncomfortable by exaggeratedly looking everywhere but at my face, punctuating this gesture with a prolonged silence.

Conversation analyst Anita Pomerantz claims that a speaker's assessment of someone or something known to participants invites a response of either agreement or disagreement. According to Pomerantz, "When no overt disagreement is made, the self-deprecating party tends to treat the self-deprecation as implicitly confirmed by the recipient."[27] Teri illustrated this point when she explained during an interview that she had experimented with various responses to thin and healthy-weight friends who called themselves fat. In an effort to discourage fat talk among her friends because she found it annoying, Teri sometimes changed the subject when friends called themselves fat. Teri said when she had tried responding to one friend's initiation of fat talk with silence, her friend expressed concern that Teri agreed with the self-deprecatory statement.

Earlier in this chapter I argued that clothing simultaneously represented a site of competition and a means for building rapport among girls at Desert Vista. Within female friendship groups, sharing clothing communicated in-group status, and girls who wore larger clothing sizes than their friends were excluded from this rapport-building activity. My research suggests that fat girls were similarly excluded from participation in fat talk, once again placing them at the margins of their friendship groups.

One variation on fat talk that emerged during interviews with girls was a focus on specific body parts as opposed to the whole body. Cory, the notably insightful Goth/Punk girl explained, "Some [girls] will be like, 'My legs look too fat,' 'My stomach isn't tight enough,' 'My boobs aren't big enough, 'My this, my that.' Just tons of stuff." This scrutiny of individual body parts reflected body-image goals of the teen girls I interviewed, most of whom wanted flatter stomachs and thinner thighs. The low-riding, tight jeans and fitted, cropped shirts that girls described as being stylish highlighted the legs and stomach, which were primary areas of concern for girls.

Wish Conversations

Another variation that emerged was what Allie called "wish conversations." She explained by providing examples: "Um, 'I wish I was skinnier,' 'I wish I didn't look like this,' 'I wish I looked like her,' 'I wish I had her hair, her eyes, her lips,' stuff like that." Another girl explained, "We just start talking, and I usually say that I wish I could be skinnier and my face was cleared up and that's about it." Another Goth/Punk girl said, "I mean, if a movie star person is on TV they'll be like, 'Oh, I wish, um, my legs looked like that' or 'I wish my stomach looked like that,' you know."

Other girls said wish conversations occasionally expanded beyond physical appearance. Sarah, a petite, quiet Latina cheerleader with delicate facial features, and long brown hair, explained that sometimes when she and her friends were at the mall and they saw a pretty girl with her boyfriend, they might say to each other, "I wish I looked like her" or "I wish I had that [referring to the girl's boyfriend]." During an interview, I asked Mary, a soft-spoken, overweight girl, whether or not she and her friends talked about body image, and she replied, "Yeah, like when we're walking and we see a crowd and we're, like, 'Ooh, wish we could be pretty like them' or 'skinny like them.' If they have more friends or they have boyfriends it's like, 'We wish we could have those.'" Like so many of the girls I interviewed, Mary viewed being thin, pretty, having more friends, and having a boyfriend as a package deal.

This concept of linking body-image goals to a lifestyle package lends support to previous research findings that advertising works through metonymy, which is the linking of a product with its features as well as with a lifestyle package.[28] In this way, consumers are not simply purchasing a product but are buying into a lifestyle. Similarly, the girls in my study believed that by attaining the perfect body they would gain access to the perfect life. As discussed earlier in this chapter, girls who could "pull off" wearing tight, revealing clothing received the most positive attention from boys. Girls viewed their bodies as gatekeepers that either restricted or allowed access to an ideal lifestyle package, which included an abundance of friends, a cute boyfriend, and the ability to wear, and look good in, the most stylish clothing.

"I'm so Ugly! You're so Fat!"

Boys engaged in fat talk differently from girls, and their style of fat talk depended on the audience. Boys called themselves fat and ugly in the presence of girls to solicit compliments and gauge girls' interest in them as romantic partners, but rules disallowed engaging in this type of exchange with other boys as a way of seeking emotional support. Teens said boys would call themselves "fat" and "ugly" in the company of girls and call other boys "fat" and "ugly" in the company of boys. Mia described how boys engaged in fat talk among girls:

Nicole: Do guys ever say, "I'm fat?"
Mia: You know, I never thought they did, but this year I have met, like, a hundred guys who do. Like, this guy Rubin is like, "I'm so fat. I'm so fat." I'm like, "You're like a toothpick." He's so skinny. And this guy named Jared, he's like, "Yeah, I'm so fat" you know. And this guy named Josh is like, "Yeah, I'm fat."
Nicole: Are they saying it to other guys, or are they saying it to girls?
Mia: To girls. When a girl's like, "Yeah, I'm fat" or something they'll be like, "No you're not. I'm ugly and I'm fat," you know [laughs].

Both boys and girls said boys called themselves "fat" and "ugly" in front of girls to gauge girls' level of interest in them. During an all-boy focus group, Tim, a healthy-weight participant, explained that a guy will say, "I'm so ugly" or "I'm so fat" to a girl as a way of determining whether or not a girl finds him attractive. According to Tim, if the girl disagrees with his self-deprecatory statement, he interprets it to mean that she finds him attractive; however, if she changes the subject or responds with silence, then he knows she does not find him attractive. Engaging in this version of "fat talk" is a way for guys to avoid potential rejection by girls.

During an all-girl focus group, Mia and Jen described a typical "fat talk" exchange initiated by a guy with a girl:

Mia: You'll be on the phone with a guy, and he'll be, like, "You wouldn't like me. I'm ugly."
Jen: Yeah. "You wouldn't like me."
Nicole: Okay, replay a typical conversation because I can't imagine it.
Mia: They'll just somehow bring up, "Who do you like?"
Jen: Yeah. "Who do you like?"

Mia: And then they're like, "You wouldn't like me," you know. "I'm ugly. I'm fat."

Jen: Or "Do you think I'm cute?" And you're like, "Yeah." And they're like, "No you don't. I'm ugly" or "I'm not you're type."

Teens said guys call themselves "fat" and "ugly" to girls to elicit compliments, and girls claimed it was usually "the guys who are hot" who engage in this sort of fat talk. As Mia explained, "They know they're cute. They just want to hear it."

Teens said that it is only appropriate for guys to call themselves fat with girls. If guys called themselves fat in front of other boys, they would risk being called a girl or gay. One girl said she had a male friend in PE class who sometimes called himself fat, and other boys responded by saying to him, "You're such a girl!" Another girl explained: "Guys aren't gonna say, 'Hey dude, I look really fat, don't I?' I mean they're not gonna say that to their guy friend, or their friend's gonna think they're gay or something."

Boys said when a guy calls himself fat in front of other guys the response is never to disagree. Reggie explained that he had a friend who was "a little chunky," and his friend sometimes said to his male friends he wished he could lose his "pudge." Reggie said the guys in their group usually laughed and told him jokingly that he could do sit-ups. During an all-girl focus-group, participants explained that guys would never call themselves fat with other guys because "if they said it to a guy and the guy's like, 'No you're not,' they'll be all, 'Whoa, gay.'"

Some teens said guys call each other fat. One girl explained that she often heard guys jokingly say to each other, "You're fat" or "You're ugly." She said a typical response was, "Yeah, I know" or "Give me a cheeseburger." During an interview, Demi talked about this form of joking among guys:

Demi: Um, they call each other fat all the time.

Nicole: So the opposite of girls.

Demi: Yeah. [Laughs loudly].

Nicole: So how have you seen guys respond when someone calls them fat?

Demi: Um, some guys are like, "I know" and stuff. They just kind of take it. Um, yeah, they just kind of mess around with it.

Nicole: Are the guys fat?

Demi: No. It's just what guys do now. It's what they do.

This kind of joking among guys served a rapport-building function within very close friendship groups, but was taken as an insult in all other social contexts, a topic discussed at greater length in the next chapter.

The tension between efforts to shape body-size perceptions through language and the undeniable biological reality of body fat emerged in this chapter. Some teens were able to approach body-image ideals to varying degrees, but none could achieve a truly fat-free physique. In the face of this material truth, teens tried to strategically hide their fat with clothing while their peers shaped perceptions of their bodies through gossip and critique. Teens negotiated and socialized each other into the boundaries of acceptable gendered body image and presentation norms through gossip sessions that also momentarily deflected attention away from their own bodies.

Girls and boys were both faced with body-image-related challenges. Girls were more harshly scrutinized and critiqued and thus felt pressured to attend to every detail of their appearance in an effort to look perfect all of the time. However, they had access to socially acceptable strategies for seeking emotional support, including fat talk and clothes sharing. These practices provided a safe space where girls could share their body-image insecurities and receive messages of acceptance and support from their friends, but they also represented sites of competition where girls competed to be prettier, thinner, and more attractive than their friends.

Boys were able to hide their bodies beneath loose-fitting clothing and were afforded a broader body size range than girls. However, boys felt anxious and self-conscious about the way their bodies looked underneath clothing and competed with each other over who was stronger and had better muscle tone. Though ritual body-image insults among boys who were close friends served a rapport-building function, this was the extent to which they were able to receive emotional support from male peers. Boys were not allowed to show vulnerability by expressing their appearance-related insecurities in the presence of other boys for fear of being called "gay" or "girly." Seeking body-image reassurance from girls was risky as well, for girls would only contradict boys' self-deprecating statements if they were interested in the boys as romantic partners.

Boys and girls across social groups had unrealistic body-image expectations for themselves and their peers. Education in media literacy is an important step toward teaching youth to think critically about the narrow ways in which beauty, bodies, masculinity, and femininity are portrayed in the media. Youth also need a better understanding of what real, healthy bodies look like to recalibrate and broaden their gendered body-image expectations. In the next chapter I continue to explore body image by focusing on fat stigma to show the everyday consequences faced by teens who failed to conform to normative standards.

Notes

1. Pascoe, 2007.
2. Bordo, 1993; Brumberg, 1997.
3. Brumberg, 1997.
4. Bordo, 1993; Brumberg, 1997; Nichter and Nichter, 1991.
5. Coates, 1999:125.
6. Coates, 1988.
7. Cameron, 1997; Johnson and Finlay, 1997; Kiesling, 2002.
8. Eckert, 1993:35.
9. Foucault, 1975/1977, 1980.
10. Eckert, 1993; Goodwin, 1990, 1999, 2002; Mendoza-Denton, 1996, 1999a, 1999b; Nichter, 2000.
11. Eckert, 1993.
12. Grogan and Richards, 2002; Kehler, 2010; Ryan, Morrison, and Ó Beaglaoich, 2010.
13. Pope, Phillips, and Olivardia, 2000.
14. Eder, Evans, and Parker, 1995.
15. Bourdieu, 1972.
16. Eckert, 1993; Eckert and McConnell-Ginet, 1995.
17. Eckert and McConnell-Ginet, 1995:484.
18. Brown, 1998:123.
19. Bordo, 1993; Brumberg, 1997; Heilman, 1998; Nichter and Nichter, 1991; Wolf, 1991.
20. Brownell and Horgen, 2004:100.
21. Eckert, 1993.
22. Nichter, 2000.
23. Nichter, 2000:51.
24. Nichter, 2000:48.
25. Nichter, 2000; Tannen, 1990.
26. Nichter, 2000.
27. Pomerantz, 1984:93.
28. Nichter and Nichter, 1991; Nichter and Vuckovic, 1994.

3
"GUYS, SHE'S HUMONGOUS!"

Ricky, a fourteen-year-old freshman at Desert Vista, self-described "gansta," and member of the Mexicans, was a study in contradictions. On the one hand, he said he did not care about appearance, body image, and others' opinions of him. On the other hand, he talked about carefully choosing clothing and accessories to wear, yelling at and beating up teens who called him fat, and exercising to lose weight and ameliorate food-related guilt.

Wearing the right clothing and accessories was very important to Ricky. He wore a thick gold chain around his neck, an earring in his left ear, baggy T-shirts and jeans, and white leather tennis shoes with wide laces tied very loosely. He kept his hair short, like a buzz cut. Ricky was well aware that clothing brand and style communicated meaningful information about an individual's identity and social group affiliation:

> I wear, like, the more hip clothes, you know, just name brands and all that. I cut my hair a certain way and wear jewelry cause a lot of kids have jewelry now, and if you don't have jewelry you're not one of them. Jewelry, clothes, and shoes. Shoes is a big thing. You just gotta wear the right shoes, like. And it depends how you wear em. You can just untie em, keep em loose. Like, if you tie em real tight, people are gonna look at you like, "Oh, you're a geek" and all that.

Ricky talked at length about exactly how guys should wear their clothes, explaining what it meant to wear them baggy but not too baggy. He also listed specific brand names that he and his friends considered cool. However, in the same interview, he said he did not worry about what he wore to school and would often just "throw on sweats and whatnot." But I never saw

Ricky wear sweats or "looking scrubbed out" (slang for not caring about one's appearance). His outfits always appeared to be carefully coordinated and styled.

Ricky told me he was five feet ten and weighed 226 pounds, which is considered obese for a boy his age by the Centers for Disease Control and Prevention. When I asked Ricky to rate how satisfied he was with the way his body looked on a scale of one to five with five being the most satisfied, he responded "three and a half" or maybe "four," explaining that while he could be a lot thinner and should probably work out more, he's pretty satisfied with the way he looks. Ricky liked that he was tall and that he had a good personality, which he described as "nice" and "sensitive." He wished he were thinner and had more muscle tone but repeatedly insisted that he really didn't care about body image, saying things such as, "Well, it doesn't really matter what I look like. I don't care what people think."

Ricky was mostly sedentary and lacked motivation to exercise. Several times a year, he would go through phases where he worked out at the gym or played basketball with friends regularly, and then after a few weeks he would quit. Getting teased for his weight helped motivate Ricky to work out:

> Well, people will just make fun of you, and it makes you want to go to the gym. Like, sometimes they'll be like, "Oh you're fat" and all this. And it doesn't really offend me that much, but I'll be like, "Oh yeah, I should go to the gym." And then, like, I don't know, it's kind of fun working out and lifting weights. It gives you a thrill to work out and see who can bench press more with your friends and stuff.

Ricky genuinely enjoyed exercising with his friends but said that after a while he would lose the motivation to continue: "Yeah, I'll work out for, like, a month or so and then after a while you get tired of it and you're just like, 'No, I'm not gonna go today.'"

Friends, family, and strangers teased Ricky about his weight. He said that when friends and family teased him, he took it as playful banter:

> Yeah, like, my friends, we'll just be teasing each other, and they'll be like, "Oh you're fat" and I'll be like, "Oh you look like a twig" and all this. Or we'll say to each other, "You're ugly" and we'll just be messing around, you know. And when someone says that to me, I'll just be like, "Oh yeah, I know that already." Me and my dad mess around, too. Like when we're playing basketball together, he's like, "Come on fat boy, catch up to me" and all this. He's just messin around, though.

In contrast, when teens who were not his friends teased him for his weight Ricky admitted that it hurt. For example, when guys he didn't know called him fat, Ricky said that he "gets mad and explodes," cussing at them, pushing them, and sometimes fighting them. He responded similarly to girls he didn't know calling him fat. For example, in eighth grade a new girl walked up to him at school and loudly exclaimed, "Don't you know you're fat?" He responded by "exploding on her." Ricky recalled, "I got in her face and yelled, 'You're ugly' and I was all, 'You think you're all bad cause you're here, but you're nobody. No one wants you here.' After that she just stopped. She didn't say anything else. She was just quiet and walked off."

Ricky was equally contradictory in responding to questions about his eating habits. He claimed he didn't watch what he ate and "just pigged out" a lot. At the same time, he said he avoided chocolate and soda because they caused weight gain, consuming sports drinks instead because he thought they were healthier and less fattening than soda. After eating a big meal or a lot of junk food, Ricky felt guilty, which motivated him to work out. He said, "I'll just eat like it doesn't matter. And then, like, after that I'll go to the park and play basketball or somethin' and try to lose it all. I think, 'Dang, I just ate a lot, and I should go at least try to lose some of it.'"

Even though Ricky was medically obese and felt angry about getting teased for his weight by people he didn't know, he admitted to teasing and gossiping about fat people with his friends: "Sometimes with a big kid, we'll be like, 'He's fat' [laughs]. We'll just like dog em and be like, 'Oh he's fat.' And when we see big girls, we'll be like 'Whoa, she's pretty big' and stuff." Ricky also said that he would never date an overweight girl because he finds them unattractive and because it would hurt his image.

* * *

The kinds of contradictions expressed by Ricky were also expressed by many other teens I interviewed at Desert Vista. Ricky's experiences with getting teased for his weight influenced his exercise practices, his relationship with food, and his self-image. The teasing motivated Ricky to exercise, and his desire to be thinner resulted in feelings of guilt when he overate. Ricky claimed not to care what others thought about his appearance, yet he responded angrily when strangers teased him for his weight. Despite the fact that he was fat and did not like being teased for it, Ricky admitted to teasing and gossiping about other fat people and said he would not date a fat girl because of what people might think. Such contradictions represented sites of tension between the powerful influence of dominant media-driven narratives that stigmatize and blame fat people for their condition on the one hand and the realities of the teens' own body sizes, eating behaviors, and exercise practices on the other hand.

This chapter explores fat stigma and teasing among teens at Desert Vista. It focuses on how these teens defined the boundary between acceptable and unacceptable body size and how they circulated that knowledge and policed the boundary through teasing and gossip. It also illustrates how the teens used fat teasing and gossip to draw attention away from their own body fat and present themselves as thinner-than their peers. In the absence of actually achieving thinness, teens created a relative reality in which they constructed thinner-than identities through teasing and gossip and circulated each other in a network of hierarchical relations based on these discursively created body-size perceptions.

Embedded in behaviors of policing boundaries related to the fat body and distancing oneself from fatness is an acute awareness that excess body fat is stigmatized in the United States. Despite the fact that the United States is in the midst of a so-called obesity crisis, Americans continue to idealize thin, toned, fat-free bodies and detest bodies that display excess fat, however that gets defined. Feminist philosopher Susan Bordo writes, "Ultimately, the body ... is seen as demonstrating correct or incorrect attitudes toward the demands of normalization itself."[1] Obesity represents an incorrect "attitude," a willful failure to adhere to the norm, and is therefore a source of social stigma. In popular media, obesity is predominantly framed as a public health crisis and an issue of personal responsibility, which places the blame squarely on individuals who fail to manage their weight effectively.[2]

What does this mean for people in their everyday lives? A major consequence of media discourses that frame obesity and fat people as a threat to our economy, health-care system, and national security is the institutionalized stigmatization of body fat.[3] That is, many people have bought into the media-generated hype that fat people are at fault for the problems associated with obesity and should be shamed into engaging in "healthy lifestyle behaviors," such as exercising and eating healthfully, an attitude that leads to teasing, bullying, and discriminating against individuals perceived to be overweight or obese.

According to sociologist Erving Goffman, stigmatized individuals display "stigma symbols," which he defines as, "signs which are especially effective in drawing attention to a debasing identity discrepancy ... with a consequent reduction in our valuation of the individual."[4] In some cases, the "stigma symbols" are discrete and readily identifiable (e.g., physical deformities or skin color). However, when body fat, something all people possess, is the stigma symbol, determining the boundary between stigmatized individuals and "normal" people can be challenging. How much body fat is too much and how do people distinguish between "normal" and "too fat" moment-to-moment as they make value judgments about others' bodies in the course of everyday life?

And now that the majority of Americans are medically classified as overweight or obese, the perceptual boundaries delineating "normal" and "too fat" have become increasingly blurred. How does stigma work when the stigma symbol, in this case excess body fat, is the norm rather than the exception? This chapter explores teens' attitudes about obesity and how they negotiated body-size boundaries and the stigma associated with excess body fat through teasing and gossip.

The Obesity Blame Game

Media coverage of the nation's so-called obesity epidemic emphasizing personal responsibility peaked in 2003,[5] the year I started fieldwork for this project. Teens at Desert Vista were clearly influenced by the media hype stigmatizing and blaming fat people for their weight. In response to interview questions about the nation's obesity epidemic, some teens acknowledged the role of a social environment where fast food was plentiful and physical activity was replaced by labor-saving devices and sedentary forms of entertainment, such as television and video games. No one mentioned or acknowledged genetic- or metabolic-related causal factors, probably because these are not a focus of obesity-related media attention.

Most teens I interviewed, like Kenny in the excerpt below, stressed individual responsibility and people's ability to control their weight through discipline.

Kenny: I mean, in our class there's this guy, huge. I mean, it kind of like makes me angry because it looks like he doesn't do anything about it.
Nicole: Huge like overweight or muscular?
Kenny: Like, really, really overweight. I mean, you know, with breasts.
Nicole: So it makes you mad?
Kenny: Well, it doesn't really make me mad. It just makes me kind of sad for him because, I mean, he has the power to make it go away. But, I mean, he doesn't care and it's sad.

Similarly, when I asked Kirk, the quarterback of the freshman football team, about his thoughts on why so many kids and adults were getting fat, he said, "I think that if you get overweight it's your fault and that it's your problem, not anyone else's. It's your problem to deal with. I don't feel bad because you got yourself there." Whereas Kenny felt torn between anger and compassion, Kirk was clear in his disdainful judgment of fat people. The common thread through both responses was the belief that fat people are responsible for their weight and that they have the power to slim down. This is similar to what anthropologist Carol Counihan found in her research on college students' relationships with food and body image.[6] Young adults in her study expressed the same beliefs about self-control and individual choice as the teens I worked with.

It was not uncommon for teens at Desert Vista to express disbelief and sometimes anger when they perceived that a fat person did not appear to want to lose weight. For example, when I asked Leslie, the slightly over-weight self-identified "non" (for non-popular), what she thought about the obesity epidemic, she responded with a description of a fat person she had seen eating at the McDonald's across the street from the high school:

> Usually when we have band practice, we head over to McDonald's, and there is this person I see there all the time and they're gettin' bigger and bigger. And they have, like, four things of fries and two hamburgers and a slushee and a drink and they're just eating away perfectly, like [makes loud, piggish noises to imitate the sounds this person makes while eating]. You're like, "Why are you doing this to yourself? You don't need that much food." And even then, if you really wanted that much couldn't you start doing something about it and getting maybe better food, not McDonald's every day for lunch?

Leslie was offended by the sight of the fat person at McDonald's eating large amounts of fattening food because she perceived it as a lack of concern for managing body weight. It seemed that for many teens I interviewed demonstrating concern about their weight was more important than actu-ally managing it effectively.

Some teens I talked with about the obesity epidemic articulated a more balanced view of the issue, acknowledging influences in the social environ-ment as well as emphasizing the role of individuals in weight management. For example, in the following interview excerpt, Jill, the plainspoken, over-weight Latina introduced earlier, blamed not only the failure of individuals to manage their weight-related behaviors but also the prevalence of fatten-ing foods and a fast-paced, demanding modern lifestyle:

Nicole: Why are Americans getting fatter?
Jill: Um, I think a lot of it has to do with fast food. They're coming out with, like, more different fast-food places to go to and that has a lot to do with it because the more fast food that's out there, the more people can go get it when they're on the run. Instead

of making the nice dinner, they go to McDonald's or Taco Bell. And some people don't have that high of a metabolism, so when they do eat it, it just sits there and it turns into fat and then a lot of people become obese. And they don't watch what else they eat. Like if you have McDonald's, maybe you have something else the next day, something healthier.

Overall, teens' responses to interview questions about high rates of obesity in the United States reflected conflicting public discourses in the media, whereby public health researchers tend to blame individuals who "refuse to do what is good for them,"[7] and nutritionists and social psychologists blame the food industry for their role in creating an ever-increasing "toxic" food environment.[8]

Stereotypes of fat people as lazy, slovenly couch potatoes who do not care about their appearance or health were prominent throughout teens' responses to interview questions about body image and the obesity epidemic. Fat stereotypes are predicated on the dual assumptions that individuals have full control over their body weight and fat people do not care enough about their appearance and/or health to maintain a socially acceptable body weight. Research shows that children as young as three years old attribute negative stereotypes to fat people, characterizing them as ugly, mean, dirty, lonely, and stupid.[9]

The adjective most frequently used by teens during interview discussions about why so many Americans are overweight or obese was *lazy*. Not only were fat individuals described as lazy, Americans in general were accused of laziness. For example, I asked Alex, a tall, slender, and articulate Goth/Punk boy who usually wore black T-shirts with punk band logos, "When you see a fat person, what are your first thoughts?" The following conversation ensued:

Alex: Average American [laughs].
Nicole: Tell me more about that. What do you mean?
Alex: Well, because America's a fat country. We're suing McDonald's
           for it. It's kind of sad.
Nicole: What do you think is making Americans fat?
Alex: Because we are just lazy. Like, if you look at the kids, I mean, none
           of us wants to go to school, and in some countries kids would
           kill to go to school. They would, you know, be ecstatic about an
           education. But we're like, "No, that's work, you know. I just want
           everything handed to me" and that sort of thing. Also fast food
           and stuff. You know, it's easier than sitting down and making
           yourself a decent meal. You know, it's easier to go up the
           drive-through at McDonald's and get yourself that super-size

fry and a Big Mac and a Diet Coke [laughs]. We're in a fat lazy epidemic right now. Way worse than SARS (severe acute respiratory syndrome).

Although Alex used the inclusive pronoun *we* to discuss the ways in which Americans in general are lazy, the underlying assumption in his commentary is that, while all Americans struggle with tendencies toward laziness, it is fat people who lose the struggle.

Closely tied to the stereotype of fat people as lazy was the perception among teens that they are also slovenly. Descriptions of fat people as lazy and slovenly were prevalent throughout interview transcripts as illustrated in the following excerpt:

Leslie: There's some people who let their bodies slip. I don't care how big you are, you need to take care of yourself.

Nicole: What are you seeing that indicates that they're not really taking care of themselves?

Leslie: Well, their hair first of all. That's the first thing I see. Like, it would look oily. And their face would just be … like, people can have a dirty look to their face. You know, when you see somebody and think, "Oh wash your face, dude." And their clothes are kind of dirty and hanging off them.

In another interview, I asked Demi, the girl with a maroon bob, to describe the kinds of guys she was attracted to. When she said she would not want to date an overweight guy, I asked her to explain, and she responded:

Cause maybe if the guy's chubbier he doesn't care about appearance. You can tell when people try to look good and stuff. Like, there's this guy in my PE class and he's chubbier, and you can tell he doesn't care at all and he doesn't want to do anything to fix it. Like, I work out, but I'm still not skinny, so that's being lazy and just not caring, too. It just bothers me. I don't like the fact that you have no interest in what you look like. I don't like that at all.

I asked Demi how she could tell the boy in her PE class did not care about his appearance, and she said, "Like, maybe his hair isn't brushed or his clothes are all wrinkly. You can tell he just picked em out of the laundry or something. Just stuff like that." Demi compared the fat boy with herself, saying that she could stand to lose some weight as well, but in her view, the key difference between the two of them was that she cared about her weight and he didn't seem to mind being fat.

Such stereotypes were further expressed during interview discussions about obesity through teens' descriptions of fat people as couch potatoes who lie around eating all day in front of the television. For example, when I asked Kirk why he thought more and more people were becoming overweight, he said, "Just goin' home, eatin', layin' on the couch the whole day." Similarly, Jesse, a tall, thin boy who hung out with the Mexicans, said about obese people, "They just sit around and do nothing." The image of the couch potato has become an iconic symbol associated with obesity in American culture. Not only is this image evoked again and again in the media, it was also frequently invoked by teens at Desert Vista. Education scholars Michael Gard and Jan Wright argue,

> The visual and verbal imagery of the "couch potato" are significant because they sum up what appear to be widely held understandings of the "obesity epidemic." In short, the "couch potato" reminds us that we are fat because we are lazy.[10]

Narratives of personal responsibility and moral failing were consistently expressed by teens at Desert Vista, illustrating the socializing power of the media and everyday discourse. Through these narratives, adolescents were able to construct their own identities in opposition to fat people. That is, criticizing others for being lazy, slovenly, and fat allowed teens to take the moral high ground and deflect attention away from their own body fat. Even if the persons taking the moral high ground were fat, they could distinguish themselves in other ways, by claiming to care about their appearance or watch what they ate, for example.

"Lose Some Weight, Tubby!"

In addition to narratives of personal responsibility, another crueler means of critiquing and blaming fat people that teens at Desert Vista engaged in was teasing and gossiping about their overweight peers. Teasing and gossiping about other people's body fat enabled many teens to draw attention away from their own bodies and construct a "thinner than" identity in comparison to the object of critique. Most on-campus teasing consisted of indirect, behind-the-back gossip, but direct, face-to-face teasing occurred as well. Both types of fat shaming were socially and emotionally damaging to the targets of such teasing.

The prevalence of obesity stigma and fat teasing among adolescents in the United States has been widely documented.[11] Adolescents report that weight-related teasing and bullying happens more frequently at school than teasing related to race, religion, or ethnicity and occurs at a similar rate as teasing for perceived sexual orientation.[12] Research shows that peers and friends are the worst perpetrators of teasing and bullying, which most commonly takes the form of verbal teasing and relational victimization (e.g., being excluded from social groups or activities, being the target of gossip and rumors) followed by cyberbullying and physical aggression.[13]

Emotional consequences associated with fat teasing among youth are serious and can reach into adulthood.[14] Overweight youth who are teased by peers are at greater risk for developing a negative body image and low self-esteem[15] and tend to have greater body dissatisfaction as adults.[16] Research also suggests that fat teasing and negative body image among youth are correlated with depressive symptoms, suicide ideation, and suicide attempts.[17]

Fat teasing was ubiquitous at Desert Vista and was not restricted to teens who were very large.[18] I was surprised to learn that anyone who displayed body fat was fair game. Teens I interviewed identified two types of fat teasing at school: direct teasing, which involved criticizing someone within their earshot and usually loudly enough for others to hear as well (e.g., "You're fat!"), and indirect teasing, or "gossip," which meant making derogatory comments about someone's appearance, behavior, or character behind that person's back (e.g., "Look at her. She's so fat.").

According to teens I interviewed, most teasing at the high school was indirect. A common scenario described was that of a group of friends commenting on the appearance of individuals who walked by them during lunch. Allie, from the Chapter 2 vignette, explained:

> We'll be at lunch and, um, my friends will notice girls that are bigger than average … and, um, sometimes they'll be like, "Well, what is she wearing?" or "Does she not know that you're not supposed to step out of the house like that?" or just stuff like that.

Another girl I interviewed also explained how most teasing was indirect: "Like, if we see a fat guy walking by and eating chips we might whisper to each other that he should stop eating those chips." Cory, the thin Goth/Punk girl with green eyes and freckled complexion, described a similar scenario: "Like, if you're with your friends, they'll be like, 'Oh look at that girl. Look how heavy she is.' It's kind of thinking out loud basically." Teens described this type of indirect teasing as a normal part of everyday conversation at the high school, behavior in which both boys and girls across social groups engaged.

Although indirect teasing appeared to be less publicly and immediately humiliating than being teased directly in front of peers, the emotional effects could be just as damaging. The targets of indirect teasing often ended up hearing what had been said about them as it spread through social networks. Cory explained, "If they're eating something, it's like, 'Look how much she's eating' or something like that. And the person a lot of times doesn't hear it, but sometimes it'll get back to em and you can tell they take it to heart a little bit."

The following interview excerpt represents a typical description teens gave of teasing that occurred at the high school:

Nicole: What about teasing? Do kids on this campus get teased for appearance, body size, or that kind of thing?

Leslie: No one will, like, go into a circle and go, "Ha ha ha you're fat!" But people will talk behind their backs.

Nicole: Tell me about that.

Leslie: Like you'd be in a circle, and let's say Suzi, the really fat girl, walks by. Everyone will get silent, and they won't go, "Ha Suzi's fat!," you know. They'll go in the circle and whisper, "Guys, she's humongous!" And the other one will go, "Yeah, I know" [whispered].

Nicole: So it's more like whispering behind the back.

Leslie: Yeah, and then you end up hearing it. So I guess it's teasing. But it's not people trying to purposely make you feel bad, I guess. It's teasing indirectly you could say.

During an interview about personal teasing experiences, Jamie, the soft-spoken overweight Goth/Punk girl, described her firsthand experience with being the target of indirect teasing: "Like, we were at this church camp or whatever and I guess he told one of his friends that I was fat and he hated me, and then I found out and I felt, like, really bad about it." Tears welled in her eyes as she recounted this painful story.

Several teens told me that teasing had been more direct in elementary and middle school than in high school, an observation supported by research on bullying behaviors among youth.[19] Leslie explained:

In elementary school, definitely it was teasing. I remember there was this one girl named Andrea, and she was this fat girl and nobody liked her because she just didn't have, like, a personality. But she just did things and the boys would throw cupcakes at her and everyone would laugh and go, "Ha ha ha ha!" It was horrible in elementary school. Kids would go home and cry. And in seventh grade it didn't really change, but nobody threw things at you. It was just like, "Oh, you're fat!" In high school it's not teasing, it's what other people say about you.

Allie described a similar transformation in teasing behavior from middle to high school:

Like, one of my friends Marissa, she gets teased, um, about being over-weight and she's, um, obese. But they call her like "the Dairy Queen" and, um, just different stuff. Now I don't see it as much, but last year [in middle school], like they'd call people "Jell-O" or stuff like that and, um, her in particular, they wouldn't let her go into certain places. Like, if we were walking they'd make her go back or turn around."

Kenny explained that when direct teasing occurs at the high school, it is often subtle to avoid teacher reprimands:

Most people nowadays, like, they're kind of afraid to do it because they're afraid to get in trouble because teachers are starting to crack down on it and make sure people don't do it. So I see people will, like, walk next to a person and whisper in their ear, and then all of a sudden the person's happiness or their face expression would just totally change. I mean, you see that in somebody's face and their eyes get kind of sad.

Others gave similar examples of disparaging comments made quickly and quietly so that teachers did not notice. Students were adapting to teachers' bullying and harassment prevention efforts by taking a more careful and subtle approach to avoid reprimand. For this reason, it was necessary to rely primarily on teens' interview accounts of both direct and indirect teasing experiences in collecting data on this topic.

Despite teens' assertions that most teasing on campus was indirect, many described vivid and brutal accounts of direct teasing they had witnessed or experienced firsthand on the high school campus. For example, one girl explained during an interview that she had seen a guy wave at a fat girl as he walked by her during lunch and say, "Do you want a wave to go with that roll [referring to her rolls of fat]?" Similarly, a boy told me that during lunch people would yell things to fat kids as they walk by, such as, "Do you know you're fat?" and "Why don't you do something about your weight?"

When I asked Kenny if he could give me examples of direct teasing on campus, he said, "Well you got 'Wide Load,' you know, that's kind of popu-lar and, um, mostly jokes like, 'You're so fat you fell through the Grand Canyon and got stuck' or something like that." Teens also described inci-dents where people would yell out, "Fat ass!" or "Lose some weight, tubby!" as a fat kid walked by. One girl told me in an interview that in her English class a boy had pointed to an elephant in an educational video the class was watching and said, "Hey, Joey looks like that elephant." This sort of public fat shaming is emotionally devastating to the victim; it demands that everyone within earshot stop whatever they are doing to closely scrutinize and judge the victim's body.

I did witness a few examples of direct teasing among teens at the high school. For example, one day while observing PE class, as students were standing around the gym waiting for directions from the teacher I heard a boy named Joshua repeatedly and loudly call his overweight classmate Kyle "Pillsbury Dough Boy." Although Kyle laughed in response, I was not convinced he thought it was funny as his laughter sounded forced. I sometimes heard students yell out insults such as "Fat ass!" during lunch or PE class. However, it occurred so quickly and in the midst of such large crowds of students that I was never able to determine who had said it to whom, a challenge I imagine teachers faced as well.

Despite these examples of direct teasing, it appeared that most fat teasing at Desert Vista was indirect, which meant that it largely went unnoticed by teachers and administrators, who might otherwise have been able to intervene or at least seek information and training on how to handle the problem. Implications of this finding suggest that schools may not realize teasing is an issue on campus or may underestimate the severity of the problem. Given previously cited research on the prevalence of fat teasing at school and the serious, long-lasting emotional impact such teasing can have on victims, school administrators should be proactive in finding ways to address verbal aggression on campus to ensure a safe learning space for all students.

The Fat Foil

At Desert Vista, I found that boys engaged most frequently in direct, weight-related teasing, with girls usually the targets. For example, during an interview about teasing, Jamie described an emotionally painful incident that involved being teased directly by a boy she liked:

> He was talking with his friends, and I walked by and he started making fun of me. I just joked around with him and made fun of him back. Cause at first he was just joking around, I guess. He probably was still joking around at the end, but then he just, like, called me fat, and I just laughed and walked away and took it to heart later on. At first I just found it funny cause that's what I usually find things like that as. But later on I just was thinking about stuff, and it made me feel kinda bad cause I didn't feel like I was accepted.

This example is illustrative of the emotional impact fat teasing can have on the person targeted.

Nicky, the overweight Latina who felt self-conscious about her double chin, explained that she had several large friends who had been teased for being fat. In particular, one of Nicky's "really big" friends had been teased a lot by boys saying things such as: "You're like the Empire State Building, just extra large!" "You hippo!" and "Get away from the vending machine!" Another of her girlfriends had been called "short and stout," "short and fat," and "love handle maker" by boys at the school.

Teens at the school primarily associated girls with indirect teasing; the concept of "mean girls" emerged as a prominent theme in interview discussions about teasing, which supports research findings about the widely held stereotype of girls as deceitful gossips.[20] Rachel Simmons, founder of the Girls Leadership Institute, writes, "Since the dawn of time, women and girls have been portrayed as jealous and underhanded, prone to betrayal, disobedience, and secrecy."[21] Though many of the teens I interviewed had, unfortunately, bought into this stereotype, I found it to be untrue. Both boys and girls at Desert Vista participated in the type of mean gossip about friends and classmates for which girls were primarily blamed.

During focus-group discussions about how boys and girls tease differently, teens often said that girls were meaner than boys and readily provided examples, as in the following excerpt from an all-girl focus group:

Anna: Girls are *terrible* to other girls.
Abbie: Like, if you wear short shorts one day then you're a slut automatically.
Linda: Yeah or they won't like you because you wear a shirt to school that they have or that they wore the same day or because supposedly one of your friends doesn't like em. Really stupid stuff. And then they just start spreading really evil rumors.

The concept of mean girls also emerged during an all-boy focus group in the context of a conversation about teasing on campus:

Reggie: I think girls can be more mean than guys at times.
Ricky: Yeah.
Reggie: Towards each other I'm sayin'. Like, starting rumors.
Ricky: Yeah.
Reggie: And sometimes movies make it seem, I don't know, but it seems like girls start a lot more rumors, and they'll make up stuff about other girls.

Although teens I interviewed overwhelmingly associated gossip with girls, some noted that boys also gossiped. Jen, the cheerleader introduced in an earlier chapter who was friends with Mia, explained:

My boyfriend has a friend named Drew, and Drew is also my best friend. Drew is just tiny, and he has no muscle. And my boyfriend will tell me, "Drew's just too small. Tell him to go to the gym and work out or something. He's just so skinny." And I'm like, "Why do you care?" [laughs] "Why do you care if he's skinny?" Or he'll tell me, "Yeah, but Jeremy's kind of fat."

A handful of teens, mostly girls, provided similar examples of how boys gossiped about each other's bodies. The stereotype of "mean girls" unfairly focuses attention on girls' behavior and obscures boys' prominent role in weight-focused victimization. Both boys and girls at Desert Vista gossiped about their classmates' bodies, but it was primarily boys who engaged in public shaming of fat teens.

Not only were girls the most frequent target of direct, weight-related teasing by boys, but girls also said that it was sometimes their own boyfriends who teased them about their bodies. Lacey, a petite blonde Goth/Punk girl who wore heavy pancake makeup and thick black eyeliner, told me during an interview that boys would sometimes say things like, "Your boobs aren't as big as hers" or "Why don't you get a tan like hers?" to their girlfriends. Sociologist Donna Eder and her colleagues argue that anxiety incited by boys' evaluation of girls' appearance fuels girls' gossip, which exacerbates girls' insecurities about the way they look,[22] something I found to be true among girls I interviewed at Desert Vista.

Sarah, the petite, quiet Latina cheerleader introduced in an earlier chapter, told me during an interview that boys sometimes tell their girlfriends to go on diets. She said that her boyfriend once said to her, "Why can't you look like your sister?" Sarah explained that her sister was very thin and that her boyfriend's comment had hurt her feelings because she felt like he was telling her to go on a diet. Jen, also a cheerleader, similarly explained that her boyfriend once grabbed the side of her stomach and said, "Look at that roll." When she told him that his comment was rude, he claimed he was just joking. Later in the interview, Jen told me that she worked hard to strengthen her stomach muscles by doing sit-ups because she wanted a "good stomach." I wondered to what extent Jen's goal to improve the appearance of her stomach was influenced by her boyfriend's comment and what the lasting effects of his "joke" would be on Jen's self-esteem.

Boys did not just give girls a hard time about their body fat; they teased each other as well. During interviews about teasing, boys often recounted direct teasing behavior they had seen in the boys' locker room. They told me that short, thin boys are called "small penis" because "the assumption is that their penis is proportionate to their body size" and that overweight boys are called "tittie boys" and told that they need to wear "man bras" because they have breasts. Boys said they have seen "scrawny" boys crammed into trashcans and lockers by larger boys and that smaller boys are routinely shoved, pushed, and tripped by larger boys as well.

One day, while observing a PE class, I noticed that all the boys had their backpacks in the gym. This was unusual as they generally stored their belongings in the locker room. One of the boys told me that the previous day during class about thirty lockers had been broken open, their contents placed in the urinal, and "peed on." The PE teacher later told me that she was not surprised by the incident because she had heard about some very cruel "hazing" incidents that had occurred in the boy's locker room.

After class that day, I was chatting with two female PE teachers in their shared office about the latest hazing incident in the boys' locker room, and one of the teachers said that earlier in the week an older boy had poured soda down the back of one of her "scrawny" freshman students in the boys' locker room. The freshman's mother called one of the assistant principals to complain about the incident and said that her son was crying all afternoon. Another of her male students had been bullied so badly in the boys' locker room that he refused to dress out for PE. The student would not reveal what had happened, just that it had been painful and embarrassing.

This kind of hazing, which occurred on a regular basis and went unchecked, made the boys' locker room an unsafe space and kept some boys from participating in PE class. It isn't only the victims who are negatively impacted by a culture of hazing. There was an air of capriciousness to the locker room aggression at Desert Vista that suggested anyone could become the next victim, causing fear and anxiety among all those who used the space. Boys told me they either avoided the locker room or tried to get in and out as quickly as possible.

When I asked girls during interviews whether or not teasing occurred in the girls' locker room, they unanimously said they had never experienced or witnessed teasing in there. My observations confirmed what they had to say, as I spent a lot of time in the female PE teachers' offices, which were located inside the girls' locker room. In fact, a few girls told stories of positive comments they had received about their bodies while dressing out. For example, one girl said other girls had told her they "wanted her abs," a comment she had clearly taken as a compliment. The female PE teachers were proud of the fact that they closely monitored the girls' locker room and attributed this to the calm, respectful culture of that space.

Although multiple pathways existed through which girls offered each other support around body image, including fat talk, clothes sharing, and occasionally complimenting each other's bodies as in the girls' locker room example cited above, in general, girls' bodies and overall appearance were harshly evaluated by both male and female peers. The widespread scrutiny and judgment of girls' bodies resulted in girls experiencing fat stigma to a greater degree than boys. Ricky from this chapter's opening vignette, explained:

Nicole: Who do you think it's worse for, fat girls or fat guys?
Ricky: Fat girls [laughs nervously].
Nicole: Why?
Ricky: Cause girls, they have to impress somebody to get guys and stuff. I think it's worse. Like, I'd rather be a fat guy than be a fat girl.
Nicole: Okay. How come?
Ricky: Just cause you'll get made fun of more by girls and guys if you're a fat girl. And it could be guys you like and stuff.

Similarly, Susan, a petite, introverted redhead with an hourglass figure and bright, blue eyes, told me that fat guys can still "get girls," explaining that Ricky always had "girls hanging off of him." She further noted that in the media "you see all of these fat rap guys who have beautiful, thin women all around them."

In general, boys were afforded a broader normative body-image range than girls. Tim, the lanky, quiet boy introduced in an earlier chapter, stated, "It's more normal for guys to be overweight. I mean, if you play football you can't be skinny. You've gotta be kind of overweight." Additionally, boys wore loose-fitting clothing that hid the details of their bulk underneath, leaving people guessing as to whether it was muscle or fat and giving them the option of showing off their bodies by lifting their shirts or flexing their muscles if they chose to do so. In contrast, girls felt pressure to wear tight clothing that showed every detail of their shape, which invited scrutiny and judgment, and there was no social space within which it was considered normal or attractive for girls to be large.

Girls faced a classic double bind in which they felt strong social pressure to wear tight, revealing clothing but were likely to be punished for doing so. They were forced to choose one of two body presentation options, neither of which positioned most of them favorably within the school's social hierarchy. Girls could either wear loose-fitting clothing that hid their body fat and risk being categorized by their peers as "boyish," or they could wear the tight clothing deemed appropriately feminine and risk being the target of teasing and gossip for allowing body fat to show.

Girls, as the primary target of weight-related critiques, were essentially the fat foil against which teens, both male and female, contrasted themselves as thinner and therefore closer to the discursively defined ideal. Since it was nearly impossible for most girls to wear the tight, revealing clothing they deemed stylish and feminine without displaying some amount of body fat, the boundary between "acceptable" and "too fat" was unclear and had to be constantly renegotiated. Most girls were potential targets for their peers' critical gaze and could be cast in the role of fat foil, which meant that girls had to constantly position themselves in contrast to this stigmatized identity category by focusing attention on other girls' body fat.

Engaging in fat gossip enabled girls to secure a higher social position but only within the context of a particular, localized conversation. Because disciplinary power situates individuals as both object and enforcer,[23] girls had to constantly reassert their "thinner-than" identity. Groups of adolescents throughout the high school were simultaneously critiquing the bodies of their female peers all day, which meant that at the very moment a girl was negotiating a "thinner-than" identity by contrasting herself with a fat foil, she could be the fat foil for another group of teens having a similar conversation only a few feet away. Thus the "thinner-than" identity was fleeting, requiring persistence to maintain.

My observation of fat as a fluid, momentary identity among most teens at Desert Vista is similar to sociologist Pascoe's finding that, for adolescent boys, the fag identity was like a hot potato that no one wanted to be left holding.[24] Like the boys in Pascoe's study, teens at Desert Vista continually hurled the stigmatized identity onto their peers for the purpose of deflecting negative attention away from themselves. They did this primarily through teasing and gossip. Though teens associated gossip with girls and direct teasing with boys, in reality the behaviors were not so clearly segregated along gender lines. While it was true that boys engaged in more face-to-face fat shaming, boys and girls both engaged in critical gossip about their peers' bodies.

"You're Fat! Just Kidding"

Teens said that among friends it was okay to "joke around" about each other's body fat. Interpreting critical commentary about one's body fat as either teasing with cruel intention or "just kidding" depended on the relationship between the speaker and object of the verbal jab. Claiming to just be kidding, however, was also a strategy used by teens to say anything they wanted without being perceived by their peers as mean. And it was a way to retreat from an awkward interaction when a teen had inadvertently gone too far and hurt a friend's feelings.

For example, one day during lunch I was sitting with a group of sophomore girls and boys in the main commons area. Two of the boys in the group were laughing as they recalled earlier comments they had made to their friend, Shelly, an average-sized sophomore girl who was also present. One of the boys, Ray, laughingly said to Shelly, "Yeah, and you freaked out when I called you fat the other day." Shelly, sounding hurt and defensive, shot back, "I can't believe you said that to me!" To which Ray, sounding uncomfortable and confused, responded, "I can't believe you are still hung up on that. You aren't fat."

Then Ray turned to me and explained, "Last week we were walking to class, and as she was going through the door I told her she wouldn't fit because she was too fat. But I was totally kidding." Shelly challenged him further by asking, "What does being fat mean to you?" He frantically scanned the courtyard to find an example of someone who was fat, but the bell signaling the end of lunch had already rung and most people were heading to their classes. After failing to find a concrete example of a fat person, Ray turned to Shelly and said, "Someone whose stomach goes out farther than their chest." She stormed away looking hurt and angry. Two days later I sat with Shelly and her girlfriends during lunch. As the girls each announced what they were going to buy for lunch, Shelly said, "I shouldn't eat because Ray called me fat" as she slumped forward over the table with her head bent down.

During interviews when I asked teens to describe teasing they had seen or experienced on the high school campus, many distinguished between teasing and "joking around." In-group fat teasing among friends was considered joking and described as "all in fun." Teasing was thought to be mean-spirited when it involved either gossiping about or teasing directly a target outside of one's social group. I found that the distinction between teasing and joking emerged primarily during interview discussions about teasing behaviors among boys.

For example, when I asked boys whether or not they had ever been teased by peers they would often qualify stories about friends teasing them with a phrase such as, "but it was all in fun" or "I knew they were just joking." This led me to wonder, were boys just joking around when they teased their friends about their body size and was this really how boys who were teased by friends interpreted their words? Or were boys who got teased by their friends putting up a brave front and pretending not to care? In individual interviews, boys shared their body-image concerns with me and sometimes admitted that getting teased about their size by friends was hurtful. My sense was that even if boys laughed along when their friends joked about their weight it really stung.

During an interview, Eddie, the Goth/Punk boy who styled his hair with a straightening iron, said he had been "a lot bigger" in the beginning of the school year than he was currently. I asked Eddie whether or not anyone used to tease him about being bigger, and he explained:

Eddie: Yeah. Like, my friends would give me a hard time about that. But it wasn't something I took serious or anything. You know, it was just something that they joked around with during lunch and stuff.

Nicole: Okay. Like, what would they say? What are some examples of how they would joke with you?

Eddie: Just, like, sometimes when I would say something that was just totally out there and just really stupid, they would just say, "Shut up. You're fat" or just somethin' stupid like that.

Nicole: Okay. So what motivated you to lose weight?

Eddie: Even though I know they didn't mean anything by it, just the fact that they were calling me fat. And I know they didn't mean anything by it at all, but that also kind of, you know, just made me want to try to lose some weight.

Nicole: You knew that they were just joking?

Eddie: Yeah.

Nicole: But does it also kind of register, too?

Eddie: Yeah, it still gets you sometimes.

Thus Eddie went to great lengths to emphasize that when his friends called him fat they were "joking around" but ultimately admitted that it hurt his feelings sometimes.

There was a widespread perception among teens that teasing was emotionally hurtful for girls but that boys could "take it." Ricky explained: "And guys, they can take it. They'll just be like, 'Yeah, whatever,' you know. Like, they don't care. And girls, they get all emotional and start crying and all that." However, my research suggests the boys were not as impervious to fat teasing as they claimed.

In this chapter's opening vignette, Ricky talks about how his friends and family jokingly call him fat, and he claims to be fine with it. Later, during an all-girl focus-group interview that included two girls who were friends with Ricky, they brought him up during a conversation about teasing. Mia and her cheerleader friend, Jen, were discussing girls gossiping about each other when I asked, "What about guys? Do they give each other a hard time?" The following exchange ensued:

Jen: Mm hm. Some guys do, like Ricky. All his friends are like, "Yeah, fat na na na." They call him fat, but he doesn't mind. He jokes around.

Mia: Yeah, he doesn't let it get to him. Like, it was me and Ricky and his cousin and they were like, "Ricky, you're leaning the car to one side." They were all like, "Get out and walk. Maybe by the time we get there you'll look like me," you know. And Ricky was all, "Shut up!"

Jen: [Laughs] I mean, they give him a hard time, but he doesn't care. Or maybe he cares, you know, but he doesn't show it. He doesn't say anything. He jokes around with them.

Mia: He's all, "I'm a fat Mexican" [laughs].

Mia and Jen acknowledged that while Ricky might feel hurt by his friends' teasing he did not "show it." Even Ricky, in this chapter's opening vignette, claimed that getting teased by friends did not bother him; instead, it was commentary about his weight by strangers that angered him. Ricky and other boys may have felt pressure to laugh along when friends made fun of them or risk being teased for taking themselves too seriously and being too sensitive.

In the following transcribed excerpt from an all-girl focus group, the participants talked about why they thought boys and girls respond differently to fat teasing:

Demi: Like, in PE class guys will just be like, "You're fat" to other guys.

Leslie: But some guys just don't take it personally. You know, it's like if you call a girl fat she'd be like [mimics a shocked and upset facial expression]. And guys, you go, "You're fat" and they go, "I know" and they, like, lift up their shirt.

Lori: I think guys are just as self-conscious about it as girls are.

Demi: Yeah.

Nicole: So what's the deal with them seeming like they're not?

Leslie: Because that's, like, the guy image.

Demi: Yeah, they don't want you to know that it hurts them, or whatever. If you call a girl fat, they'll go cry. If you call a guy fat, they're like, "Huh." Like, they just laugh about it.

Eder and her colleagues assert that the code of normative masculinity requires boys to "deny pain and suppress feelings."[25] In fact, they found that if boys responded emotionally to being teased by another boy "the exchange would immediately escalate to more serious insulting."[26] The pressure boys feel to "play it cool" when teased may have contributed to the verbally and physically abusive culture of the boys' locker room discussed earlier in this chapter. It prevents boys from reporting teasing incidents to teachers for fear of being perceived as "girly" or, even worse, "gay."

During a focus group comprised of two boys and two girls, all of whom were good friends, I witnessed firsthand friends "joking" about each other's weight:

Laura:	Tyler, you're fat enough for me.
	[All except Tyler laugh loudly. Tyler looks hurt.]
Laura:	I'm just kidding. I'm just kidding, Tyler. Tyler, I was just kidding.
Tyler:	[Pointing to his full calorie soda] Wait. I don't need this. I need to diet. I'm fat.
Laura:	If anyone's fat, it's this Cheeto [referring to a cheese flavored snack].
Tyler:	Annoying.
Laura:	What did you say?
Tyler:	Annoying.
Laura:	You're so mean.
Tyler:	You called me fat.
	[Kira and Eddie laugh.]
Laura:	I was just kidding.
	[Kira and Eddie laugh.]
Tyler:	Who's the mean one? Do I always run around and call you fat? No.
Laura:	I was just kidding.
Tyler:	Another thing that annoys me is when a girl will turn around and look at another girl that's fatter than her and then think that that girl's skinnier. Like Kira probably thinks that Laura is skinnier than her when honestly she's not.
Laura:	What?
Tyler:	No offense.
Eddie:	[To Laura] See? Now you've become a fatty all of a sudden.
Laura:	Tyler, just shut up. I'm gonna cry. When I called you fat, I was just kidding, and you're all serious.
Tyler:	Hey, I didn't call you fat. I just said–
Laura:	–Yes you did.
Tyler:	I just said you're bigger than Kira. It's just a fact of life. And then look at white skirt [referring to a girl standing nearby]. You probably think that she's skinnier than you.
Laura:	No. She's fat.
	[Everyone laughs.]

This exchange led me to wonder whether or not fat teasing was ever really interpreted by the target as just a harmless joke. Tyler was clearly very hurt by his friend's "joke" stating that he was fat. It was rare for a boy to acknowledge his pain as a result of fat joking in front of other guys. It might have felt safer for Tyler to admit hurt feelings in the face of fat joking while in the presence of girls who were close friends.

Leslie, the self-identified "non" (for non-popular); her friend Demi with a maroon bob; and her other friend Lori, a slender, tanned girl with bleach blonde hair, said the following about teasing versus joking during a focus-group interview:

Lori: I think all teasing is really mean. Like, I don't think there's anything fun about it. I mean it's just not fun. It's not nice.

Leslie: Yeah, but people do joke around. Like, people joke around with me all the time, and they're not serious.

Lori: Well, we can joke around with each other, and we'd be fine.

Nicole: Because you're friends?

Leslie: Yeah.

Demi: I think people have taken the joking around thing out of proportion cause it's bull crap if someone says something about someone else then they're like, "Oh I'm just joking." Like it probably really hurt their feelings. Do you know what I mean? Like there's joking and there's just saying you're joking. Everybody's like, "I'm just joking," but they're not.

Leslie: People can say exactly what they mean and then follow it up with, "I'm just kidding."

Communication scholars Carol B. Mills and Amy Carwile assert that ambiguity in teasing stems from the interplay between challenge and play, two necessary elements of a tease: "The ambiguity created by the juxtaposition of play and challenge creates the possibility for teasing to operate on multiple levels, and with multiple potential outcomes created by the participants of the tease themselves."[27]

Joking with friends by making jabs about sensitive, hot-button topics, like body image, is probably going to result in hurt feelings, whether teens show it or not. In this culture of hyperawareness about body image combined with media-generated idealized images that are unachievable, widespread stigmatization of fat people, and messages that body size is a choice, I imagine very few individuals are truly impervious to jokes about their body fat.

Teasing is also an example of "personalist" linguistic ideology,[28] which prioritizes the speakers' intentions over the meaning and effect of utterances, resulting in the speaker's ability to deflect responsibility for offensive utterances. That is, people can get away with calling someone fat as long as they frame the utterance as "just a joke." At this point, if the listener continues to take offense then she can be accused of taking herself too seriously. This allows someone to say anything and then avoid responsibility for the consequences by calling it a joke as the earlier exchanges between Ray and Shelly and Laura and Tyler illustrate.

In her research on girls' aggression, Rachel Simmons found that girls used humor to insult each other indirectly. She writes, "Humor is an especially popular way to injure a peer indirectly. Joking weaves a membrane of protection around the perpetrator as she jabs at a target."[29] Simmons further explains that girls who are targets for such "joking" feel pressure to hide their hurt feelings for fear of being thought of as hypersensitive. As discussed earlier in this section, teens associated this type of stoic reaction to "joking" with boys. Interview and observational data from my study reveal mixed findings. For example, girls reported voicing hurt feelings when their boyfriends made negative comments about their bodies under the guise of "just joking." Similarly, in the example above, Tyler became visibly upset when a female friend "jokingly" called him fat during a mixed-gender focus-group interview. However, I have also presented a number of examples where boys and girls both indicated that they smiled through the "joking" incident, even though it made them feel badly about themselves.

The many nuances of group dynamics likely influence how adolescents react to teasing or joking that hurts their feelings. All teens felt some degree of pressure to "play it cool" and laugh along in the face of fat teasing, but it depended on the social context. For example, close friends, such as Laura, Tyler, Eddie, and Kira from the example above, may feel more comfortable letting each other know when their jokes are hurtful. Boys may also feel freer showing emotion and vulnerability in the presence of girls. However, just as boys risked being called "gay" if they engaged in fat talk with other boys, it was also unacceptable for them to admit hurt feelings among male friends who joked about their body fat. Many teens acknowledged that jokes were often not truly meant to be playful. Couching an insult as a joke allowed the speaker to express a harsh opinion or observation about someone without being judged for it, regardless of the consequences.

Blending In

Social cliques served as protective buffers against teasing because they provided a means for teens to blend into the crowd. The degree to which an individual would get picked on when not in the presence of their social group was an indication of the social status of the group with which they affiliated. For example, it was unlikely that a Jock/Prep would get picked on while walking alone on campus because the Jocks/Preps were a powerful, high-status group. In contrast, a Goth/Punk would be a more likely target for teasing when separated from their group because the Goths/Punks were looked down on for their counterculture style and beliefs.

Consider the following two interview excerpts, the first with Kenny, the

outspoken, red-headed, Goth/Punk, and the second with Ricky, introduced in this chapter's opening vignette, along with his friend, Reggie:

(1)
Nicole: Tell me about teasing that happens on campus.
Kenny: Most people, they won't pick on anybody unless they're alone.
Like, if somebody's big and they're walking alone, they'll be like,
"Lose some weight, tubby" or they'll call em "fat ass" or some-
thing.
(2)
Nicole: Okay. Tell me which kids have the hardest time in school in terms
of getting picked on or teased.
Reggie: Like, I'd say if you hang out with people at lunch in your group,
you wouldn't really get picked on. But it's when you're walking
around just by yourself, like you're alone.

These two examples illustrate the importance of being part of a social group
and running with one's herd as much as possible to avoid standing out.

Clearly, the high status of some social groups, such as the Jocks/Preps,
provided protection for members. Kirk, the freshman quarterback who hung
out with the Jocks/Preps, explained to me during an interview why he had
never been teased at school:

Nicole: Have you ever been teased by anyone at school?
Kirk: I don't wanna be cocky or anything, but, like, I'm kinda a big-time
athlete. I'm, like, a starter on the football team. I'm the starting
quarterback, and in basketball I'm a starter. And I just don't think
people wanna say stuff and then, if they do say stuff, I think
they're probably scared of my friends.

For the Jocks/Preps, their high-status position in the Desert Vista social
hierarchy acted as a strong protective shield from direct teasing regardless
of whether they were alone or with their friends. This was true for the
Mexicans as well because their classmates perceived them as "tough," a
stance that they may have consciously enacted for this purpose.

In contrast, members of the Goths/Punks were frequent targets for direct
teasing because their group was socially marginalized, did not project a
"tough" identity like the Mexicans, flouted normative fashion trends,
appeared unconcerned with body-image ideals, and embraced difference
in general. Goth/Punk teens I interviewed recounted experiences where
their classmates called them "fat," "ugly," or "gay." Cory, the thin, freckle-
faced Goth/Punk introduced earlier, said that in PE the Jocks/Preps

sometimes called her guy friends "ladies" for being thin and lacking muscle tone.

The Goth/Punk social clique functioned as a safe space for social misfits who did not easily fit in with other groups. The Goths/Punks were also physically isolated from other major social groups, which may have provided an added layer of protection from teasing by outsiders when they gathered during lunch and other break times throughout the school day. However, during much of the school day, which required students to follow their individual class schedules, Goths/Punks were dispersed. Luke, a Goth/Punk boy who claimed not to have combed his hair in three months and sported black polish on his fingernails, explained to me during an interview that people in his group were frequently teased for being "different." He said it happened most often when they were in class "with a bunch of jocks" and did not have the protection of their group.

It is important to note that fat teasing was only part of a broader range of teasing of teens who did not align with narrowly defined appearance and behavior norms. Anyone who stood out from the crowd, both literally and figuratively, was teased by their peers, including loners, nerds, gay and bisexual teens, and people who had mental and physical disabilities. Even minor aspects of a person's behavior or physical appearance that teens perceived as "different" could incite teasing, such as wearing glasses, having a big nose, carrying the wrong type of backpack, laughing too loudly, trying too hard to fit into a group, or wearing the wrong style of shirt.

For example, Allie told me about an incident she witnessed where the teasing escalated into physical violence toward a boy simply because he was "nerdy":

Allie: Um, guys get teased because they're short and they're not cute. They get, like, pushed around and beat up. And one time this kid, they'd always make fun of him because he had a rolling backpack and because he, um, wore the strap sandals all the time. They'd always make fun of him. And one time this kid just started beating him up on the bus.

Nicole: What kind of backpack did he have?

Allie: One of those ones that you roll around.

Nicole: Oh, I see. So why were they making fun of him?

Allie: Cause he was nerdy, and he wasn't dressed right and, um, nobody liked him because of his image and so this kid just started beating him up.

In this case, the boy was not just teased but physically assaulted by another boy simply because he projected a "nerdy image."

The life of one freshman boy at the high school named Trey, who was teased relentlessly and physically assaulted by classmates for being "different," even ended tragically. A member of the Goth/Punk group, Trey was not a participant in my study, although several of his close friends were. Trey's friends described him as quiet, shy, and a little nerdy. He was short, thin, wore glasses, and had brown hair that fell over his forehead, earning him the nickname "Harry Potter." Trey was teased and physically assaulted by other boys on a regular basis for "being different." It is unclear why Trey became such a focused target of bullying, but his friends cited numerous examples of verbal and physical abuse he endured at the hands of his classmates at school, on the bus, and even in his neighborhood.

On Valentine's Day of the year I conducted fieldwork at the high school, Trey committed suicide. The day after Trey's suicide, the campus community seemed to be in a collective state of shock. Counselors were on hand in the office to offer grief counseling; groups of teens waited their turn, slouched over and silent. I sat near the Goth/Punk teens during lunch and saw a lot of spontaneous crying and hugging. A student band performed nearby in honor of "Appreciate Diversity" week and they played an REM song called "Everybody Hurts" about holding on to life in the face of despair. I listened to lyrics urging students to "hang on when you're sure you've had enough of this life" because "everybody cries and everybody hurts sometimes." I felt incredibly sad as I remembered stories these teens had told me during interviews about their experiences with being teased, and I thought about the suffering many of them probably endured in silence as a result. Trey's suicide was a powerful reminder of how turbulent and painful adolescence can be for many teenagers.

Though Trey's friends grieved his loss and continued to lean on each other for support during the remainder of the school year, I was surprised by how quickly the school community moved on from this tragedy and the minimal impact it seemed to have on campus culture. At the very least, I expected some degree of self-reflection by school teachers, counselors, and administrators to explore what could have been done to protect Trey from the relentless bullying he experienced, most of which happened on campus and on the school bus. When I asked a couple of staff members about this they leaned in, furtively looked around as if to see if anyone was within earshot, and whispered that this was not the first time a Desert Vista student had committed suicide. In fact, three students had killed themselves in the past five years, all loners who were bullied by classmates.

I asked what efforts the school was making to improve its policies on bullying and harassment as a result of these deaths and the staff members said they were not aware of any such efforts. Instead, they described a culture of silence and denial, explaining that no one talks about the suicides or the ways in which the school could have intervened to prevent them. At the time of my fieldwork, teachers and administrators at Desert Vista were focused on incidents that created obvious, major disruptions, such as fighting and physical assault. With approximately 2,000 students roaming campus during passing periods, the daily mid-morning break, and the single student lunch period, adults were mostly unable to pay attention to or address incidents of verbal harassment. During classes, teachers sometimes chastised students for teasing their classmates when they overheard the exchange, but there were no policies or procedures in place for handling teasing or bullying on campus. No narrative about the problematic nature of these kinds of behaviors existed and awareness of school bullying as an issue to be addressed had not yet infiltrated the consciousness of Desert Vista's school culture.

At the time of my study, there were few safe spaces on campus for students who were teased or bullied by their peers. The school had made some effort, such as providing Gay Alliance's SafeZone training for all staff several years prior to my research, but the resulting impact was minimal. For example, surprisingly few classrooms displayed the SafeZone sticker meant to communicate the school's commitment to ensuring a culturally competent and supportive environment that values diversity, equality, and inclusion.[30] I asked several teachers why so few of these SafeZone stickers appeared on campus and was told that many staff opposed gay rights on religious or moral grounds and therefore refused to support the program. It remains unclear to me how supporting a school culture of safety and respect for all students is a choice rather than an expectation for all school staff. Teachers who refused to support the SafeZone program and school leaders who allowed them to do so failed the students of Desert Vista. Trey's story illustrates how important it is for the entire school to be on board with maintaining a safe learning environment for every student. It is not a SafeZone if staff members get to opt out.

In 2011, seven years after Trey's suicide, the School Board formally adopted a policy defining bullying and harassment and outlining procedures for reporting and addressing incidents. In 2013 Desert Vista created an action plan to improve school climate that included reducing the percentage of students who report harassment and bullying as an objective. In 2015 the school implemented a twenty-four hour tip-line enabling students and parents to anonymously report campus incidents related to bullying, drugs, alcohol, weapons, and violence. These are all steps in the right direction but also exemplify the painfully slow process of enacting change within institutions.

Teens at Desert Vista stigmatized divergence from narrowly constituted gender and body-image norms, especially fatness, often drawing on media-generated stereotypes of fat people as lazy and sloppy. They teased and gossiped about their classmates' bodies as a way of marking difference and drawing attention away from their own body fat. Earlier research has illustrated how girls define and reinforce ideas about what it means to be a socially appropriate girl through gossip[31] and how boys gossip as a way to assert themselves as heterosexual males.[32] Gender studies scholar Barrie Thorne claims teasing also functions as "borderwork" by maintaining boundaries and asymmetries between social groups.[33]

My findings align with these theories on teasing, social norms, and "borderwork." Teens at Desert Vista used direct and indirect teasing to negotiate and define the perceptual boundaries between bodies that were "acceptable" and bodies that were "too fat." Direct teasing functioned as a very explicit and public way for adolescents to mark someone who displayed too much body fat as "other," while indirect teasing allowed teens to more subtly co-construct and circulate knowledge about body-size norms among their friends through constant surveillance, evaluation, and verbal critique of their peers. By engaging in running commentary about their peers' bodies, teens continually negotiated body-fat norms against which they measured themselves and each other.

Fat stigma is another area where education in media literacy is needed. Youth must learn how to think critically about the patterned ways in which fat people are represented in the media and the negative stereotypes that become codified through these representations. The teens in my study were largely unaware of the ways in which they reinforced unrealistic body image norms and punished themselves and their peers for failure to adhere to narrow, unattainable ideals. The daily appearance-based gossip and teasing that students engaged in was such a normal part of conversational chatter that it was rendered practically invisible. One way to bring awareness to these harmful dynamics is through explicit counter messages to mainstream media images that set the impossible standard and demonize those who deviate from it. In the next chapter I expand the discussion on body image to explore how it impacts teens' willingness to participate in physical education class, a space where bodies are the focal point and scrutiny extends beyond appearance to include performance.

Notes

1. Bordo, 1993:203.
2. Boero, 2012; Kwan, 2009; Kwan and Graves, 2013; Lawrence, 2004; Saguy, 2013; Saguy, Gruys, and Gong, 2010; Saguy and Gruys, 2010.
3. Boero, 2012; Kwan and Graves, 2013; Greenhalgh, 2015; Saguy, 2013; Sobal, 1995.
4. Goffman, 1963:43–44.
5. Lawrence, 2004.

6. Counihan,1992.
7. Gard and Wright, 2005:7.
8. Brownell, 1994; Horgen and Brownell, 2002; Schwartz and Brownell, 2007; Wadden, Brownell, and Foster, 2002.
9. Harriger *et al.*, 2010; Holub, Tan, and Patel, 2011; Lehmkuhl, Nabors, and Iobst, 2010; Margulies, Floyd, and Hojnoski, 2008.
10. Gard and Wright, 2005:22.
11. Eisenberg, Neumark-Sztainer, and Story, 2003; Griffiths and Page, 2008; Puhl and Latner, 2007; Neumark-Sztainer, Story, and Faibisch, 1998; Strauss and Pollack, 2003.
12. Puhl, Luedicke, and Heuer, 2011.
13. Puhl, Peterson, and Luedicke, 2013.
14. Thompson *et al.*, 2005.
15. Crocker and Garcia, 2005; Eisenberg, Neumark-Sztainer, and Story, 2003.
16. Grilo *et al.*, 1994.
17. Dave and Rashad, 2009; Eisenberg, Neumark-Sztainer, and Story, 2003.
18. See also Taylor, 2011.
19. Macklem, 2003.
20. Brown, 1998; Eder, Evans, and Parker, 1995; Nichter, 2000; Simmons, 2002.
21. Simmons, 2002:16.
22. Eder, Evans, and Parker, 1995.
23. Foucault, 1975/1977.
24. Pascoe, 2007.
25. Eder, Evans, and Parker, 1995:72.
26. Eder, Evans, and Parker, 1995:74.
27. Mills and Carwile, 2009:286.
28. Duranti, 1993; Hill, 2008.
29. Simmons, 2002:78.
30. Gay Alliance, 2012.
31. Coates, 1999; Eckert, 1993.
32. Cameron, 1997; Johnson and Finlay, 1997; Kiesling, 2002.
33. Thorne,1992, 1993.

4

"WHEN I RUN MY LEGS JIGGLE"

Jamie, a fourteen-year-old freshman at Desert Vista who hung out with the Goths/Punks, had endured fat teasing from friends, family, classmates, and boys she liked since the sixth grade. Jamie had very low self-esteem as a result. She usually sat hunched over the table as we talked, her dark blonde hair hanging down over her face, gaze cast downward, mumbling her answers to questions, and often second guessing herself, especially when she expressed a strong opinion. Jamie almost always wore skin-tight faded blue jeans with an oversized sweater or sweatshirt and white tennis shoes.

Jamie told me that she was five feet four and weighed 150 pounds, which is considered overweight for a girl her age by the Centers for Disease Control and Prevention. Jamie hated her stomach because she said it "jiggled" when she moved and flowed over the waistband of her pants. When I interviewed Jamie and asked her to rate how satisfied she was with the way her body looked on a scale of one to five with five being the most satisfied, she responded "Three," explaining that she liked her hair, face, and small hands but disliked her "chunky" stomach and thighs and her big feet. She felt like she was fatter than most of her close friends and was self-conscious about wearing larger clothing sizes than they did. Earlier, on the screener, Jamie had penciled in "negative 100" next to the question about her level of body satisfaction.

Jamie explained that she had been about ten pounds heavier at the beginning of the school year when she had completed the screener. She had lost weight by eating less. In fact, she endeavored to cut out meals entirely and only eat snacks throughout the day. For example, she skipped both breakfast and lunch most days, instead snacking on a bagel and cream cheese or cookie, a soda, and a bag of chips at school. Other snack favorites included pizza, ice cream, peanut butter and crackers, salad, and fruit. Instead of buying lunch, Jamie would often eat bites of her friends' food as a strategy for consuming fewer calories. Sometimes she would try to avoid eating at school altogether. On those days, Jamie was so hungry by the time she got home after school she would binge on whatever she could find to eat in the house.

Jamie had also started exercising more since the beginning of the school year. At the suggestion of one of her girlfriends, Jamie occasionally did sit-ups and push-ups at home in the evenings. She found these exercises boring and therefore had a hard time sticking with the routine. Jamie was trying to walk more instead of sitting around the house so much. On the weekends, she found friends to walk with her to the convenience store or stroll around the mall. Jamie played in a roller-blading hockey league during the spring. They practiced once a week and competed against other teams once a week. She had played hockey since she was seven and really enjoyed it.

Jamie had earned a "D" in PE class the first semester of ninth grade because she had never participated. She had felt self-conscious running or moving her body in shorts because she had been concerned that the fat on her thighs and stomach would visibly jiggle and that she would mess up her hair. She had PE class in the middle of the day and didn't want to have sweaty, stringy looking hair all afternoon. The second semester Jamie participated a little more actively for several reasons. First, she really wanted to lose weight and understood the importance of regular exercise in achieving that goal. Jamie's best friend, Alyssa, was also in the class with her second semester and encouraged her to participate more actively. Having a good friend to exercise alongside made Jamie feel safer and more comfortable participating. Finally, the teacher expressed concern about Jamie's failing grade and met with her several times to brainstorm ways for her to be more active that felt reasonable for her.

Jamie felt that losing weight could open up possibilities for a whole new way of life; she would get teased less, be treated more respectfully in general, attract positive attention from boys, and feel freer to try new things:

> Like, I've had my eye on this one guy and I just figured that if I lost weight he'd see me better or whatever. Like, I don't know, it seems like a lot of thin girls get a lot more respect than big girls do and with more respect they get more guys attracted to them. And, like, if I was thinner I could be more open to things and try a lot of new stuff cause whenever I wear any kind of clothes I kind of try to hide my stomach in any way possible so I'm not really open to doing that much stuff. And, like, just the other day I heard somebody make fun of me,

or whatever, behind my back; they called me fat. My friend told me.
So, that kind of made me want to lose weight, too.

In the last chapter, two instances in which Jamie had been teased by boys
she liked—once behind her back at church camp and another time to her
face in front of a group of friends at school—were described.

Jamie's mom, who was also overweight, had purchased diet products for
Jamie and criticized her for her body size. Jamie described one particularly
painful incident:

> Like, I was just wearing this shirt that I used to wear all the time and
> I was just outside my house hanging out with my friends. I was outside
> talking to one of the guys I used to like a lot, and then my mom
> came out from the house and pulled me away and just told me that I
> looked fat and I should, like, watch out what I wear and so the rest
> of the night I didn't talk to her cause I was really mad.

I asked Jamie how her mom's words had made her feel, and she responded,
"Pretty bad. Like, when my mom said it I felt really bad cause I didn't
think she'd ever go so low as to say that."

Even Jamie's best friend's parents had been critical of her body size.
Jamie's best friend, Alyssa, also a Goth/Punk, was petite and thin with
long dark hair, big brown eyes, and a wide smile that lit up her whole face.
Jamie said that recently she had been hanging out at Alyssa's house and
overheard the girl's parents talking in the next room about how they wanted
their daughter to "have friends who were more her size." Jamie felt crushed
by this and worried that she might lose her best friend, so she asked Alyssa
about it the next day. Alyssa admitted that her parents had been pressur-
ing her to hang out with a different crowd but assured Jamie that her parents
were "just going through a rude phase" and that it would pass.

When I asked Jamie how she handled the emotional pain around getting
teased and criticized for her body size, she said she had learned to preemp-
tively make fun of her body fat in front of others to beat them to it:

> Like, in sixth grade they would say something mean, and then I'd
> run off and start crying. And since then I learned—I don't know
> where. I don't know if it was my parents or just experience—that,
> like, when I put myself down more I protect myself against rude
> comments toward me cause I'm used to them already. So I make fun
> of me cause then when people laugh and joke around about it, it does-
> n't really hurt me anymore. If I make fun of my stomach first and then
> they say something mean, I can just laugh and make fun of them,

too, and then usually we all laugh and stuff. It just hurts less if I say it first.

* * *

Jamie's story, like those of other teens highlighted in chapter vignettes, provides a window into the interconnectedness of body image, self-esteem, fat teasing, food consumption, and exercise practices. For Jamie, her body-image concerns and getting teased for her weight resulted in low self-esteem and impacted many aspects of her life. Jamie believed that if she lost weight she would be happier, have more friends, and be treated with more respect. To that end, she tried to watch what she ate and exercise more but faced challenges at school that impeded her progress. Additionally, Jamie did not participate in PE class the first semester because she felt too self-conscious about how her body looked while she exercised. Her inability to control junk food consumption and manage her body fat through exercise negatively impacted the way Jamie felt about her body.

This part of my study focuses on teens' perceptions about, and participation in exercise, how it differed for boys and girls, and how their beliefs about and participation in exercise were related to body image, gender stereotypes, and fatness. I also consider how differences in the degree to which boys and girls felt motivated, encouraged, and entitled to occupy physical space translated to their participation in exercise and sports and the extent to which these ways of moving were reproduced and resisted by teens. Many teens I interviewed were not able to exercise outside of school due to lack of transportation and other obligations, such as after-school jobs, baby-sitting younger siblings, house chores, and homework, making PE class their only opportunity to engage in physical activity.

It is estimated that only about half of youth get the recommended sixty minutes of vigorous- or moderate-intensity physical activity every day. Since rates of physical activity decline with age, teens are much less likely to meet the recommended guidelines than younger children. Moreover, physical education requirements in schools have been on the decline since the passage of the No Child Left Behind Act in 2001. As a result of increased demand for better standardized test scores coupled with fiscal pressures resulting in teacher layoffs and a lack of equipment and other resources, nearly half of school administrators have reported cutting significant time from PE classes and recess to devote more time to core subjects, such as English and math.[1]

According to the Institute of Medicine (IOM), high school students across the nation average two PE classes per week with each class providing only ten to twenty minutes of vigorous- or moderate-intensity physical activity at best. The IOM has recommended that the US Department of Education make PE a core subject and that schools add additional opportunities for physical activity throughout the school day in the form of recess, classroom activity breaks, intra and extra mural sports, promotion of active commuting to and from school, and "open gym" or walking programs before school.[2]

Many states have policies requiring PE as part of the curriculum, but schools seldom adhere to time allocation guidelines and these policies are not well monitored or enforced.[3] Federal policy has focused less on physical education than on school food, which may be one reason why fewer gains have been made in improving physical education in schools nationwide. For example, in 2004 the US government issued a mandate requiring schools districts that receive funds under the Child Nutrition and WIC Reauthorization Act of 2004 to establish a school wellness policy. This mandate required districts to develop specific goals for improving nutrition education, school food, and physical activity, but not physical education specifically.

Increasing opportunities for exercise at school is an important first step in helping youth achieve the recommended 60 minutes of physical activity daily, but we also need to understand how youth feel about exercising in front of their peers at school, the degree to which they are willing to engage in such activities, what facilitates their participation in physical activity at school, and what stands in the way. I found that boys and girls participated very differently in PE and this chapter explores what teens had to say about that.

Hogging the Ball

At Desert Vista, all freshmen were required to take one year of PE. Beyond this requirement, students could choose to take elective exercise classes, such as aerobics, strength and conditioning, and dance. All of the freshman PE classes were co-ed, with an enrollment of twenty-five to thirty-five students. Five of the six PE teachers followed a traditional curriculum that focused on team sports such as softball, football, basketball, lacrosse, team handball, and tennis. One teacher replaced team sports two days a week with "body-sculpting" exercises, which consisted of running a mile or more and doing strengthening exercises, such as sit-ups, push-ups, leg lifts, squats, and lunges.

Much of my time at Desert Vista High School was spent observing and participating in PE classes. Early in my field research during a series of "open gym" days, I noticed that boys and girls tended to participate in PE quite differently. "Open gym" usually occurred when it was raining outside, forcing all of the PE classes to converge in one gymnasium. During "open gym," teachers brought out various types of balls and equipment and set up the gym for a couple of sports options, usually basketball and volleyball. Students were allowed to engage in any activity they chose for the duration of the class period.

During "open gym," what initially appeared to be random, frenzied activity turned out to yield important information about the ways in which boys and girls engaged differently in PE class. Once I was able to tune out balls flying through the air, kids dashing around the floor, and headache-inducing noise levels, I began to discern a pattern whereby the majority of girls would sit, stand, or stroll around the edges of the gym talking in small groups while most of the boys actively played basketball and volleyball in the middle of the gym.

During organized sports activities throughout the year, I also noticed that boys participated more actively than girls, especially during team sports. While boys focused intently on the game and physically exerted themselves, often working up a sweat, girls tended to stand around watching and flirting with the boys. PE teachers' frequent encouragement of girls who were just standing around to participate more actively often went unheeded as girls either responded with excuses or simply ignored their teachers.

During team sports activities, I frequently observed girls giggle or squeal as they tried half-heartedly to obtain the ball or prevent the other team from scoring. More often, I saw girls moving aside to avoid an approaching ball rather than trying to catch or block it. Sometimes girls employed unconventional techniques to gain the upper hand in a game. For example, during a mixed-gender game of lacrosse I observed several girls flirting with boys from the opposing team in an attempt to distract the boys from the game so they could obtain the ball more easily. The girls would pat boys' rear ends with their lacrosse sticks and place their sticks between boys' legs, making the boys laugh. They would then take advantage of the distraction they had created to get the ball. When the girls caught the ball, they would hold it to their chests or cradle it like a baby and giggle while running away from opposing team members.

Boys and girls participated differently, in part, because of societal expectations and gender norms that teach girls and boys to occupy and move through space differently. Gender scholars such as Iris Young,[4] Sandra Lee Bartky,[5] and R. W. Connell[6] argue that gender norms are literally embodied in how we move through the world and occupy the space around us. Young's classic study on gendered bodily comportment in sports participation suggests that girls' body movement tends to be more restricted than that of boys. Young asserts, "Women tend not to reach, stretch, bend, lean or stride to the full limits of their physical capacities."[7] Moreover, Young observes that women do not occupy the entire physical space available to them, which further limits their range of motion and engagement in physical activity. She writes, "For many women as they move in sport, a space surrounds them in imagination which we are not free to move beyond; the space available to our movement is a constricted space."[8]

Feminist scholar Sandra Bartky expands Young's analysis to explore gendered bodily comportment more broadly. She describes a 1979 art exhibit by photographer Marianne Wex in which thousands of candid photographs of people in their daily lives depicted the ways in which men and women occupy space differently:

> Women sit waiting for trains with arms close to the body, hands folded together in their laps, toes pointing straight ahead or turned inward, and legs pressed together ... Men, on the other hand, expand into the available space; they sit with legs far apart and arms flung out at some distance from the body.[9]

Both Young and Barkty discuss the ways in which women are socialized to occupy space and move their bodies in ways that limit and constrain their engagement with the world around them.

In contrast, scholar R. W. Connell focuses on how boys are socialized through participation in sports to feel entitled to engage actively and assertively with the world around them. She writes: "To be an adult male is distinctly to occupy space, to have a physical presence in the world."[10] Connell points out that sports help socialize boys into heteronormative masculinity by teaching them how to demonstrate force, which she defines as "the irresistible occupation of space" and skill, which she defines as "the ability to operate on space or the objects in it (including other bodies)."[11] My observations of mixed-gender sports activities during PE class at the high school resonate with Young's, Bartky's, and Connell's assertions about gender differences in bodily comportment. Boys seemed less inhibited, more confident, and more entitled to actively and competitively engage in activities than girls, who stood around fidgeting, chatting, and appearing uncertain about how to participate.

Yet the ways in which boys and girls are socialized to move through and occupy space differently tell only part of the story. When I interviewed girls about their attitudes toward PE, I learned that most felt marginalized and excluded during mixed-gender sports activities. Many girls told me that boys would only pass the ball to other boys, making it difficult for girls to get involved in the game. When I asked Allie from the Chapter 2 vignette how she felt about having boys and girls together in PE class, she replied, "Sometimes the guys leave the girls out a lot. Like the girls really want to play and they leave us out because they don't think that we can handle it." Allie's comment is representative of what most of the girls I interviewed said about their experiences in PE class.

Both boys and girls frequently expressed the stereotype that boys are more skillful than girls when it comes to sports and athletics. In the following transcript excerpt, Demi, the confident girl with a maroon bob introduced earlier, explains why she thinks girls do not participate as actively as boys:

Nicole: What would you change about PE if you could?
Demi: I think there should be just girls' PE and just guys' PE cause you've got, like, the big guys that wanna play all tough and stuff and you've got, like, the girls that wanna play, but they can't because the guys are all over the ball and stuff.
Nicole: Okay. So do you think that the co-ed nature of classes kind of discourages girls from participating?
Demi: Yeah.
Nicole: What is it about the guys' presence in PE that causes girls to participate less do you think?
Demi: They just feel less qualified I guess.

Demi initially explained the difference by drawing on the stereotype of tough, aggressive guys who take over the game, but upon further reflection she added that girls tended to hold back because they lacked confidence in their athletic ability.

Australian sociologist Lois Bryson argues: "Negative evaluations of women's capacities are implicit in the masculine hegemony in which sport is embedded. This has the effect of promoting male solidarity through the exclusion process, which provides support and fuel for negative male attitudes towards women. Women themselves finish up accepting that men are more capable than they are."[12] At Desert Vista, boys' explicit exclusion of girls from mixed-gender team sports in PE was a contributing factor for why girls felt "less qualified" to play.

When I asked boys whether or not there were differences in how boys and girls participated in PE, most reiterated what girls had said about boys engaging more actively:

Nicole: Do the guys and girls in your PE class participate differently?
Tim: Yeah.
Nicole: How so?
Tim: Uh, like, all the girls won't run all the time.
Tad: Yeah.
Tim: Like, they won't play basketball. They don't always participate,

and the guys always wanna play. We'll be playing, and they'll be watching.

Tad: Yeah, they'll just sit there and talk to each other.

In contrast to the girls I interviewed, who blamed their lack of participation on boys' domination of the ball during games, boys blamed girls for their own passivity. As in the transcript excerpt below, boys often claimed that girls did not want to participate:

Nicole: Do guys and girls participate differently in PE?
Reggie: Yeah.
Ricky: Guys are more active. We're more into the sports than girls.
Reggie: Yeah.
Ricky: Like, some girls are into it, but some girls are just like, "Oh, no I don't wanna play. I can't hit the ball" [spoken in high pitched, mock whiny tone].
Reggie: They're like, "I can't do that." Cause we had to run eight laps, you know, in Miss Wyatt's class and some girls will be like, "Oh I can't do it. I'm not gonna do it" and stuff.

In this focus-group transcript segment, the boys suggest that girls choose not to participate in PE because girls feel inept when it comes to sports.

Earlier, I quoted Demi as saying that girls participate less actively than boys in mixed-gender sports activities because girls feel less qualified in the presence of boys. While Reggie, Ricky, and Demi all appear to be saying the same thing, there is a subtle and important distinction. Whereas Demi attributed girls' feelings of athletic ineptitude to boys' domination of the games, boys I interviewed did not acknowledge their own role in girls' lack of participation. Boys did not appear to be aware that girls felt excluded by them; instead, boys thought girls did not want to participate and drew on stereotypes of girls as whiny and unskilled with sports to explain the phenomenon. PE teachers could address this issue early in the year by teaching girls how to actively engage in the game and encouraging, or even requiring, boys to pass the ball to girls. Team-building activities that emphasize sportsmanship and healthy competition are an important strategy for facilitating greater inclusion of all students in PE activities.

"It's Just a Game!"

Another reason girls cited for not actively participating in PE was that they did not view it as a forum for serious competition. According to Jill, the plainspoken, overweight Latina introduced earlier, playing a team sport in

PE was "just a game for a grade," while boys treated it as serious competition:

Nicole: Are there, like, patterns of participation with guys and girls?
Jill: Guys really participate more and take it seriously. Like, they get mad if you miss.
Nicole: And how do you feel about that?
Jill: I mean, I don't really think it's necessary to get all mad because, I mean, it's not like you're playing professionally or anything. It's just a game for a grade. I think they take it a little too seriously.
Nicole: Has anyone ever gotten mad at you for missing a point or a goal or anything like that?
Jill: Not really. No, usually the guys get mad at the guys for doing that.
Nicole: Why do you think that is?
Jill: I think they think the girls don't really care about the game and that they're not into it. Like, in basketball guys only pass to each other and not really to the girls.

Although girls appeared to lack competence and competitive drive during mixed-gender sports, on the rare occasions when boys and girls were separated in PE I saw girls actively and skillfully compete against each other in an effort to win.

During an interview discussion about gendered differences in PE participation, Cory, the petite, insightful Goth/Punk girl introduced earlier, explained that girls are capable of excelling in sports, but they do not take PE seriously and therefore do not put forth much effort:

Nicole: Do boys and girls participate in PE differently?
Cory: Boys just kinda play, and, I don't know, they don't hold back, I guess. Whereas, like, if a girl doesn't want to do something she'll just sit there and won't do anything.
Nicole: So, like, the girls don't necessarily play as hard?
Cory: Yeah. Although in track they do.
Nicole: Do you think for girls it matters whether or not it's a school-sponsored sport or PE class?
Cory: Well, yeah, if their heart's really in it and if they really want to do it then they'll push themselves. But just for PE they don't think it really counts I guess.

Cory differentiates between competing in PE and competing in extracurricular sports. She contrasts the girls on her track team, who "push themselves" with girls in her PE class, who "won't do anything." Here,

Cory reiterates what Jill said earlier about girls seeing PE as "just a class" and not a forum for serious competition.

In contrast, boys clearly viewed PE as a forum for showing off their athletic skills and competing against one another. Jesse, the tall, thin Latino boy who hung out with the Mexicans, told me boys were competitive in PE, which is similar to what most boys said. When I asked Jesse why, he replied, "I don't know. It's fun to show off your skills, just show each other up." Another boy said that while girls run as little as possible in PE "guys try to run the mile as fast as they can and try to push themselves." Girls observed similar competition among boys during PE, often describing boys as "trying to impress everyone" and "showing off" in an effort to athletically outdo other boys.

The intense competition with which many boys approached PE sports activities was immediately apparent to me. In contrast to girls, who typically did not exert enough physical effort to break a sweat, boys were often sweaty, flushed, and out of breath by the end of PE class. During games, I often heard boys make comments to each other, such as, "You suck," "You run like a girl," and "I bet you can't hit that." After a game, boys on the winning team would gloat to boys on the opposing team, saying things like "Ha, we beat you!" to which I once heard a boy reply, "Oh, that was just my practice round."

In addition to actively competing in organized sports activities during PE, I often saw boys devise various impromptu competitions during free time in PE, an observation that resonates with previous research on gendered play.[13] For example, one day in Mrs. Wyatt's PE class, students finished a written exam about the rules of basketball early and had fifteen minutes of free time at the end of the period. While most of the girls stood around talking with each other, a group of boys competed to see who could climb to the highest part of a peg-board on the wall. Another group of boys competed to see who could jump up and touch the highest point on a nearby basketball hoop, and a third group of boys competed to see who could run up the gym bleacher steps the fastest.

For many boys, even those who hung out with non-mainstream groups like the Goths/Punks, demonstrating athletic skill was an important part of constructing heteronormative masculine identities. Despite the fact that some Goth/Punk boys appeared to reject normative gender ideals by wearing black clothing, having longish hair, and sporting black nail polish, these same boys admitted to me that they wanted to be physically strong, lean, and toned. This is an example of the complex and often contradictory nature of identity construction. These contradictions represent sites of struggle between aligning with and deviating from social norms.

My observation data suggest that girls felt freer to compete during

PE sports activities when boys were not involved in the game. When girls only played with and competed against each other they actively engaged without fear of being scrutinized and judged for their athletic performance or how their bodies looked. Girls' sense of self was not tied to the outcome of their performance in PE as it was for boys, which resulted in competitive play that had a much more relaxed, fun feel to it. PE teachers I talked with told me that their students performed better in class when boys and girls were separated during activities. For this reason, the teachers occasionally separated boys and girls during team sports.

One day I walked out to the soccer fields to observe Mrs. Roy's final PE class of the day. As I approached, I saw her assembling groups for team handball and passing out equipment to students. I noticed that she had separated the boys and girls and had sent the boys to the other side of the field to play. She excitedly told me that this would be a fun class for me to watch because the girls "get really feisty with this game." In fact, she warned me to stay clear of the field because "they get rough." I was intrigued by her words and a bit skeptical because I had yet to see girls "get really feisty" during any PE activity.

I witnessed a considerable change in the way the girls played team handball that day. The girls engaged in genuine athletic competition, chasing each other in an effort to obtain the ball, diving for the ball, and throwing themselves in front of the goal to block the other team from scoring. They were alert and focused, calling out directives to team members, such as "pass me the ball," "watch out on your left," and "go right!" I was struck by the confidence these girls exuded as they played team handball, all of the self-consciousness that I had previously witnessed gone. At the end of class, the girls' faces were flushed. They were sweaty, some of them had grass stains on their clothes, and they were laughing as they recounted highlights from the game.

Later that spring I interviewed Mia, who had played team handball in Mrs. Roy's class that day. I asked her if she preferred to exercise with girls or guys, and the following conversation ensued:

Mia: Girls.
Nicole: How come?
Mia: Like, in PE if Mrs. Roy will put all the girls in a game then the girls actually participate. Like, I don't remember what game we were playing, but we wouldn't do anything cause, you know, the guys would only pass to the guys, and the girls don't wanna embarrass themselves. But when she put all of the girls together we were, like, tackling each other during the game.

Nicole: I saw that.
Mia: Yeah.
Nicole: When you were playing team handball, right?
Mia: Yeah, that's what it was. And, like, we'd all go attack Marie and
          she'd fly down. We got all rough. It was, like, so much funner than
          with guys. With guys, you know, you're prepping up to make
          sure you still have the lip gloss in your pocket and stuff.

Mia's sentiments about co-ed PE are representative of what most girls said. Only a few girls told me they liked co-ed PE because it allowed boys to see that girls can be good at sports, the same girls who attempted to actively participate in PE activities on a regular basis.

Girls' comments that PE was "just a class" and not a forum for serious athletic competition may have functioned as a defensive strategy against boys who accused them of "doing nothing" and being "lazy" in PE. During a mixed-gender focus group, I asked participants whether or not boys and girls participate differently in PE. Eddie, the Goth/Punk boy who straight ironed his hair, said, "Girls, for the most part, refuse to run too much. They refuse to do anything too much. Girls will do the bare minimum to get passed." As a result, the majority of girls missed out on an important opportunity to get some exercise.

Kira, the lanky Goth/Punk girl with red and black hair, replied, "I have an 'A' in there, stupid! Anyway, what's the point? What are we running for? Absolutely nothing." Kira justified her passive participation in PE, portraying herself as smarter and more practical than the boys in her class because, while they exerted effort unnecessarily she exerted minimal effort and still earned an "A" in the class. The implicit message in Kira's argument is that she could compete if she wanted to, but she chose not to because the payoff was not sufficient to merit her effort.

Girls and boys approached PE very differently because they were invested differently in athletic competition. For boys, showing skill in sports was an important part of displaying heteronormative masculinity. PE represented an arena for boys to show off, outperform each other, and prove their manhood. Given this, it is not surprising they did not pass the ball to girls; incorporating girls into the game would get in the way of showing off their skills. Girls enjoyed competing for fun when they were separated from the boys. They had less to prove on the field because athletic skill was not tied to normative feminine identity. Instead, girls competed more fiercely with each other off the field to achieve the best body and look more attractive than their friends in clothes.

"Does My Hair Look Okay?"

My research showed that concern about messing up their hair and makeup and anxiety about how their bodies looked while exercising kept girls from actively participating in PE, a finding that is not surprising in light of the pressure girls felt to look cute constantly. I became aware of these possibilities one particularly hot afternoon in September as I stood outside watching students run around the track. It was one of those blazing hot days when the temperature was above 100 degrees and the air was completely still with no breeze to offer relief. Sweat began to dampen my hair and trickle down the sides of my face, and I dreaded feeling sticky and gross for the rest of the day. Given these conditions, I wondered whether students, especially girls, worried about messing up their perfectly applied makeup and carefully styled hair while exercising in PE.

Consequently, as part of the second interview, I asked teens what kinds of things they worried about during PE to understand the extent to which appearance- and hygiene-related concerns might impact their level of participation. Boys and girls who had PE early in the morning told me they did not worry about sweating because it was still fairly cool at that time of day. Those who had PE during the last period of the day also said they did not worry about getting sweaty because they could go home and shower right after class. However, students who had PE during the middle part of the day expressed concerns about sweating, smelling for the remainder of the school day, and messing up their hair.

The potential for hair becoming messed up during participation in PE seemed to be the primary concern for girls. Some girls said they rushed to change back into their school clothes as quickly as possible after PE so they would have time to restyle their hair before going to their next class. However, by the time students walked back to the locker rooms from the playing fields or gym at the end of PE they typically had less than ten minutes to change clothes and primp before heading out to their next class. During the year I conducted fieldwork, stick-straight hair was in vogue, which meant that many of the girls spent a great deal of time and effort each morning styling their hair with flat irons. For example, Allie, from the Chapter 2 vignette, spent over an hour each morning straightening her long, wavy hair.

Demi said her hair was "her thing." She explained that she colored it regularly, taking great care to touch up the roots, and straightened it every morning with a flattening iron. When I asked Demi if she worried about anything during PE, she responded, "Um, I usually don't wear makeup, so that's not really an issue. Like my hair, I'm really picky about that, so yeah. Like, if my hair gets messed up I freak out." I asked Demi whether or not her hair-related concerns ever affected her level of participation in PE and she replied, "Sometimes. It depends. Like, if it's windy and my hair's going everywhere, I'll stop and fix it. I don't care if the ball's coming. Like, [laughs] that's just kind of how I am."

Regarding implications of such dogged attention to details of appearance, feminist philosopher Sandra Bartky writes:

> The woman who checks her makeup half a dozen times a day to see if her foundation has caked or her mascara has run, who worries that the wind or the rain may spoil her hairdo, who looks frequently to see if her stockings have bagged at the ankle or who, feeling fat, monitors everything she eats, has become, just as surely as the inmate of the Panopticon, a self-policing subject, a self committed to a relentless self-surveillance.[14]

The Panopticon in the quote above refers to a type of prison architecture developed in the eighteenth century marked by an elevated watchtower at the center from which all prisoners could be seen. Prisoners were segregated under the watchtower, unable to communicate with each other or guards and never certain about whether or not they were being observed.

French philosopher Foucault co-opted the Panopticon as a metaphor for disciplinary power in the modern state, a process involving the differentiation of individuals, hierarchical observation, and normalizing judgment that is initially imposed externally and eventually becomes internalized by individuals who police themselves.[15] Influences like media-generated, airbrushed images of thin, seemingly flawless women as well as medical standards like the body mass index that define "normal" body weights, are examples of externally imposed appearance standards. These girls' concerns about their hair, makeup, and body image during PE illustrate the extent of their unconscious commitment to the "relentless self-surveillance" about which Bartky has written.

Although getting hair messed up during PE was the primary concern for girls I interviewed, some girls did worry that their makeup would get messed up. Mia, for example, told me that she reapplied makeup "nonstop" throughout the day and rarely let anybody see her without it. She explained to me during an interview that she worried about her makeup smearing during PE:

Nicole: What do you think of PE?
Mia: I think it'd be better if, during games and stuff, they'd put, like, all of the girls on one side. Also in the summer here it's so hot and they make you run.

Nicole: So you don't want to have to run outside when it's hot?

Mia: Yeah. Cause then girls don't wanna put all their effort into it cause then their makeup's gonna smear.

Nicole: Is that something you worry about during PE?

Mia: Yeah. I don't really care about my hair. My hair is just, like, whatever. But makeup is important.

Another girl described an elaborate beauty ritual she engaged in daily that involved applying makeup in the morning before school, washing it off right before PE, and then reapplying it after PE.

Girls also worried about how their bodies would look while they exercised in front of their peers, especially in front of boys. Jamie told me that in addition to being concerned about her hair during PE she worried about how her stomach looked when she ran:

Nicole: What do you worry about during PE?

Jamie: I'm sometimes worried about hair cause my hair's usually a mess in PE. And then, I don't know, like, when I run I can feel my stomach go up and down. So that bothers me.

Nicole: Do you not like the way it feels for your stomach to go up and down, or are you worried about the way it might look?

Jamie: Probably both.

Nicole: Um, do you think that worrying about your stomach affects your participation in PE?

Jamie: Yeah. That's probably the main reason why I don't like to run.

Mia said she worried about the way her legs looked when she ran in PE: "I don't like when we do the testing. Like, I hate running across the floor when you do the sprints back and forth. I feel like when everyone's sitting on the ground, you know, my legs are jiggling and the floor is moving, and I get really embarrassed." PE made the personal management of fat difficult for girls, because when they moved their bodies, they worried that their body fat would visibly move as well.

Wearing baggy T-shirts and sweat pants would appear to be a simple, straightforward solution to the problem of hiding fat. However, to be considered fashionable girls felt the need to wear tight, revealing clothing even in PE because the ability to "pull off" this fashion trend greatly increased girls' social status within the adolescent hierarchy. Additionally, the intense Arizona heat made it virtually impossible to wear long pants during PE because this would cause girls to sweat more, which, in turn, would cause their hair and makeup to become even messier.

In contrast to the girls I interviewed, most of the boys I talked with did not express concern about sweating or messing up their hair in PE. Instead, boys were concerned about their athletic performance, impressing their peers, and helping their team win the game. When I asked boys during interviews if they worried about anything during PE, most simply replied, "No." As a follow-up question, I often asked boys, "What about getting sweaty or messing up your hair? Do you worry about those kinds of things?" A typical response to this question was, "No, that's what deodorant, cologne, and hair gel are for" or "No, I just throw on some cologne and deodorant."

Although I did not have access to the boys' locker room for obvious reasons, I can attest to the fact that a number of boys employed these methods for combating sweat-induced body odor. After PE, students who had finished dressing early, mostly boys, often stood just outside the locker rooms while waiting for the bell to ring. On the days I stood outside the locker room socializing with students at the end of the period, I was often assaulted by the overpowering smell of cologne and spray-on deodorant every time a boy emerged.

Instead of being worried about appearance and personal hygiene during PE, boys I talked with expressed concern about their athletic performance. For example, one boy told me he did not like PE because he felt like he was "not good at it" and worried what his classmates might think or say about him. When I asked another boy during an interview whether he worried about anything during PE, he responded,

> When we jog, I like to make sure that I'm ahead of everybody else. I don't like to lose. And if somebody's ahead of me it lets me know that somebody's better than me, and I want to be the best.

Yet another boy I talked with said he enjoyed competing with his classmates during PE and explained that it only occurred to him to worry about being sweaty from exercising when he returned to the locker room at the end of class. As discussed in an earlier chapter, boys associated concern about appearance with femininity. Just as boys talked about "throwing on" whatever clothes they could find in the morning before rushing out the door to school, boys also said they "threw on" deodorant and cologne to mask body odor that might be caused by sweating during PE.

Though boys did not admit to worrying about getting sweaty during PE, they were aware that this was a concern for girls. For example, during an interview about differences in the way girls and boys participate in PE Kirk, the freshman quarterback, said that girls "just stand around" most of the time. When I asked him why he thought girls did not actively participate, he replied, "Cause they don't wanna get all sweaty."

Similarly, during an interview with Eddie, he initially admitted to worrying about getting sweaty during PE but immediately and self-consciously retracted his statement:

Nicole: Do you ever worry about getting sweaty and stinky during PE and then having to go through the rest of the school day like that?
Eddie: Yeah, definitely.
Nicole: Does it affect your participation at all?
Eddie: Um, sometimes it does. But I kind of wouldn't say that. It's more girls that worry about getting sweaty as opposed to guys.
Nicole: Do you hear them talking about it?
Eddie: Um some of the girls when we have to run a mile or something like that, they sit there and they, like, yell out that they don't wanna get sweaty and stuff like that.

During interviews about PE, boys contrasted their own lack of concern about body odor or appearance with girls, who were so worried about their hair, makeup, hygiene, and body image that it affected their participation in PE. As a result, most boys were getting a good workout during PE, while girls passed up what might have been their only opportunity for daily exercise.

Girly Girls and Competitive Boys

Girls and boys both drew on gender stereotypes to explain why girls did not participate in PE, why girls lacked athletic ability, and which types of sports were appropriate for girls and boys, but subtle distinctions emerged in their beliefs about gender and athleticism. Boys viewed girls in general as primarily being concerned with their appearance and lacking athletic ability. Girls, on the other hand, described one type of girl this way, referred to as the "girly girl," but did not believe this depiction accurately characterized girls in general.

After hearing the term "girly girl" several times during interviews with girls, I asked an all-girl focus group what it meant:

Nicole: What does it mean to be girly? I keep hearing that word.
Anna: Worrying about the way she looks and her makeup all the time.
Linda: Yeah, just caring about themselves in terms of physical attributes.

Girls also described "girly girls" as being "wimpy," "fussy," and "prissy" when it came to participation in sports. When I asked one girl to describe differences in how girls and boys participate in PE, she responded by giving her impression of "girly girls" in an exaggerated high pitched, whiny voice:

"It's kind of like you see in movies. 'Girly girls' are like, 'I don't wanna throw the ball. I don't wanna catch it. I don't wanna.'"

Boys performed similar imitations of the way girls behaved in PE, but the difference was that boys perceived all girls as "girly." For example, during a mixed-gender focus group one of the boys said that girls "refuse to do much of anything" in PE. To illustrate his point, he performed his interpretation of how girls are in PE class, also in an exaggerated high pitched voice: "Well, I'm kind of girly, and I just do the bare minimum because I hate physical education. I'd rather have my rolls [referring to rolls of fat]."

During interview discussions about PE, a few girls criticized "girly girls" for making all girls look inept at sports. Kerri, the petite, pragmatic Latina with a boyish figure, said, "Girls have kind of built up a bad reputation for themselves when it comes to sports cause they don't like to do em all." When I asked Kerri how she felt about co-ed PE, she exclaimed, "It drives me crazy when girls play softball and dodge the ball or when they play with press on nails!"

Allie, on the other hand, explained that she liked co-ed PE because it provided girls with an opportunity to counteract negative stereotypes:

> I like it cause you get more of a chance to compete against the opposite sex. And I like that frankly because they [boys] get to know that girls aren't just spazzes and ditzes who don't know what they're doing.

A handful of girls, like Kerri and Allie in the examples above, said they tried to challenge the unfair stereotype that girls were "wimpy" and "whiny" when it came to physical activity through their active engagement in sports.

Despite some girls' attempts to counteract the "girly girl" image, negative stereotypes about girls' athletic abilities pervaded teens' discourse. For example, when I asked a boy whether he preferred working out with guys or girls he responded, "Girls are good to work out with when you want to be slow. You can be slow with girls." Similarly, another boy said that he would rather exercise with girls when he wanted to "just mess around" but with guys when he wanted a serious workout. The implication in these boys' statements was that girls are not serious athletes and therefore not worthy opponents or teammates on the playing field.

In fact, most of the boys I interviewed did not see girls as competitors in PE sports activities. For example, during an interview with Kirk about teasing during PE class, the following conversation ensued:

Nicole: Do kids get teased in PE?
Kirk: Yeah. Like, if they're not any good [laughs].

Nicole: Okay, like what would someone say?
Kirk: "You suck!"
Nicole: Do more guys or girls get teased for not being very good.
Kirk: Only guys.
Nicole: By girls or other guys?
Kirk: Guys.
Nicole: What about girls who aren't very good? Like, do the guys pick on
          them, too?
Kirk: Not really.
Nicole: Why do you think that is?
Kirk: Cause I think that guys expect other guys to be good at sports
          and they don't expect girls to be as good.

In an article about gendered interaction in high school athletics, gender and language scholars Penelope Eckert and Sally McConnell-Ginet write: "Male camaraderie excludes women and includes other men as fellow 'tough guys,' to be slapped on the back, playfully punched around in certain contexts."[16] This was certainly true at Desert Vista. Boys not only excluded girls from participation in games, but from competitive banter as well. Boys I spoke with readily admitted that they did not view girls as competent athletes, which is why they excluded their female classmates from playing in PE sports activities. Again, what boys did not acknowledge during interviews was their role in girls' non-participation.

Gender stereotypes about athletics extended beyond PE. Teens classified particular sports as being culturally appropriate for either girls or boys. In response to the question, "Are there sports you associate with boys?" the most frequent responses were football, hockey, baseball, and wrestling. When I asked teens which sports they associated primarily with girls, most cited volleyball, softball, and cheerleading. In addition, some participants made gendered distinctions between power walking, jogging, and running, explaining that girls power walk and jog, and boys run. These participants' classifications of masculine- and feminine-associated sports are similar to findings from other studies exploring gender stereotyping and sports.[17]

When I asked one boy why he associated football and wrestling with guys, he replied, "They're more physical." Another boy told me that he associated football and baseball with boys because these two sports were "aggressive and involve hitting." Others said that boys play "rougher" and can handle getting hit, whereas if girls were to get hit during a sport "they'll start complaining and cry." Similarly, a girl explained to me during an interview that contact sports are for boys because girls would be afraid of getting hurt.

Jennifer Hargreaves, a sociologist who studies gender and sports, asserts,

"In sport 'masculine' identity incorporates images of activity, strength, aggression and muscularity and it implies at the same time, an opposite feminine subjectivity associated with passivity, relative weakness, gentleness and grace."[18] Teens' comments regarding socially appropriate sports for girls and boys reinforce the stereotype that boys are serious athletes while girls are athletically inept and uninterested in sports. As one girl so aptly put it, the popular perception is that "guys wrestle and girls put on makeup."

Despite teens' perceptions that contact sports are for boys and that boys play sports more aggressively than girls, a number of girls I interviewed said they participated in traditionally male sports activities, such as boxing, hockey, and football. Five of the girls who participated in my study said they sometimes play football with neighborhood boys on the weekends, three were taking boxing lessons after school, and one played in a competitive co-ed hockey league. Allie had begun working out at a boxing gym when I interviewed her for the second time in the spring, telling me that she enjoyed the challenge and competition that boxing provided.

When I asked Allie to tell me more about why she enjoyed boxing, her eyes lit up as she said, "Like, now when I go to boxing, there's a lot more guys there than girls, which is all right. And I think it's kind of fun cause you get to kind of, um, box with somebody that usually would be out of your league." Another girl explained during an interview that she liked taking kickboxing classes because it helped her to work off some of the anger and aggression she felt.

A surprising number of girls expressed their desire to play tackle football. Out of the thirty girls I interviewed, six told me they wanted to try out for the school's football team. Three of these girls did not pursue trying out for the team either because they felt intimidated since it was an all-male sport or because their parents forbade it. However, the other three actively pursued trying out for the team by expressing their interest in playing to the football coach and/or showing up for tryouts.

According to these girls, the coach would not allow them to try out. Lacy, a petite blond girl, described to me her thwarted attempt to try out for the team:

Lacy: I usually play football with just a group of guys at the park that's down the street. Like, every once in a while after I finish my homework I'll go down there and play tackle football or touch football. And I tried out for football this year.
Nicole: Really?
Lacy: Yeah, but the coach said I couldn't play cause I was a girl.
Nicole: What?
Lacy: He's very sexist.

Nicole: So, tell me what happened.

Lacy: Well, I told him the day before tryouts, "I'm gonna try out for football" and he said, "Football's not a girl's sport." That's what he told me when I was in the gym cause he's in there second hour when I have PE. And my friend Heather was gonna try out, too, and my other friend Lily. And he said, "Football's not a girl's sport," and we said, "Well, we're gonna show up." And when we went down there for tryouts, he said, "Football's not for girls." We were like, "Okay."

Nicole: So did you go to tryouts anyway?

Lacy: Yeah we went down there, but then he just kinda said, "No."

The idea that contact sports are only appropriate for boys is tied to previously discussed gender stereotypes that associate boys with aggression and girls with fragility. Girls I interviewed who played tackle football with male friends on weekends, took boxing and kickboxing lessons after school, played in a competitive hockey league, and expressed a desire to try out for the school football team challenged these gender stereotypes.

Previous studies have documented girls' struggles to negotiate participation in sports with maintaining a feminine identity.[19] Physical education scholars Claudia Cockburn and Gill Clarke, for example, discuss the "double identity" that athletic girls must negotiate in an attempt to maintain a normative feminine identity and participate in sports. They assert, "It is highly unlikely that girls can achieve being both physically active *and* [heterosexually] desirable, so they are often obliged to choose *between* these images."[20]

Most girls I interviewed similarly told me that although they thought a girl could be both athletic and feminine they did not think most people would agree. The majority of boys said that girls were usually either feminine or athletic but not both. As one boy put it, "Normally girls are one or the other. It's hard to be two styles at once." These stereotypes of girls as athletically inept, weak, whiny, and only concerned with appearance limited their access to active engagement in PE. Boys did not view girls as capable or willing participants in PE activities and therefore ignored and excluded them. Girls who participated in extracurricular sports, especially those traditionally restricted to males, resisted these narrow ideas about femininity.

Athletic Girls

Girls tended to feel less qualified than boys in PE class, frustrated that they were excluded by boys from participating, and reluctant to participate due to appearance-related concerns. This left girls who enjoyed playing sports but did not have the time, money, transportation, or parental support to do so beyond the school day with no opportunity to exercise, hone their athletic skills, and engage in fun, healthy competition.

Those girls who had both the desire and access participated in extracurricular sports, such as hockey, boxing, track, and football. They felt empowered through participation in sports, enjoyed the sense of accomplishment, and liked being part of a team. At the same time, narrow, deeply held ideas about femininity meant that athletic girls were not considered sexually desirable or attractive by boys at the high school. Consequently, girls who chose athleticism paid a social price.

As discussed in an earlier chapter, most of the teens I interviewed associated having muscle tone with looking like a guy. Boys described girls who displayed muscle tone as "mannish" and "intimidating." Many girls stated during interviews that they did not want to acquire muscle tone because it would negatively affect their social status. Most of the boys I interviewed associated the attributes of athleticism, strength, and muscle tone with normative masculinity in such an interwoven way that they could not be disentangled. For these boys not only were girls with muscle tone masculine, so too were athletic girls by virtue of their physical strength, skill, and agility—all traits associated with boys.

Sociolinguists Eckert and McConnell-Ginet argue that girls' varsity athletics does not carry the same high level of status as boys' athletics partly because "the association of the athlete with physical prowess conflicts with feminine norms, with notions of how a [heterosexual] girl 'should' look and behave."[21] This assertion aligns with my findings at Desert Vista. For example, when I asked Kirk, the quarterback of the freshman football team, whether or not he would be attracted to a female athlete, he explained that those are not the kind of girls guys typically want to date because they are usually "manly, like lesbians."

Kirk's response was typical of what boys had to say about female athletes, who were often described as having "guy features" and being "ugly." Jesse, the tall, thin Latino who hung out with the Mexicans, similarly noted, "Most girls that are really pretty, they don't do sports. They just, like, hang out with their friends all the time." Jesse made it clear, as did many boys, that the competitive sports realm is reserved for boys and unattractive girls.

When I asked Ricky, the obese boy introduced in the Chapter 3 vignette, whether or not he found female athletes at school attractive, he replied, "If she's pretty then yeah [laughs] it's cool. But most of em are kinda ugly [laughs]." Later, during an all-boy focus group in which Ricky was a participant the topic of female athletes arose again in the context of a discussion about gendered appearance norms. In response to the question, "Are girls or guys more concerned with their appearance," Ricky said,

Mostly girls. They always have to look good, put on their makeup, do their hair. But some girls don't care. Like athletic girls, they really don't care. Like girls that play sports, they'll just come in with their hair up and shorts and a shirt.

Gendered appearance norms at the school required girls to go to great lengths to look attractive, while boys could get away with "scrubbin it." In fact, boys associated spending time and effort on appearance with girls, claiming that boys just "throw something on" in the morning before school. Because girl jocks violated gender norms requiring them to prioritize beauty regimens over athletics most boys considered them unfeminine and, therefore, unattractive.

In addition to describing athletic girls as "ugly" and "manly" because of their reported disregard for feminine appearance norms, boys associated athletic girls with power, strength, and skill, all qualities they considered masculine. For example, during an all-boy focus-group discussion about female athletes, one of the participants said he would not want to date an athletic girl "because they're athletic, they're muscular, and I wouldn't want a muscular girl. I don't want a girl that's stronger than me." The other participants emphatically agreed with this statement, one adding that he would "rather have her be my friend than my girlfriend."

In fact, most boys I talked with said they would want to be friends with female athletes but would not be involved in romantic relationships with them. Such views reflected the fact that, according to Cockburn and Clarke, constructing normative feminine identities involves

more than just appearance; girls need to behave in a certain way, too. In order to be socially acceptable as a "teenage girl" they are required neither to take part in sport—especially "boys' sports"—nor to physically exert themselves in any other way.[22]

In another all-boy focus group, the participants similarly agreed that they would not want to date an athletic girl. When I asked them why not, one of the boys explained, "Looks and, um, power. They have more of, like, lesbian or guy features and more power strength wise." This boy's response to my question is quite revealing because he explicitly links power and strength with degree of attractiveness in girls. His response implies that not only are athletic girls unattractive romantic partners because they violate feminine beauty norms by failing to wear makeup, style their hair according to the latest fashion trends, and wear tight, revealing clothing, but also because they are strong and powerful.

Underneath boys' rejection of girls who displayed strength and athletic skill lay a fear of the potential for a girl to beat them in an athletic competition. Earlier in the book, I discussed gender norms requiring boys to be bigger and stronger than girls. This gender imperative extended to athletic ability as well. Boys talked about the fear of competing against female athletes and the humiliation they would feel if they were beaten by a girl. For example, Jerry, the short, thin, nervous boy who constantly fidgeted, told me during an interview that he would rather exercise with guys because "girls might be better at the sport and show me up."

I conducted an all-boy focus group in which two of the participants were members of the school wrestling team. At one point during the interview, I asked them if they had ever wrestled against girls in competition, and the following conversation ensued:

Robbie: Yeah.
Reggie: Thankfully not [laughs].
Nicole: Robbie, how was it?
Robbie: Well, it's like really, really, really scary cause you're thinkin' man, if you ever lost you have the whole team watching. But I've never, ever, ever seen a girl beat a guy.
Reggie: Like, if you have a girl in your weight class, you're all scared cause then you'd be like, "Oh is she gonna wrestle me" and then you're like [groan].
Nicole: Would it be worse to lose to a girl than to lose to a guy?
Everyone: Yeah [laughter].
Nicole: Why?
Robbie: Because you'll never see girls win in all the tournaments that I've ever been to.
Reggie: Yeah, I've never seen a girl win.
Nicole: So what would it say about you if you lost to a girl? What would that mean?
Reggie: You would get dissed on pretty hard I would think.
Ricky: Yeah. I would be scared to walk around school.
Reggie: Yeah, it'd seem kinda–
Robbie: –Awkward.
Ryan: Weak, yeah.

Sociologist Donna Eder and her colleagues assert that aggression and toughness are socialized and reinforced through male sports culture. In their study of middle school peer cultures, the authors found that boys policed the boundaries of toughness through ritual insults: "Names such as 'pussy,' 'girl,' 'fag,' and 'queer,' associate lack of toughness directly with femininity or homosexuality. These names are used when boys fail to meet certain standards of combativeness."[23] If girls are considered weak when it comes to sports, then, as Robbie and Ryan explain in the example above, a boy who gets beaten by a girl in sports competition would also be thought of as weak and would likely be teased by his teammates for transgressing a crucial gender boundary.

For boys, an even worse prospect than losing to a girl is losing to a girl with whom they are romantically involved. Boys I talked with said they would not want to date an athletic girl for fear that she might outperform them in sports. John, a lanky, nerdy boy with fluffy red hair and glasses explained to me during an interview that, although athletic girls can sometimes be pretty, "if she's better than the guys, then the guys get embarrassed and don't want to go out with her." Sammy, an affable, easygoing Latino with an athletic build, similarly explained that he would not want to date a girl who has muscle tone because that probably meant she was athletic: "She could beat me in arm wrestling, and if you can beat me in arm wrestling it's over [laughs]." I asked Sammy what it meant to him if a girl beat him in sports, and he replied, "I need to work harder" [laughs].

One way in which boys displayed heteronormative masculine identity was to be seen with girls who displayed heteronormative feminine identity, which is why boys were attracted to girls who were weaker and smaller than them. Eckert and McConnell-Ginet write, "Heterosexual femininity is constructed as directly contrasting with the superiority in physical strength embodied in hegemonic masculinity."[24] For boys at Desert Vista, athletic girls explicitly challenged feminine norms by being strong, adept at sports, and sometimes rejecting beauty practices associated with traditional femininity, all of which functioned as an implicit challenge to normative masculine identity.

Girls I interviewed knew how boys felt about female athletes. When I asked girls, "Which girls on campus get the most positive attention from boys?" most responded that boys prefer "girly girls" who are petite, wear tight, revealing clothes, and participate in "feminine" sports activities like cheerleading and dance. For example, Jamie explained:

> Basketball girls at school are more on their skills and their muscles than they are on their looks. And those cheerleader girls are all about looks and, of course, they have skill, but they're mostly about looks. And usually guys want girls that will always look good for them and look good at school.

Similarly, Allie, who had unique insight into this topic because she worked in the male-dominated athletic training room after school and overheard boys' conversations about girls, did not think guys were attracted to athletic girls:

Like, being in the training room, you hear it a lot. Like, guys don't think the girl basketball players are very attractive. I mean, they can be pretty face-wise, but the guys will be too intimidated to go out with them. Like, they don't want a girl that can beat them at basketball [laughs].

Another girl also told me that girls in sports do not have boyfriends because boys are too intimidated: "They're like, '[I] don't want my girl to beat me.'"

The take-home message for girls who understood the negative stereotypes associated with female athletes was that they must choose between pursuing romantic relationships with boys and excelling in sports. In a social environment where girls gained status primarily through their relationships with high-status boys, athletic girls, like fat girls, apparently needed to sacrifice the potential for upward social mobility.

However, despite the double identity dilemma girls face there are payoffs for girls who actively and competitively engage in sports. Research suggests that many female athletes feel empowered by their participation in sports and proud of their accomplishments.[25] I similarly found that some of the girls in my study expressed pride in their physical abilities. For example, Jamie told me she had been involved in a co-ed hockey league since she was seven years old. When I asked her how many girls were in the hockey league, she explained:

There's a few girls. But right now I'm the only girl on the team and that's how it's been my whole life except for one season where we got a bunch of girls and had a girl team. We whipped everybody's butt cause we were just a lot better.

Jamie spoke about her hockey accomplishments with an air of confidence; she looked me in the eyes and sat up straight, in contrast to the way she usually hunched over the table with her gaze cast downward.

Similarly, Allie surprised me when she told me she was taking boxing lessons, explaining that, although she had initially signed up for boxing lessons to lose weight she now enjoyed the competitive aspect of it. Allie's eyes lit up as she said,

I really want to get in the ring and fight, which would be awesome to me cause I think that's like the greatest thing. Yeah, so I'm just trying to get trained for that and see if they'll put me in the ring.

All of the girls I interviewed, including Jamie and Allie, expressed body-image concerns during interviews and appeared to be insecure about their appearance in general. However, when these two girls talked about their involvement in sports they seemed to forget about their body-image concerns, if only momentarily, as they expressed pride and excitement about their athletic accomplishments.

Girls' involvement in sports despite the potentially negative social ramifications may be viewed as resistance to normative feminine ideologies. Gender philosopher Judith Butler proposes that disruptions in routinized gender performances, where gender norms are questioned and subverted through practice, are the spaces within which individual agency resists dominant ideologies.[26] These girls' participation in hockey and boxing, and the enthusiasm and pride with which they spoke of their athletic accomplishments, represented an interruption to the ways in which their peers expected them to move through the world and occupy space, as their athletic empowerment temporarily subsumed their concerns about body image and social status.

Social theorists remind us that gendered embodiment influences more than behavior, appearance, and desires; it also has the potential for physically transforming the body.[27] Robyne Garrett, a scholar of gender and physical activity writes:

> Through continuous bodily practice, gender is "performed" and it is through the ongoing process of gender performance that the nature and meaning of people's bodies are physically altered. Knowledge of gender becomes deeply inscribed in muscle and skeletal systems, posture, gaits, and styles of movement.[28]

For teens at Desert Vista, body size and shape helped determine students' places within the school's social hierarchy and how their peers treated them.

The idea that active engagement in sports was narrowly associated with normative masculine identity to the extent that female athletes were labeled "butch" and "manly" could have serious social and health consequences for girls at the school. The message girls at Desert Vista received was that they must choose between being "girly" and athletic. Either way, they lose. Getting involved in sports can provide girls with a sense of pride, accomplishment, and empowerment. However, in an adolescent environment driven by a social hierarchy, largely based on appearance and adherence to normative gender identities, pride and empowerment about athletic achievement might hold less value than the potential for upward social mobility.

Studies show an ongoing gender gap in physical activity participation among teens, with girls continuing to lag behind.[29] Multiple factors contribute to this gap, including the degree to which schools and communities provide opportunities, level of parental encouragement, and peer influence. For physical activity participation to be empowering for girls, they must see themselves as competent and skillful, develop and sustain positive social relationships, and enjoy themselves.[30] One study found that peer acceptance strongly mediated the self-esteem boys and girls attained from participating in sports, which helps explain why boys, who are celebrated for their athletic achievements, seek out sports participation at a higher rate than girls, who are more likely to be stigmatized for embracing an athletic identity.[31]

The girls in my study reported feeling "less qualified" to play sports than boys, frustrated that boys excluded them from team sports in PE, and self-conscious about how they looked while exercising. Moreover, girls who genuinely enjoyed engaging in physical activity refused to participate in PE because they understood that if their peers thought of them as athletic it would negatively affect their social status. These findings are consistent with those from recent studies reporting that pre-teen and teen girls struggle with gender stereotypes associating athleticism with boys, concerns about how their bodies looked while exercising, fear of being teased and thought of as "butch" for participating in sports, and frustration about boys dominating the playing field.[32]

As a result of these challenges, most girls I interviewed at Desert Vista felt discouraged from engaging in physical activity even while they aspired to achieve thin, toned, fat-free bodies. Moreover, they understood that the consequences associated with being considered overweight by their peers included teasing, harassment, and poor positioning in the adolescent social hierarchy. This was yet another arena in which they faced the material realities of their bodies. The physical nature of PE class drew attention to teens' bodies both on the field and in the locker room, which opened them up for critique and fat teasing.

The heightened focus on bodies is inevitable in PE class but some key procedural changes could ease the body angst a bit and shift student dynamics around it. For example, PE uniforms that are baggy and provide ample coverage of sensitive areas, such as thighs and stomachs would possibly alleviate student anxiety about their body fat jiggling during exercise. In addition, separating girls and boys during team sports might encourage girls to engage more actively, as it did in Mrs. Roy's class. Emphasis on sportsmanship, teamwork, and inclusion by the PE teacher can also help shift the interpersonal dynamic in team sports. However, for this strategy to work teachers must be supported through professional training, reasonable class sizes, and a broader school culture that cultivates such values. In the next chapter I continue to explore the central thematic threads of body image and gender among youth at the high school by shifting focus to their food-related practices.

Notes

1. Institute of Medicine, 2013.
2. Ibid.
3. Institute of Medicine, 2013; National Association for Sport and Physical Education and the American Heart Association, 2010.
4. Young, 1980.
5. Bartky, 1990.
6. Connell, 1983.
7. Young, 1980:149.
8. Young, 1980:143.
9. Bartky, 1990:68.
10. Connell, 1983:19.
11. Connell, 1983:18.
12. Bryson, 1987:350.
13. Thorne, 1993.
14. Bartky, 1988:81.
15. Foucault, 1975/1977.
16. Eckert and McConnell-Ginet, 1995:484.
17. Hardin and Greer, 2009; Klomsten, Marsh, and Skaalvik, 2005; Koivula, 1995; Koivula, 2001; Thorne, 1993.
18. Hargreaves, 1986:112.
19. Cockburn and Clarke, 2002; Garrett, 2004b; Krane *et al.*, 2004.
20. Cockburn and Clarke, 2002:661.
21. Eckert and McConnell-Ginet, 1995.
22. Cockburn and Clarke, 2002:653.
23. Eder, Evans, and Parker, 1995:63.
24. Eckert and McConnell-Ginet, 1995:485.
25. Krane *et al.*, 2004; Hargreaves, 1993; Theberge, 1997.
26. Butler,1990.
27. Connell, 1995; Garrett, 2004a; Young, 1980.
28. Garrett, 2004a:143.
29. American Association of University Women, 1998; Centers for Disease Control, 2012; Deaner *et al.*, 2012; Lenhart *et al.*, 2012; Sabo and Veliz, 2008.
30. Deem and Gilroy, 1998; Garrett, 2004b; Taylor, Beech, and Cummings, 1997.
31. Daniels and Leaper, 2006.
32. Clark and Paechter, 2007; Jeanes, 2011; Slater and Tiggermann, 2010.

5

"IT'S ALL GOING TO TURN INTO FAT"

Jackson, a soft-spoken, Latino freshman at Desert Vista, had acne and wore his hair short and spiked on top, a popular style for boys at the time. He was a social misfit who struggled to fit in with his peers and had only a few friends at school. Having attended middle school in another district, Jackson did not know anyone at the high school when he started ninth grade.

Jackson told me he was five feet eight and weighed about 165 pounds, which is considered overweight for a boy his age by the Centers for Disease Control and Prevention. When I asked him to rate how satisfied he was with the way his body looked on a scale of one to five with five being the most satisfied, he responded, "two and a half or three," explaining that he was larger than he wanted to be. He had been teased all through middle school for being fat.

Jackson self-identified as gay and had been picked on and beat up for it when he came out in eighth grade. He said he had begun to "act out," fighting back and "taking it out" on other kids who were smaller and weaker than him. Without providing details, Jackson said that his behavior had been "totally out of control." As a result, he had been suspended from school a number of times. In August, right before he had started ninth grade, Jackson's parents had decided to move him into a group home where he would get the support and counseling he needed.

Jackson struggled with overeating and secretive eating, saying,

> Last week I ate a lot of junk food all at once. I ate, like, a brownie with ice cream, and then I wasn't full so I went to Baskin Robbins and had three scoops of ice cream. Then I talked my dad into going and buying some donuts, and I ate those.

Jackson further told me he would buy a bunch of junk food at school in the morning and eat it in the bathroom during passing periods so no one would see. In seventh grade, he had started collecting candy and chips, hiding them in his room, and eating from his stash at night after dinner. In eighth grade, he had developed a habit of binging and purging in an effort to lose weight and ameliorate the guilt he felt after consuming large amounts of food.

Jackson stated that, with the help of his therapist he had been able to stop purging, but he still struggled with binging on junk food at school, where it was available in abundance:

> It's hard here because you've got junk food whenever you want it and you have money to spend and you want to eat the candy and stuff. It's hard not to spend your money on the bad food, and there's no one telling you not to.

At the beginning of the year, Jackson's parents would give him twenty dollars every Monday to spend on lunches for the week, but he would spend it all on candy, chips, ice cream bars, sodas, french fries, and pizza on Monday and Tuesday, leaving no money for food Wednesday through Friday. Consequently, Jackson's parents soon began doling out his lunch money, giving him five dollars a day, to ensure he had money for food all week long. Nevertheless Jackson said the five dollars was usually gone before lunch period, spent on snacks from the vending machines.

Jackson had taken a culinary arts class in school and had learned about the importance of eating a balanced diet. He clearly understood the concept of healthy foods and good nutrition. He knew he should eat a mixture of lean protein, fruits, vegetables, and whole grains and was even able to provide examples of healthy meals that incorporated each of the necessary food components. He also realized that junk food should only be consumed occasionally and in small amounts. Nonetheless, if junk food was available, he felt compelled to eat it until he either ran out of money or felt sick from being overly full.

Jackson wanted to be seen as someone who was strong, in control, and had "his act together." He said, "I want people to think I'm presentable, um, outgoing, but mostly that I have control over stuff and that I can control everything that happens in a situation wherever I am. And, like, strong—I want to be strong, calm, and in control." Jackson also wanted to be lean, toned, clean-cut, and well dressed and believed if he could achieve these qualities he would be popular, drive a cool car, and have a lot of friends. For Jackson, this image of a calm, collected, traditionally good-looking man represented the key to elevated social status.

When I interviewed him at the beginning of the year, Jackson proudly announced that he was exercising at least four times a week, alternately running a quarter of a mile, swimming five laps in the group home pool, or practicing dance moves after school in his room. Even though he often felt unmotivated to exercise, he did it anyway. The exercise routine helped Jackson feel more in control of his emotions and his body. It also lessened the guilt he felt from overeating—exercise was a much healthier counter behavior to binging than purging.

However, when I interviewed Jackson in the spring, he was no longer exercising regularly outside of school. He said the boys from the group home all went to the park together every Friday afternoon to play a team sport like baseball or soccer, but he participated only minimally because he "hated team sports." Occasionally, the boys in the group home would practice yoga together and sometimes Jackson would follow along, but he did not stick with it because he thought it was too hard—he would get out of breath or have sore muscles the next day. Jackson could not explain why he no longer practiced dance moves, ran, or swam regularly, only that he did not feel like it.

Jackson liked stretching and doing calisthenics in PE class but did not enjoy team sports activities. He participated enough to move around a bit but not enough to break a sweat: "I don't want to sweat because I always like to be clean, not dirty. So sometimes when it's hot and we're having class outside I will get all panicked and start freakin' out. I don't want my hair to be messed up, and I don't want to smell bad."

Jackson said no one took showers after PE because "the locker room is not a positive environment." His goal was to change in and out of his PE clothes and get out of the locker room as quickly as possible because boys "get pushed around" if they take their time. Jackson said sometimes boys would throw each other into the showers while they were still dressed and turn the water on or stuff each other into lockers and close the doors.

During the second interview, Jackson, who by then had been living in the group home for about seven months and missed his family, said he was looking forward to earning weekend home visits soon. He missed his mom's cooking, reminiscing about the traditional Mexican dishes she would prepare for the family. Jackson's cousin, who had been in the military, was currently living with his parents, and Jackson hoped his cousin would help him get back into an exercise routine. If the weekend visits went well and he continued to engage in healthy behaviors, Jackson would get to move back in with his family by the end of the school year.

* * *

Jackson's body-image ideals, his relationship to food and exercise, and his interactions with peers were all influenced by his identity work. That is, Jackson had difficulty managing his appetite, exercise habits, and emotions but strived to become, and be perceived as, someone who was calm, collected, and in control. Being lean and toned, eating healthfully, engaging in exercise, and keeping his cool in the face of getting teased for being both fat and gay were achievements Jackson believed would lead to a happy life. Like most students I interviewed, Jackson experienced intermittent successes and failures as he worked toward these goals. The school environment worked against Jackson on every front; he was surrounded by junk food he could not resist, was teased for being overweight and gay, and refused to participate in PE because he did not enjoy team sports and worried about his appearance and hygiene. In particular, Jackson's story illustrates how body image and food are enmeshed.

This chapter focuses on the school food environment and ways in which boys and girls negotiated and reconciled consumption of fattening "junk foods" with their body-image goals, sense of self, and personal beliefs about weight as a matter of personal responsibility. I also discuss strategies teens used to limit food consumption at school, differences in how boys and girls approached food, and how teens used language to express food-related guilt and present themselves as body-conscious even as they gorged on fattening foods.

The prevalence of low-nutrient, energy-dense foods and beverages in many US public schools has been well documented, and contentious debates about school food continue to play out in the media.[1] Based on recent media coverage of school food policies now in place, it seems like things have improved quite a bit in the last decade. We have all heard about the increasing popularity of farm-to-school programs as well as recent federal legislation designed to improve the nutritional quality of what students eat and drink at school. For example, the Institute of Medicine (IOM) reports that twenty-one states have stricter school meal standards than the US Department of Agriculture requirements as compared to only four states seven years ago. And twenty-seven states have farm-to-school programs as compared to only one state five years ago.[2]

These are noteworthy improvements and signal an important shift in public awareness of the problem and willingness by lawmakers to take action. However, follow-up studies evaluating the impact and effectiveness of some of these policies illustrate how messy and slow such change can be, showing us that we still have a long way to go in making meaningful, sustainable improvements to foods available in schools. Before presenting my findings, I will briefly discuss school food policies to assess where we are as a nation in addressing student wellness through improvement of school food environments.

The Child Nutrition and WIC Reauthorization Act of 2004 (Public Law 108-265) required all school districts participating in the National School Lunch Program to adopt a wellness policy that includes nutrition guidelines for all foods available at school, including school meals and competitive foods (e.g., junk foods like candy and chips). This program was phased in during the 2006–2007 school year. A follow-up study in 2010 examining a nationally representative sample of school district wellness policies concluded that three years after the Child Nutrition and WIC Reauthorization Act of 2004 took effect, nutritional guidelines for competitive foods were weak, especially at the middle and high school levels, and competitive foods and beverages continued to be highly accessible to students in all grade levels.[3] A second follow-up study found that five years after the law took effect there had been progress to implement, strengthen, or increase the comprehensiveness of school district wellness plans in general. However, the report concluded that wellness policies remained weak overall, especially in the area of competitive food guidelines.[4]

Another noteworthy policy breakthrough was the voluntary removal of full-calorie sodas from schools by the three top-selling beverage companies, which took effect in fall 2006.[5] A follow-up study assessing the change and impact of this policy found that between 2004 and 2010 the beverage industry reduced calories shipped to schools by 90 percent and reduced shipments of full-calorie soft drinks to schools by 97 percent.[6] Still, results from studies assessing whether or not a reduction in the availability of sugar-sweetened drinks at school resulted in a reduction in students' overall consumption of sugar-sweetened drinks are mixed.[7]

Most recently, the Healthy, Hunger-Free Kids Act of 2010 required the USDA to improve nutrition standards for school lunches over a three-year period beginning in fall 2012. The new standards required more fruits and vegetables, whole grains, fat-free or low-fat dairy products, and lean protein. Guidelines specified limitations on fat and sodium content, as well as calorie ranges and portion sizes by age group and prohibited the use of trans fats altogether.[8] A February 2014 US Government Accountability Office study that received national news attention found 1.2 million students and 321 school districts across the nation had stopped participating in the National School Lunch Program as a result of the new guidelines after participation had steadily increased over a decade.[9]

According to the report, students were dissatisfied with how the food tasted and they complained about the increased cost of meals coupled with decreased portion sizes; not only were students paying more for less, but the new lunches left them feeling hungry. School officials also complained about the increased cost associated with implementing the guidelines, as well as decreased morale of cafeteria staff who watched students throw away much of the food they worked hard to prepare. Forty-eight out of fifty states cited food waste as a major challenge of implementing the new guidelines.

The report also found that portion requirements and calorie limits did not align, which led some schools to add foods to their menus that did not improve the nutritional value of the meal (e.g., pudding, potato chips) to meet minimum calorie requirements. The 1.2 million students who stopped participating in the National School Lunch Program went instead for their lunch to vending machines, à la carte snack bars at school, and off-campus restaurants.[10]

In 2013, Do Something, a nonprofit organization that aims to empower teens to take action around social issues about which they care, launched a project called "Fed Up" that collected photos submitted by teens of school lunches around the country and survey data from those teens about what they thought of their school lunches.[11] The online project showcased more than 7,000 photos of school lunches across the United States and reported that students who perceived their school lunch to be healthy threw away food less frequently than those who thought their school lunch was unhealthy. Two in five students reported feeling sick after eating school lunch, and 58 percent had nothing positive to report about their school's food. Teens were invited to vote either "toss it" or "eat it" for each food photo posted. The study reported, "Overall, 70 percent of lunches were deemed trash-worthy by our users."[12] Several 2014 meal photos were submitted from students at Desert Vista, all of which had an overall vote of "toss it." It appeared from the photos that Desert Vista school lunches had not changed much in ten years.

Even now, with this legislation in place, efforts to reform the overall landscape of school food have a long way to go, which is why the issue remains in the forefront of public health and policy discussion. At the heart of the "food and obesity" debate is the question of whom to blame. The food industry insists that individuals are responsible for their food consumption choices, while nutrition experts and social psychologists argue that it is the responsibility of industry and government to improve the type and quality of foods available to consumers.[13]

Public policy scholar Kelly D. Brownell and his colleagues assert that rising obesity rates are primarily the result of a "toxic environment,"[14] which is defined as "unprecedented exposure to energy-dense, heavily advertised, inexpensive, and highly accessible foods . . . combined with an increasingly sedentary lifestyle."[15] Health advocates cite the following as examples of the toxic environment: large portion sizes; the proliferation of fast-food restaurants and gas station mini-marts; school contracts with soda companies; fast-food franchises located in school cafeterias; and aggressive food advertising.[16]

Despite research showing that food environments likely have a greater impact on obesity rates than individual factors, such as knowledge about healthy eating and motivation to lose weight and make healthy lifestyle choices,[17] popular obesity discourses highlighting the role of the individual remain predominant. The food industry promotes personal responsibility discourses and has responded to toxic environment claims by denying health problems and costs associated with obesity and supporting a "market choice frame" that emphasizes individual responsibility and personal choice.[18]

The phrase "junk food," used throughout this chapter, refers to how teens described foods they associated with weight gain. Students I interviewed were predominantly concerned with body image and managing their body weight and less concerned with the nutritional value of food as it relates to overall physical health. As such, they conceptualized foods and beverages they perceived to be high in fat and/or calories and therefore likely to cause weight gain as "junk foods." Conversely, students conceptualized healthy foods as those they perceived to be low in fat and/or calories and therefore less likely to cause weight gain. My findings are similar to those of anthropologist Counihan who researched college students' ideas about food and body image and learned that their "overall interest in food was not in its intrinsic properties, but in their relationship to it and through it to their bodies and to a standard of beauty based on extreme thinness."[19]

Improvement of school food has at long last become a focal point among policy makers. Strides have been made in the past decade but not much has changed as a result. Findings from my study provide a rare look at the everyday consequences of offering junk foods at school from the perspectives of teens at Desert Vista.

Curly Fries Everywhere!

Students at Desert Vista were surrounded by junk food all day long and therefore many found it impossible to resist. Most wanted to make healthy choices to work toward their body-image goals but felt unable to do so at school. They were instead provided with opportunities to purchase and consume sugary, fattening foods and beverages all day long. Healthy foods, like fruit and salads, were available, but they were offered in small quantities and displayed in obscure areas of the cafeteria, which rendered them invisible to most teens.

In contrast, the most prominently displayed food and beverage options were those available in brightly colored vending machines located throughout campus. Vending machines contained an assortment of candies, cookies, pastries, bottles of soda, sports drinks, fruit juices, and water and were strategically placed so that students could not walk from one class to the next without passing at least one. The machines were reportedly locked during lunch so that the school lunch program did not have to compete for revenue. This meant they were available to students before and after school, during the twenty-minute mid-morning break, and during passing periods between classes, which provided plenty of opportunity for students to stock up on soda and snacks that they could eat throughout the day, even during lunch.

I often saw teens rushing to buy candy, chips and soda on their way to and from classes throughout the school day. According to Mrs. Wyatt, one of the PE teachers, food and drinks were strictly prohibited in the locker rooms. However, the placement of vending machines inside the gym directly in front of the locker rooms made this rule nearly impossible to enforce. One day, as I walked by the vending machines located in front of the locker rooms, I saw two boys holding the door of a soda machine open while other students grabbed bottles of soda, shoving as many into their backpacks as they could fit. When Mrs. Wyatt saw what was happening, she ran out of the gym to find the vendor, who had forgotten to lock the machine after restocking it.

Once the machine was locked, I followed Mrs. Wyatt into her office, which was located inside the girls' locker room. There, her face bright red, she exclaimed, "I hate those vending machines!" as she threw a pen across the room. She explained that she does not allow soda in her house and that her son, Kirk, who was a participant in my study, grew up not drinking soda. However, now that he was a freshman at the high school Kirk was "free to drink it all day long."

She further explained that the "vending machine issue" had been debated recently during faculty meetings. Those in favor of vending machines had argued that students would be faced with junk food for the rest of their lives and that they needed to learn to make their own decisions about what to eat and drink. Mrs. Wyatt had countered by pointing out that adults who know junk food is bad for them cannot control themselves as evidenced in the high rates of obesity among adults in the United States. Exasperated, she asked me, "How can we expect kids to control themselves around it, especially when they don't know how bad it is for them?" This debate among school staff mirrored discussions that continue to play out nationally among policy makers and public health experts about obesity, responsibility, and blame.

Candy was also available all day in the school's bookstore located in the main commons area, even during lunch when vending machines were locked, and the bookstore candy was almost half the price of what vending machines charged. Many students I interviewed said they preferred buying candy from the bookstore because they could get more for their money. One girl explained,

Like, at the beginning of the year, whenever we used to sit over by the snack machines we would always get a Starburst in the morning, and now we go to the bookstore and get, like, three candies for the same price as one Starburst from the snack machine.

Another student, Linda, described her experience walking past the bookstore, where candy was sold:

Linda: I pass there between every period. So whenever I go past there it's, like, I wanna get something, but I hold myself back or restrain myself. And she does not do a good job of restraining me [referring to her friend, Abbie, who was also a focus-group participant]. Like, I tell her not to let me get certain things or not to let me get more than two candies or one candy or whatever, and then she always goes in to buy candy.

Abbie: Like, we'll be standing there, and she's like, "Don't let me get anything" and then first period she's like, "I want something" and I'm like, "No" and she's all, "No, I really want something."

Linda: I don't think they should have candy only cause it's so tempting.

During lunch, the school offered a wide variety of food and beverage items in the cafeteria as well as outside in the main commons area. Students could purchase meals sold through the National School Lunch Program in the cafeteria, which included a lot of high-fat main entrée items such as corndogs, hamburgers, burritos, chimichangas, fried chicken poppers, and *taquitos* as well as starchy or fried side dishes like french fries, Spanish rice, refried beans, mashed potatoes, and corn. Side salads, which consisted of a small amount of iceberg lettuce, a few shreds of carrot, and a generous amount of ranch dressing, were available daily as part of the school meal. I rarely saw students eating side salads during the school year but often observed them using the ranch dressing served with the side salad as a dipping sauce for french fries and fried chicken poppers.

Students could also purchase prepackaged sandwiches and entrée-sized salads in the cafeteria. One medium-sized bowl containing whole fruits (i.e., apples and oranges) was located in a remote corner of the cafeteria's food service area. During the school year, I never saw a student either buy or eat fruit on the high school campus, which is consistent with interview data about food consumption presented below. In fact, I observed students with fruit only twice, when two boys tossed an apple back and forth like a baseball during lunch, and another time when a boy kicked an orange like a soccer ball on his way to class.

A coffee bar offering a full range of Seattle's Best brand coffee drinks (e.g., mochas, lattes, cappuccinos), hot chocolate, and large assorted pastries was also located inside the cafeteria. Across from the coffee bar was an "Island Oasis" booth, where fruit-flavored "slushee" drinks were sold in flavors such as raspberry mango and strawberry. I later looked up nutritional information for these drinks and found that most are 110 calories per eight ounces (ten calories more than an eight-ounce can of Pepsi Cola).

Even with the voluntary removal of full-calorie soda from schools that occurred two years after my study, drinks like these have continued to provide similar amounts of sugar to students in schools across the nation. However, whereas students I interviewed at Desert Vista knew full-calorie sodas were not good for them, they perceived these "slushee" drinks as healthy because they were marketed as fruit smoothies.

Outside the cafeteria, in the main commons area, students could buy prepackaged, reheated mini-pizzas from a food service window called "Skinny Vinnie's." Each day, during the mid-morning break and lunch period, food carts were rolled out into the main commons area, from which students could purchase prepackaged à la carte items, such as bagels with cream cheese, mini-pizzas, french fries, chips, ice cream, burritos, bottled sports drinks, and bottled water. In short, there were a ton of options for purchasing food in and around the cafeteria.

The first day I observed lunch period my initial thought as I saw students milling around with food was, "Curly fries everywhere!" The vast majority of students who had food were eating curly fries (a type of french fry that is seasoned with spices and fried into curly shapes) out of small cardboard containers. I saw more students eating curly fries that day than any other food item, a trend I noticed throughout the school year during lunchtime observations. Indeed, curly fries appeared to be the main food staple at Desert Vista High School. Upon examining the daily menu that first day, which was posted on the wall inside the cafeteria, I saw that the meal being served was chicken tenders (small fried pieces of chicken), curly fries, and salad. This was a typical daily lunch offering.

In addition to the on-campus fare, a McDonald's restaurant was located directly across the street from Desert Vista. According to students, this was a popular lunchtime destination for juniors and seniors, who had off-campus privileges, as well as underclassmen, who regularly snuck off campus during lunch. I asked one of my freshman participants who ate there once a week how crowded it gets during lunch, and she replied, "My gosh, it's horrible! Like, you can barely find a seat."

I observed this firsthand one day when I walked over at the beginning of lunch period and found that not only was the line about twenty people long but also all the seats were taken. While there I discovered that the restaurant was attached to a service station mini-mart that offered a seem-ingly endless array of junk food, including a wide variety of candies, pastries, chips, sodas, and sports drinks. In fact, a number of high school students were purchasing their lunches from among the assorted pack-aged goods at the gas station mini-mart. It was a virtual cornucopia of junk food.

The McDonald's restaurant across the street was also a common after school hangout for students. A number of teens I interviewed who stayed late for sports, band, detention, or seventh-hour classes, said they frequented the restaurant after school. Typically, after school activities did not begin right after the final class period of the day, so depending on the activity, students had twenty minutes to an hour of free time after the school day ended before they had to return to campus.

One girl who stayed afterwards every day for cheerleading said she often walked over to the restaurant with her teammates before cheer practice to get a milkshake and fries. She expressed concern that cheerleading was caus-ing her to eat more junk food and subsequently gain weight. This student's concerns resonate with recent research showing that students with fast-food restaurants located within one-half mile of their school consumed fewer servings of fruits and vegetables, more servings of soda, and were more likely to be overweight than students whose school was not located near fast-food restaurants.[20]

"They're Like Walking Advertisements"

The availability of junk food both in school and directly across the street made it impossible for teenagers at Desert Vista to make healthy food choices. I asked Ricky from the Chapter 3 vignette to describe challenges he faced with weight loss attempts, and he replied, "There's food every-where. Like, you can't really get away from junk food no matter what." In fact, when I asked teens where they encountered the most junk food the majority said school. One girl explained:

> I think it's school because we're here every day, so we can get candy every day if we want to, which we pretty much do. At stores you have to go to the stores and buy it and then go back to your house. But at school it's easy because you have to go to school anyways.

The easy access to junk foods on campus created an environment where consumption of foods high in fat, sugar, and salt but low in nutritional value was the norm. Despite students' best efforts to "restrain" themselves, many explained that they simply could not resist eating junk food while at school.

Most of what teens reportedly consumed at school was high in fat and calories without contributing significantly to their nutritional needs.

Teens told me that seeing their friends and classmates eat junk food all day at school also made them crave it. One girl explained, "Like, you see people every day walking around eating candy and stuff, and it's like, 'Ooh, I want some!' They're like walking advertisements." Another girl similarly told me, "I crave the taste of soda in my mouth, especially when I see someone else drinking it." She said that even if she is not hungry but she sees someone eating food it sometimes causes her to crave that food:

> Like the other day at lunch we were walking past Annie, and she had a burrito, you know the ones I really like. And I wasn't even hungry, but she had it so I was like, "Can I have a bite?"

Junk food consumption on campus was not confined to lunch period, passing periods between classes, and the twenty-minute mid-morning break. According to teens I interviewed, students ate all day long, even during classes, as evidenced by the following focus-group transcript segment of Ricky and his friends:

Nicole: Robbie, you said that you try to eat healthy foods. Is this a challenge at school?

Robbie: Yeah, cause there's nothing here that like–

Reggie: –See, I couldn't do that cause, like, my friends are all around me eating good food, and I'll be like, "Oh I'm gonna buy that. I wanna go get one too." Either you won't eat or you'll have the junk food.

Ricky: Yeah. Like, if you don't eat at lunch, there'll be junk food in the classroom and stuff. Like you go up to people and say, "Oh let me have some."

Reggie: Yeah.

Nicole: Okay. So someone always has something to eat.

Reggie: Like, people eat after third period, and then they'll eat after lunch and stuff. And then in my fourth period class we eat all the time.

Ricky: And then the break kills it cause, like, at break there's food and some people just can't resist it. They're like, "Oh, I should get something to eat." And then at lunch it's, "Oh, I didn't eat that much [at break]. I should go get something to eat."

As these examples illustrate, eating healthfully was not an option at the high school, not necessarily because healthy foods were not available but because it was difficult for teens to make healthy food choices when everyone around them was eating junk food. Though the school offered prepackaged salads, sandwiches, and fruit, teens I spoke with felt overwhelmed with temptation to consume the junk food instead because it was so pervasive.

In fact, many students I interviewed did not even know the cafeteria sold fruit. When I asked an all-girl focus group what foods they would like to see added to the fare currently available at the high school, they responded:

Linda: Fruit.
Anna: Yeah, they don't have fruit here do they?
Linda: I don't think so.
Abbie: I don't think so. But they have Starbursts.
Linda: That's, like, the closest thing to fruit they have.
Anna: And Skittles.

Even students who knew about the fruit bowl and told me they wanted to see more "nutritional stuff" sold at the high school did not choose to eat fruit sold in the cafeteria. For example, during an all-boy focus group, I asked, "What do you think about the food here?" The following conversation ensued:

Tim: A lot of junk food.
Tad: Yeah.
Tim: Not enough nutritional stuff. I mean, if they have nutritional stuff students don't eat it. Nobody buys it. Like the oranges, you never see anybody buy em.
Nicole: Have you ever seen anyone with an orange at school?
Tim: No.
Nicole: Have you ever bought one?
Tim: No.

Tim told me during an earlier interview that his favorite food was oranges. He had said, "Sometimes I'll be sitting in class, and I'll crave an orange for no reason." However, when I asked Tim which foods he typically ate at school he replied, "Pizza, chips, and burritos." The prevalence of junk food on campus normalized the everyday consumption of candy, chips, soda, and fried foods to the extent that teens, even those who genuinely liked healthy foods automatically went for the junk foods instead.

"You Did It Again, Didn't You?"

Teens said they chose unhealthy over healthy food options because the unhealthy items were more readily available, more actively promoted, and more visible. The power of food advertising is well documented.[21] For example, studies have shown a positive correlation between the amount of time children spend in front of television and the amount of junk food they consume.[22] Advertising encompasses more than television and media ads; at Desert Vista, the prominent placement of junk foods, which encouraged widespread consumption of these items, was a powerful form of advertisement.

I explored this phenomenon further during focus-group interviews by asking, "Why do people choose to eat junk food instead of healthy food?" One group of girls I interviewed said they preferred junk food because it was "funner" than healthy foods:

Nicole: Why do we eat junk food instead of apples, oranges, and bananas?

Abbie: Cause it's funner when you've got, like, the flaming hot Cheetos [spoken with enthusiasm and accompanied by a smile and jazz hands] versus, like, an apple and an orange [spoken in a monotone voice and accompanied by a bored expression]. [laughter]

Linda: Yeah.

Nicole: What do you mean when you say it's funner?

Anna: It's got a better name.

Abbie: Cause you have the little tiger [referring to the depiction of an animated cheetah on the packaging and in advertisements for Cheetos].

Anna: Yeah, the tiger that's flaming hot. And you have an orange, just an orange.

Nicole: Okay. So the orange is boring next to the flaming tiger?

Anna and Abbie: Yeah.

Abbie: If you see a basket of fruit, you're like "Wow. Fruit" [Spoken in a monotone voice]. You know, we've had fruit, like, forever. And then you see Cheetos and you're like, "Wow! Food! Like, real food" [Spoken with enthusiasm]! For some reason, junk food is better.

Nicole: What do you mean? Are you saying that Cheetos and other junk food is the real food?

Abbie: Yeah. It seems more like real food cause nobody eats fruit hardly ever. Like, nobody eats fruit anymore. It's just, like, fruit.

Nicole: Why else do we go for junk food?

Abbie: Well, they advertise it a lot more than fruit. Like, have you seen the swirly commercial? The kid comes home, and his hair is all crazy cause he goes on, like, a roller coaster. And he is the

> guy that, like, makes it all fun. You know, it's like we're gonna
> go on a trip and eat these Cheetos.
>
> Anna: There are no commercials about apples and oranges. There isn't.

This interview segment further illustrates the normalizing effects of what students perceived to be the school's junk food culture. Abbie describes junk food as "real food" based on her perception that "nobody eats fruit anymore." The girls also point out that packaging and advertising for "junk food" is more colorful and exciting than for fruit. A qualitative study by public health scholar Dianne Neumark-Sztainer and her colleagues reported similar findings.[23]

Television is still the main venue for advertising to youth, and in 2011 children between the ages of two and eleven viewed about a dozen TV ads a day for unhealthy foods and beverages.[24] Food companies spend $1.8 billion each year marketing food and beverages to youth, 90 percent of which focuses on promotion of fast food, sugary drinks, sugary breakfast cereals, and candy.[25] The government's advertising budget for healthy foods is a small fraction of what corporations spend to market their junk food products,[26] the effects of which are reflected in the focus-group discussion segment. Even worse, junk food advertising in schools remains prevalent. One study found that nearly 90 percent of high school students were exposed to corporate food and beverage marketing at school via one or more of the following forms: exclusive beverage contracts, school event sponsorships, providing fast-food coupons as student incentives, serving branded fast food, and displaying poster ads.[27]

While Abbie was able to describe in detail a commercial for her favorite cheese-flavored chips, Anna pointed out that she never sees commercials for fruits. Furthermore, marketing literature focuses on the importance of making food fun, referring to this strategy as "eatertainment."[28] As a result, youth are not just eating a food product that tastes good; they are consuming the fun, interactive lifestyle that comes with the product.[29] Ironically, the exciting, fun lifestyle connected to junk food products is reminiscent of what teens had to say about the connection between achieving the ideal body image, popularity, and greater social mobility.

Although the food environment certainly contributed to the normalization of junk food for students at Desert Vista, teens told me they were surrounded by junk food in other environments as well, including at home and at the mall, a popular afterschool and weekend hangout. For example, the majority of teens I interviewed said they liked to eat at a fast-food Chinese restaurant called Panda Express, located in the mall's food court. Many specifically said that orange chicken was their favorite food from Panda Express.

Having never eaten orange chicken from Panda Express, I wondered why it was so popular among these teens. I had the chance to find out during an all-girl focus-group interview with Leslie, the self-identified "non"; Demi, the girl with a maroon bob; and their friend, Lori.

I asked the girls, "When do you go for junk food?" They immediately and unanimously told me they always eat orange chicken from Panda Express when they go to the mall, which sparked a conversation about why they crave this particular food item:

Lori: It's good.
Demi: It is addictive. Even the drink cup knows you got orange chicken cause, like, you get your cup and you sit down at the table, and it says in big letters, "You did it again, didn't you? Orange chicken" [laughs].
Lori: In orange letters on the cup.
          [laughter]
Nicole: No way [laughs].
Demi: And if you go there, you <u>will</u> get orange chicken.
          [laughter]
Leslie: Yeah, there's Orange Julius and Cousin Subs and forty people are in line–
Lori: –For Panda Express. And their orange chicken tray is always empty when we get there. We're like, "We have to wait ten minutes! What?" [spoken in an exasperated voice]
Demi: It's addictive. They, like, sprinkle salt in there.
Leslie: I think it's cocaine or something.
Lori: Oh, it's so good.
Leslie: I don't know how to say this but, like, when I see the colors of Panda Express, I sprint to it.
          [laughter]
Leslie: And it's good food. It's glistening food.
Lori: –Orange chicken. It has, like, this thick layer of juice or something on it.
Demi: Yeah.
Leslie: Yeah. And, like, you're waiting in line, and you're so hungry–
Demi: –[laughs]. You just wanna jump over the counter.
Leslie: But, I don't know, you're waiting in line, and you just look up and you see all the food and you see em, like, scooping it in there and you're like [pants like a dog].
Lori: Just can't wait. You run to your table and you're like [mimics eating fast with both hands].

The power of advertising is clearly reflected in this focus-group interview segment.

The prominent placement of junk foods at school and places where teens spent a lot of time, like the mall, was just as powerful, if not more so, than direct advertising. Margo Wootan, Director of Nutrition Policy at the Center for Science in the Public Interest argues, "Marketing helps to define what kids want to eat. It helps to define the social norm of eating for kids, what kids think of as food."[30] Together, direct advertising and prominent product placement promoted, normalized, and increased the consumption of junk food, which made teens crave it even more.

"I Shouldn't Be Eating This"

Although the majority of teens I interviewed said they struggled to eat right, most consumed junk food daily, a behavior that threatened to align them with the overweight individuals they criticized. Consequently, most of the teens I interviewed expressed concern for managing their weight. Girls expressed their anxieties about junk food consumption and weight gain with each other to seek emotional support and present themselves as weight conscious. They also shared food and left their lunch money at home to limit the amount of junk food consumed.

Boys had similar anxieties but, as discussed in earlier chapters, were uncomfortable sharing their feelings as showing vulnerability in front of their male classmates invited teasing and ridicule. To watch them eat or talk with their friends, it would not appear that they worried about weight gain at all. They voraciously consumed food, jokingly called each other "fat" and "ugly," and laughed along when they were the butt of these jokes.

Girls communicated their anxieties about body weight largely through "guilt talk" (e.g., "I shouldn't eat this because it's fattening."). Guilt talk was usually accompanied by consumption of the food item in question. Expressions of guilt before, during, or after the consumption of junk food marked it as a transgression outside the realm of what teens knew they should be eating. Engaging in guilt talk allowed girls to demonstrate an awareness of their responsibility to maintain a normal body weight and ameliorate some of the guilt they felt. Here again, language and physicality intersected. For girls used guilt talk to portray themselves as body-conscious individuals even while they consumed fattening foods that would impact their body size and shape.

However, girls did not simply engage in guilt talk to demonstrate an awareness of their responsibility to maintain normal body weight. Girls often said during interviews that eating junk food genuinely made them feel guilty. For example, an overweight girl named Katie explained that when she ate junk food she felt guilty and thought, "That's [referring to the food she is consuming] making my stomach bigger." However, Katie said she usually continued eating the fattening food despite her feelings of guilt.

Jamie, introduced in the Chapter 4 vignette, similarly explained: "Well, I eat a lot of junk food and usually feel guilty afterwards. And then, like, after a while I think, 'If I wouldn't have eaten that I wouldn't be so full' and I think about how it's all going to turn into fat." When asked to describe what kinds of foods she ate on a daily basis, one girl I interviewed began talking about junk food, saying:

> I'll be craving something fattening, and sometimes I'll be like, "No, I'm not gonna eat it. I'm not gonna eat it." And I don't eat it. But there are times when I just eat it, and then afterward I'm like, "What did I do?" and I feel guilty.

Clearly, these girls had internalized the connection between junk food consumption and weight gain. However, they felt unable to stop eating junk food, which resulted in feelings of guilt and concerns about managing their weight.

As discussed, girls' body fat was more closely monitored and criticized than boys' by both male and female peers at Desert Vista. It is not surprising that girls, who receive a steady stream of messages about the importance of being thin via media advertisements, family members, and peers,[31] would express guilt over consuming junk foods, which are linked to increasing overweight and obesity rates.[32]

Just as women are expected to control their body fat, so are they expected to limit the amount of food they consume, which was true for girls at Desert Vista. Susan Bordo writes:

> The social control of female hunger operates as a practical "discipline" [to use Foucault's term] that trains female bodies in the knowledge of their limits and possibilities. Denying oneself food becomes the central micro-practice in the education of feminine self-restraint and containment of impulse.[33]

For girls I interviewed at Desert Vista, their lack of "feminine self-restraint" around junk food consumption manifested in feelings of guilt.

Most girls expressed feeling guilt when eating junk food, but only three of twenty boys said eating fattening foods made them feel guilty. During individual interviews, some boys discussed concerns about weight gain as a result of eating a lot of junk food at school. However, most did not talk about junk food consumption and weight gain concerns in terms of guilt.

And boys did not admit to worrying about their weight in all-male group interview settings. As discussed in earlier chapters, boys associated appearance-related concerns with femininity, a finding supported by other studies on boys and body image.[34]

At Desert Vista, girls' guilt around eating junk food and concern with managing their body weight often led to sharing food with girlfriends to limit their consumption of junk food. Throughout the school year, I observed groups of two to three girls sharing one food item, such as a burrito, a pastry, or a piece of pizza, on a daily basis. During interviews, most teens, male and female, said that girls shared food to watch what they ate.

Moreover, many girls explained that they purposely left their lunch money at home to avoid purchasing junk food at school and instead took bites from their friends' food. For example, one girl told me that when she ate school food every day in middle school she gained a lot of weight and then lost the weight by abstaining from school food. Now that she was in high school she kept the weight off by taking bites of food her friends had purchased to limit how much she ate. Leslie said that girls share food "so they can't splurge and eat a lot." She explained, "They get a piece of pizza and think, 'Ooh, this is bad, but if I share it's not as bad.'"

Ricky and his friends described girls sharing food with each other in the following way:

Ricky: Some girls will be like, "Oh, I'm fat. I can't eat all this. Here, you eat it."
Reggie: Yeah.
Ricky: Or "I'm full. Eat this."
Nicole: Okay. So do you hear girls talk like that a lot?
Reggie: Yeah, all the time.

Similarly, a participant in an all-girl focus group said girls share food because "it makes them feel less fat about eating."

In contrast, I rarely saw boys share food with each other, and I sometimes observed boys guarding their food from friends to avoid sharing. For example, one day during lunch I walked into the lobby of the gym, where a group of approximately twenty boys played basketball every day and observed boys drinking from liter bottles of soda, eating family-sized bags of chips, cartons of french fries and chicken tenders, and multiple slices of pizza. I was struck not only by the ravenous nature with which these boys ate but also by the large amounts of food they consumed in comparison to girls. While some boys tried to limit their consumption of junk food in private, publicly they ate heartily, as it was not considered appropriate for boys to express concern for their weight by appearing to watch what they ate.

The intensity with which boys guarded their food was noteworthy. Some boys tried to grab food from boys who were still eating. For example, Jerry, the short, thin, fidgety boy introduced in an earlier chapter, stood in a corner hovering over his chicken tenders and french fries, glancing around nervously as he ate. Another boy approached Jerry from behind, put his arms around Jerry, and asked, "How's it going?" as he attempted to grab Jerry's food. Jerry angrily pushed the boy away, saying "Dude, get away."

At that point, a boy walked in with a large box of donuts that a friend had brought him from an off-campus location, and he was immediately surrounded by about fifteen boys. He held the box of donuts up high above his head while other boys begged him for some and tried to grab the box away from him. He announced that he would not give anyone a donut because if he gave out one then he would have to share with everyone and waited until boys began taking basketballs out to the court to eat the donuts. Although this example is an extreme version of what I observed on campus throughout the year, it accurately illustrates the difference with which boys and girls approached food in general.

Teens I interviewed said boys did not share food with each other as often as girls and that boys shared food differently. They often described similar scenarios to what I observed in the gym when boys guarded their food from each other. For example, when I asked participants in an all-girl focus group whether or not boys shared food, Leslie replied,

> Mm no. I've never seen a guy share food. I'm thinking about Sam right now. He has, like, eight taquitos and if you try to take one away he's all, "No" [Spoken in a loud, high pitch shriek]! They don't really share.

Sharing food at Desert Vista was perceived as a strategy for watching what one ate, and as such was a behavior associated with girls.

When boys did share food, it was different from how girls did it. Participants from an all-boy focus group explained:

Nicole: Do girls and guys share or, I mean, trade food differently?

Ricky: Kind of. We'll rip off a piece and be like, "Here you go" [spoken gruffly] and a girl's like, "Here, take a bite" [spoken politely, in a high pitched voice, followed by laughter].

Nicole: So guys wouldn't take bites off the same burrito after eating from it themselves?

Reggie: We just kind of rip it off. Like, I'd rather just tear it off if it's a
          guy, but if it's a girl it's all right [laughs].
Ricky: Yeah [laughs].

In the transcribed interview segment above, I self-corrected after using the word *share*, changing it to *trade* because boys I interviewed seemed really uncomfortable with the idea of *sharing* food with other guys.

When I asked boys whether or not they shared food with their friends, they often responded with nervous laughter. Sometimes, an uncomfortable silence and a simple "no" would accompany the boys' nervous laughter. However, most boys answered the question but changed the word *share* to *trade* or *jack* (a slang term meaning "to steal") in their response. "Trading food" was the most common descriptive phrase used by boys, followed by "jacking food." Boys also explained that they shared (or traded) finger foods (e.g., chips, chicken tenders, french fries) that did not require mouth contact. That sort of mouth contact was considered too intimate to occur between boys. It implied homosexuality, a label most boys wanted to avoid at all costs because of the stigma associated with it.

In contrast to the perception that girls shared food as a strategy for limiting food consumption, teens said guys shared food because they did not have money to buy their own. For example, during an all-boy focus group, I asked participants why they trade food, and Ricky responded, "Like, some days someone won't have no money, and they'll [gesturing toward his fellow focus-group participants] buy something. And sometimes our friends will lend us money, and we'll buy something and then just pick off each other's food."

Similarly, Tim told me that he and his friends trade food because "not everyone always has money. Like one of my friends has a job, so he's always got money; so sometimes he buys lunch." Most boys I interviewed said boys trade food for financial reasons, either pooling their resources to buy as much food as possible for the group or eating from a friend's lunch. None of the boys interviewed, either individually or as part of a group, claimed to trade food as a strategy for watching what they ate.

Sharing, like worrying about one's appearance, was a social practice that boys and girls associated with femininity. Thus, the way teens consumed food, how much food they ate, and even how they talked about food were related to their body-image concerns and, perhaps more surprisingly, their ideas about heteronormative masculinity and femininity.

Schools must continue efforts to provide healthy foods and beverages for students. It is hypocritical to teach students about the importance of eating healthfully and reinforce mainstream media messages about individual responsibility in the fight against obesity while making fattening junk foods readily available at school. For teens at Desert Vista, this mixed message intensified their food-related guilt and body angst. In the following concluding chapter, I discuss policies and strategies for improving school culture around issues of body image, fat stigma, exercise, and food.

Notes

1. Brownell and Horgen, 2004; Chriqui *et al.*, 2010; Nestle, 2002; Story, Kaphingst, and French, 2006; US Government Accountability Office, 2005.
2. Institute of Medicine, 2012.
3. Chriqui *et al.*, 2010.
4. Chriqui *et al.*, 2013.
5. Burros and Warner, 2006.
6. Wescott, Fitzpatrick, and Phillips, 2012.
7. Craddock *et al.*, 2011; Taber *et al.*, 2012; Yon and Johnson, 2014.
8. US Department of Agriculture, Food and Nutrition Service, 2012.
9. US Government Accountability Office, 2014.
10. US Government Accountability Office, 2014; "1M Kids Stop School Lunch," 2014; "Let's Move," 2014.
11. Sheikh, 2014.
12. Sheikh, 2014:4.
13. Brownell *et al.*, 2010; Kwan, 2009; Schwartz and Brownell, 2007.
14. Brownell, 1994; Horgen and Brownell, 2002; Schwartz and Brownell, 2007; Wadden, Brownell, and Foster, 2002.
15. Wadden, Brownell, and Foster, 2002:513.
16. Brownell and Horgen, 2004; Nestle, 2002; Schlosser, 2001; Schwartz and Brownell, 2007; Wadden, Brownell, and Foster, 2002.
17. Story *et al.*, 2008.
18. Kwan, 2009.
19. Counihan, 1992:57.
20. Davis and Carpenter, 2009.
21. Bernhardt *et al.*, 2013; Brownell and Horgen, 2004; Linn, 2004; Nestle, 2002; Nichter and Nichter, 1991; Powell, Harris, and Fox, 2013.
22. Galst and White, 1996; Hancox and Poulton, 2006.
23. Neumark-Sztainer *et al.*, 1999.
24. Powell, Harris, and Fox, 2013.
25. Federal Trade Commission, 2012.
26. Brownell and Horgen, 2004; Nestle, 2002; Powell, Harris, and Fox, 2013.
27. Terry-McElrath *et al.*, 2014.
28. Linn, 2004.
29. Nichter and Nichter, 1991.
30. Katz *et al.*, 2013.
31. Nichter, 2000; Nichter and Nichter, 1991; Taylor, 2011.
32. Kubik, Lytle, and Story, 2005; Vartanian, Schwartz, and Brownell, 2007.
33. Bordo, 1993:130.
34. Gill, Henwood, and McLean, 2005; Ryan and Morrison, 2009.

6

So What? What Now?

Mia, a fourteen-year-old freshman at Desert Vista High School, hated the way she looked, was teased by her classmates for being fat, and struggled with bulimia. When I interviewed Mia and asked her to rate how satisfied she was with the way her body looks on a scale of one to five, with five being the most satisfied, she responded, "Two," explaining:

> I criticize myself all the time. Like, I'm not happy with myself. You know, I just feel really fat in my stomach or whatever, and I bring myself down all the time cause I always compare myself to other people. My friend Angie is so pretty; every single guy likes her because of her body. She has the really tiny waist and the big butt like they talk about in songs you hear on the radio. Every time I'm with her she gets every guy, every one of them. It just like breaks my self-confidence. And when I'm with her I just feel like there's no point in even putting on makeup or anything cause it never does anything. I don't like the way I look at all. I don't like looking in the mirror cause I don't like what I see.

Mia told me that she was five feet six and weighed 142 pounds, which is considered a healthy weight for a girl her age by the Centers for Disease Control and Prevention. Nonetheless, she was teased mercilessly at school for being too big.

Mia said that girls come up to her on a regular basis and ask, "How much do you weigh?" or "What did you eat today?" to suggest that she should watch what she eats. Her peers called her "fat" and "ugly," saying things like, "Oh my God, you're such a fat ass!" During an interview, Mia described a particularly hurtful incident:

I had a pair of pants in my backpack, and this guy Joey took em out of my backpack. Angie was like, "What size are those?" and Joey's like, "A million bazillion." And he put em on, and they were falling off of him ... I was really embarrassed, and he's like, "Whose are these?" And I'm like, "Oh they're Justine's." I didn't want to tell him they were mine. And they [the boys in the group] were saying, "Oh my God these things are huge. You could fit two people in here." And, you know, they were really my pants. I just, you know, had a mask on, not letting it show. But I wanted to cry so bad.

I asked Mia why she thought her classmates teased her about her weight since she was clearly not fat. She explained that kids figure out what their peers are self-conscious or sensitive about and tease them for that.

When Mia's classmates called her ugly or teased her about her face, she could hide her emotions. However, when anyone teased her about her weight, she would become visibly upset or even cry. As a result, everyone knew that was her weakness, and whenever someone got mad at her or wanted to pick on her they would say something mean about her weight.

For example, Mia got into an argument with a girl at lunch one day, and that night the girl called her at home and said, "Hey, my mom has some diet pills if you need them, cause you kind of do." I asked Mia how this ongoing teasing made her feel, and she replied:

You know, I'll say I don't care, but then I'll look in the mirror and tell myself that it's true. And then I'll want to watch my weight, but hearing them say things like that makes me want to eat more because I get stressed out and that's like my way of feeling better.

Mia ate a lot of junk food, which she got both at school and at home, and felt guilty about it. She described an ongoing battle with bulimia, which had peaked the year before in eighth grade. With the support of family members, Mia had recently stopped binging and purging and had begun walking after school and on weekends to relieve stress.

Although Mia took PE class every day at school, she did not see this as a safe space for engaging in exercise. Mia said that girls competed to look the best in their gym clothes:

Like, for most of the girls in there, you know, it's a competition to see who can show more of their body for the guys or who is the most flexible [sigh]. And then, you know, people make fun of you if you wear the same gym clothes more than once a week. They're like, "Hey didn't you wear that yesterday?"

Mia preferred to wear sweat pants rather than shorts, but doing so made her stand out since all of the other girls wore shorts. Ultimately, it did not really matter what she wore because either way she got teased in PE for her weight.

Mia felt self-conscious about how her body looked when she exercised, and worried that she would appear to be out of shape compared to other girls. She explained:

> Like, when I run my legs, you know, jiggle, and I don't like people to watch when I go around the track and [sigh] then there's some girls who can run three laps and just be like "yeah." And then I'm dying after three laps. I hate it when we do the fitness tests, or whatever, when you have to do the sprint runs with two people at a time and everyone sits and watches you. I hate that cause the floor moves when you run. Then you're trying to beat that person you're up against.

Teasing behaviors that occurred throughout the school day were intensified in PE because teens' bodies were on display in gym shorts and T-shirts and students had greater freedom to interact without close supervision while playing games and sports in the gym or on the field.

One day in PE Mia wore shorts because it was really hot outside. The students had to run around the track for five minutes as a warm-up exercise, and as Mia ran she felt sharp pains in the backs of her thighs. When Mia turned around, she saw that one of her male classmates was shooting the backs of her legs with a BB gun. She asked him why he was doing that, and he replied, "Your legs jiggle." I asked Mia if the student got into trouble for having a BB gun in PE class, and she said that the teacher did not notice. He would pull the gun out and shoot her when they were on the opposite side of the track from their teacher. Not surprisingly, Mia dreaded PE and resisted participating as much as possible.

* * *

For Mia and other teens I interviewed, how they felt about their own bodies was so enmeshed with their relationship to food, exercise, and their peers that these issues could not be meaningfully interpreted in isolation. For example, Mia had low self-esteem, which was related to her belief that she was fat, all of which was fueled by fat teasing. Even though she was not overweight by medical standards, Mia was teased mercilessly for the way her body looked. She was an easy target because of her obvious low self-esteem and because she had few friends on campus. Feeling self-conscious about how her body looked and getting feedback that reinforced those feelings resulted in Mia refusing to participate in PE class, which had implications for her health and her body size.

Like other teens at Desert Vista, Mia worried about eating too much junk food because she knew it would result in weight gain, yet she could not resist the temptation. Mia felt the food-related guilt that many girls talked about, but unlike most teens she developed a harmful habit of binging and purging. She, like so many others, had internalized the widely held belief that body size is a choice and that individuals are responsible for managing their weight through lifestyle. All of these interrelated issues— body image, self-esteem, attitudes about fatness and responsibility, food consumption, exercise practices, and fat teasing—were largely mediated and negotiated through language.

What I Learned

I began this book by explaining what body image and obesity have to do with language. How we talk about fat does not simply reflect our attitudes but also shapes our understanding of fat, how we feel about our own bodies, and how we relate to others based on our perceptions of their body size. Feminist philosopher Judith Butler writes: "Language and materiality are not opposed, for language both is and refers to that which is material, and what is material never fully escapes from the process by which it is signified."[1] That is, language and the body are intertwined because language does not just describe the body but shapes it through the processes of naming, describing, and critiquing.

I explored how teens developed shared understandings of fat through everyday conversation, teasing, and gossip. Teens positioned themselves as "thinner than" their peers by engaging in ongoing critique of their peers' body fat. Such discourses enabled teens to divert attention away from their own bodies, display awareness of the boundary between acceptable and unacceptable body size, and construct themselves as body-conscious individuals willing to take personal responsibility for their appearance in opposition to those deemed too fat.

Direct teasing functioned as a very explicit and public way for adolescents to mark someone who displayed too much body fat as "other," while indirect teasing, or gossip, allowed teens to more subtly co-construct and circulate knowledge about body-size norms among their friends through constant surveillance, evaluation, and verbal critique of their peers. Both strategies also functioned to elevate the social status of those teasing, who deflected attention away from their own bodies and lowered the status of the person being criticized. By engaging in running commentary about their peers' bodies, teens continually negotiated body fat norms against which they measured themselves and each other, and through which they circulated each other in a network of hierarchical relations.

I discussed how teens talked about body image, food, and exercise, and how those conversations influenced not only perceptions about what looks good and how much fat is too much but also relationships among teens and their positions within the school's social hierarchy. In this way, language was a powerful influence on the material body because teasing, gossip, and everyday conversation shaped certain aspects of teens' day-to-day realities on campus, including their ideas about body image, femininity, and masculinity; how they categorized their peers in terms of body size and attractiveness; how they felt about the way their own bodies looked; and how they related to their classmates based on discursively co-constructed perceptions of their body size.

Yet language does not tell the whole story. The physical reality of the body, the materiality that Butler refers to in the quote above, cannot be denied. Teens at Desert Vista were constantly butting up against the physical reality of their bodies. For example, the ultimate goal for most teens, boys and girls, was to eradicate visible body fat. Boys wanted lean muscle tone, and girls aimed for thin, fat-free physiques. However, they could not escape the biological reality that every body contains fat. Some teens could approach the body-image ideal to varying degrees, but none could achieve the so-called perfect body. This is, in fact, the nature of an ideal—it is something one strives for but never quite achieves. There is always work to be done.

Not only were students at Desert Vista unable to achieve the ideal. Many of those whom I interviewed were overweight and a few were obese, which generally reflected national body mass index trends for youth. In the context of this material reality, teens focused on strategically hiding their fat beneath clothing. The popular style for boys was loose-fitting clothes, which made obscuring fat relatively easy. However, it was nearly impossible for girls to wear the tight, revealing outfits considered stylish and feminine without displaying some amount of body fat. This meant that almost all girls were potential targets for their peers' critical gaze and could be cast in the role of fat foil.

The boundary between acceptable and unacceptable body size was negotiable up to a point. The largest teens on campus, very fat girls in particular, were stuck with their "too fat identities" and the accompanying social stigma. For example, clothes sharing and fat talk simultaneously represented sites of competition, rapport building, and solicitation of emotional support from girlfriends. However, just as girls who wore larger clothing sizes than their friends were excluded from clothes sharing, undeniably fat girls were excluded from participation in fat talk, relegating them to the margins of their friendship groups.

Additionally, girls who were considered overweight or obese by most of their peers were excluded from discursively positioning themselves as thinner than other girls through gossip and teasing, rendering their place in the adolescent social hierarchy non-negotiable. Some overweight or obese boys could still participate in this type of discursive positioning by drawing attention to the flaws of girls and hiding their own body fat underneath loose-fitting clothing. This is where materiality becomes undeniable; for very large teens, girls in particular, could not be "not fat," even through discourse.

Students were also faced with the material reality of their bodies every day as they negotiated the school food environment and participated in PE class. Teens I interviewed clearly understood that consuming foods and drinks high in fat, calories, and sugar (e.g., soda, candy, pizza, chips) on a regular basis caused weight gain. Even teens who were overweight harshly criticized fat people who ate junk food for not seeming to care about their appearance or health, describing fat people as lazy and sloppy. Yet these same teens felt unable to resist junk food, which was readily available all day at school. Many students I interviewed, especially girls, felt guilty about eating fattening foods. Their feelings of guilt were enmeshed in beliefs about personal responsibility, body-image ideals, anxiety about fat stigma, and social positioning among their peer groups.

With regard to physical activity, most girls chose not to participate in PE class because they worried about how their bodies looked and did not want to mess up their hair and makeup. They also felt unqualified to actively participate in the presence of boys who "hogged the ball." Boys were faced with a harsh physical reality in the locker room, where some were teased and even physically assaulted for the way their bodies looked. Teens I interviewed understood the importance of exercise in achieving their body-image goals, but some chose not to participate in PE because it did not feel like a safe space. Yet, for some of these teens, PE class was their only opportunity to exercise, which meant they did not engage in physical activity at all.

In general, I found that Desert Vista's high school environment was fraught with difficulties for most teens, male and female. Both boys and girls expressed body-image concerns and worried about being teased. Girls were held to a harsher standard of beauty that required them to look cute all the time, a gendered imperative that was made difficult by the negative stereotypes associated with female athleticism and the prevalence of junk food on campus. Being held to a harsher standard of beauty was slightly moderated by various strategies girls used to support one another, including fat talk, guilt talk, and clothes sharing. Such practices provided safe enclaves where girls felt supported and accepted by their girlfriends, but they also represented sites of competition among girls who strived to be prettier, thinner, and more desirable than their friends.

Although body-image ideals for both boys and girls were unrealistic, boys were generally afforded a broader body-size range than girls. Heavier body weights for boys were more acceptable because boys were expected to be physically larger than girls, and it was considered advantageous for boys who participated in sports, such as football and wrestling, to be large. These ideas conferred a degree of acceptability and normalcy to boys who were heavier. But boys did not escape fat stigma at school. Those who were too short, too thin, too fat, or did not fit the tacit standards of masculinity in some other way were verbally teased and sometimes physically assaulted by other boys. Because these behaviors tended to occur in the boys' locker room, those who were victimized did not feel safe dressing out or participating in PE class.

Additionally, no safe emotional space existed for boys to talk with each other about their body-image concerns. They had no acceptable strategies for seeking emotional support or soliciting compliments about their appearance from their male friends. The only appropriate way for boys to talk about body image with each other was to gossip, tease, and attack others for the way they looked or objectify attractive girls by complimenting their body parts, often through sexual innuendo. Boys competed with each other over athletic performance, muscle tone, and six-pack abs. Nonathletic, fat boys were not only excluded from these masculinity-affirming practices, but were ridiculed and bullied for the way their bodies looked.

Where to Go From Here

Policy suggestions related to childhood obesity tend to focus on schools as an important site for change. The Institute of Medicine (IOM), for example, asserts that schools have the potential to play a crucial role in childhood obesity prevention because children and teens spend up to half of their waking hours and consume up to half of their total daily calories there.[2] The 2012 IOM report on "Accelerating Progress in Obesity Prevention" recommends as one goal a school-based approach requiring collaboration among multiple stakeholders: "Federal, state, and local government and educational authorities with support from parents, teachers, and the business community and private sector, should make schools a focal point for obesity prevention."[3]

The IOM report reminds us that schools have a broad mission that encompasses supporting the overall health and wellbeing of students in addition to teaching academic skills. For example, schools require immunizations, provide health screenings, offer opportunities for physical activity, and provide meal programs intended to support a healthy diet.[4] It cites research suggesting that students who engage in regular exercise and eat well-balanced, nutritious meals learn better and miss fewer days of school for health reasons.[5]

In 2005 and again in 2012, the IOM recommended that schools provide more opportunities for students to engage in physical activity, make substantive improvements to nutrition standards for all foods and beverages sold or provided through schools, and incorporate food literacy into the curriculum. Steps for implementation at the federal, state, and local levels are clearly outlined for each of these recommended strategies. This three-pronged approach that addresses physical activity, nutritional standards, and education about eating healthy is a sound model for addressing obesity-related issues in an integrative way. However, the reality of affecting social change is complex and slow going, especially in institutional settings.

The IOM reports that recent efforts to implement school food and physical education policies have gained some traction but notes that "they are neither widespread, integrated, nor strong enough to produce the needed reduction in childhood obesity rates."[6] School-based policy changes require resources such as technical assistance, training, funding, adequate staffing, and time in addition to effective communication, collaboration, and coordination among multiple stakeholders. In line with this reality, the IOM recommends that physical education and food literacy requirements be adequately supported through funding and teacher training.[7] However, even when school-based policy mandates are supported with necessary resources the process can still be fraught with unanticipated challenges.

For example, as discussed in earlier chapters, the Healthy, Hunger-Free Kids Act of 2010 required an overhaul of nutrition standards for all food and beverages available in schools over a three-year period. A follow-up US Government Accountability Office report found that school districts faced significant challenges implementing this policy mandate, including food waste, meal planning, and financial management issues, despite numerous government memos offering written guidance and site visits to some school districts.[8]

The report found a combination of rapid policy implementation and mid-process changes to federal guidance and compliance monitoring hindered the success of the program in the short term, and it emphasized the importance of technical assistance occurring in coordination with compliance monitoring. That is, technical assistance should be guided by information about what is and is not working well so that it can be targeted to effectively address problem areas.

Several years ago I contributed to the evaluation of the Alliance for a Healthier Generation's Healthy Schools Program, which was founded by the American Heart Association and the William J. Clinton Foundation in 2005 to reduce incidence of childhood obesity by improving schools in the areas of nutrition, physical activity, health education, and employee wellness. This program is not a typical grant program in that it does not award funds to participating schools or districts, but rather provides extensive technical assistance to help schools make sustainable changes. I collaborated with a team of researchers to visit twenty-one schools located in California, Florida, Michigan, Minnesota, New Jersey, and Wisconsin to learn how well the program was working.

Through our site visits we learned that schools could make simple but meaningful changes to improve the health and wellbeing of students. Examples of positive physical activity changes some schools made included: increasing time spent in recess to make up for reductions in PE class time; incorporating school wide ten-minute exercise breaks during the day; offering students incentives for participating in community fundraising activities, such as Jump Rope for Heart and National Walk to School Day; partnering with community organizations, such as the YMCA, to offer after school sports activities; making school gyms, playgrounds, and sports fields available to students before school, after school and during lunch; organizing after- or before-school walking clubs comprised of students and teachers; and obtaining grants for afterschool enrichment programs that include an exercise component from organizations like the Girls and Boys Club and 21st Century Learning Center.[9]

With regard to school nutrition, research shows that competitive foods (e.g., chips, soda, candy, ice cream) are still readily available at high schools across the country and improvement of school meals has a long way to go. Schools should to be prepared to practice what they teach, so to speak. Junk food in schools is more pervasive than we realize. In addition to vending machines, snack bars, and bake and candy sales, it is not uncommon for teachers to reward students with candy, donuts, and pizza parties. Schools may have policies that prohibit these junk food avenues, but without staff buy-in, monitoring, and enforcement such policies are worthless.

Some argue that schools need to sell junk food to make money for extracurricular programs, but research challenges that reasoning, revealing that health costs associated with selling junk food outweigh the revenue benefits. In 2003–2004, before the Healthy, Hunger-Free Kids Act of 2010, food service management for school districts nationwide reported obtaining, on average, 12 percent of revenues from competitive junk foods. Most of the competitive junk foods (80 to 90 percent) from that time would not comply with current nutritional standards, which replace items high in fat, sugar, and sodium with whole grain foods, low-fat dairy items, fruits, and vegetables. In anticipation of lost revenue as a result of stricter nutrition standards, a 2013 study conducted by the USDA recommended a combination of pricing and marketing strategies to increase sales of healthier competitive foods that comply with updated standards and expand participation in the school meals program.[10]

The Healthy Schools Program evaluation team found that schools and districts were able to implement a number of sustainable strategies to improve foods and beverages offered to students. Examples included: participating in state or federal programs (e.g., Farm to School Network, US Department of Defense Fresh Fruit and Vegetable Program) to increase the variety of fresh fruits and vegetables available; reducing the fat content of foods by using reduced-fat cheese, baking rather than frying, and draining the fat from ground beef; increasing the number of whole grain foods available by switching to brown rice and whole wheat bread; renegotiating vending machine contracts to offer healthier snacks and drinks; implementing policies restricting the sale or distribution of competitive foods on campus (e.g., candy sales, cupcake parties); and pricing healthier foods lower than junk foods.[11]

Additionally, we found that schools promoted healthy eating using simple strategies like sponsoring weekly taste tests of healthy foods, involving students in meal planning, displaying colorful posters promoting healthy eating throughout the school, offering rewards to students who ate the fruits and vegetables provided as part of the school meal, and cutting up fruit before serving it to make it easier for students to eat. Overall, the most successful Healthy Schools Program schools reported a high level of administrative support for school wellness efforts. The support of staff, students, and parents was also an important indicator of success.[12]

Examples from the Healthy Schools Program evaluation findings illustrate how schools can communicate to students that nutrition and exercise are important. Additionally, strategies used by these schools to increase physical activity and foster healthy eating shift the emphasis away from individual responsibility rhetoric and the obsession with body size toward a message of empowerment about making positive choices within an environment that nurtures healthy decision-making. This is a step in the right direction to fostering healthier body image as well as eating and exercise habits among youth.

However, findings from my study suggest that body-image concerns and weight stigma need to be factored into policy suggestions. How teens feel about their bodies and are treated by their classmates for the way they look impacts their relationship with food and exercise. Girls, even those who were considered thin and attractive, felt too self-conscious about their appearance and athletic abilities to actively participate in co-ed PE sports activities. Clearly, increasing opportunities for physical activity at school will not result in health improvements if teens are so self-conscious about the way their bodies look or so afraid of being teased in the locker room that they won't participate.

Further, students need close supervision in all areas of the school, including and especially locker rooms, where they are particularly vulnerable to body-focused scrutiny and teasing. I would also argue for the requirement of PE uniforms that are loose fitting and provide adequate coverage of the body to reduce body image-related competition among girls and concern among teens about how their bodies look during exercise. Additionally, PE teachers could begin the school year by teaching and encouraging girls how to actively engage in games and encouraging or even requiring boys to pass the ball to girls. Team-building activities that emphasize sportsmanship and healthy competition are one approach for facilitating greater inclusion of all students in PE activities. Mrs. Roy's strategy of separating girls and boys during team handball worked well in that context and is another option to consider. However, gender-segregated PE classes, though legal in some cases, remain a controversial issue.

In 2006 Title IX regulations were revised to allow schools more leeway in creating single-sex classes. Gender-segregated PE classes have received mixed reviews. Some studies show separating girls and boys during PE results in increased participation by girls.[13] However, feminist organizations, such as the American Association for University Women and the Women's Sports Foundation, have spoken out against gender-segregated classes, arguing that it invites the kind of discrimination Title IX was originally intended to address. On the one hand, I think boys and girls must learn to engage with each other respectfully in their families, communities, and workplaces throughout life. School, PE classes specifically, can be a good training ground for learning this type of collaborative spirit. For this to work, however, teachers must have the resources needed to support them in promoting teamwork, respect, and gender equality and they must be operating within a school culture that actively cultivates these values. The harsh reality is that many teachers do not operate within this kind of school environment, in which case the most pragmatic solution for encouraging boys and girls to actively engage in PE class is probably to separate them during team sports as Mrs. Roy did.

Schools are a convenient and practical focal point for addressing childhood obesity, but need for support from the community and parents cannot be overemphasized. Schools have become a virtual dumping ground for programs and policy meant to address physical and mental health, life and social skills, and behavioral issues in addition to academic proficiency, college preparedness, and vocational skills for a wide range of students, many of whom have special needs and require additional resources. Additionally, class sizes in schools across the nation continue to increase and pressures related to standardized testing remain intense.

Importantly, the IOM took a systems approach in its recommendations for accelerating progress in obesity-prevention efforts.[14] A systems approach recognizes that people operate in multiple environments (e.g., school, home, work, community) and that policy changes need to occur across those environments to have the greatest impact. For example, the IOM model connects the school environment with physical activity and food environments that address policy at the local community, state, and federal levels. Teens may spend a great deal of their waking hours in school, but they also spend time at home and in their communities.

In his book *How Children Succeed*, Paul Tough highlights the importance of communities, parents, and schools working together to support and nurture children.[15] He talks about the propensity to blame schoolteachers and administrators for student failure, citing an example from Chicago Public Schools whereby a new superintendent attempted to improve the worst-performing school in the district by cleaning house, so to speak, and hiring all new staff. But nothing changed as a result. Test scores remained the lowest in the school district.

Tough concluded that the reason sweeping changes in school staffing did not fix the problem was because the community—characterized by high crime rates, pervasive drug use, and uninvolved parents—remained the same. This is true for school-based obesity-prevention programs as well. Teaching students how to eat healthfully and prepare nutritious meals is only effective if they can actually obtain healthy foods at their local grocery stores, for example. Policy efforts must support families and communities as well as schools in order to achieve meaningful outcomes.

In addition to improving nutrition standards for school food, providing food literacy, and increasing opportunities for exercise at school, youth also need to be educated in media literacy. Counter messages that challenge dominant narratives are necessary to foster awareness of how powerful the media is in influencing our ideas about gendered body image and social norms, attitudes about fat people, food consumption choices, and exercise practices. My findings suggest that everyday language is impactful and shapes our perceptions, attitudes, and beliefs.

The IOM agrees; its model for systems change situates the school, physical activity, food, health-care, and work environments within a broader context of communication environments. Communication-related recommendations include development and implementation of a nutrition and physical activity social marketing campaign funded by the federal government and foundations. The IOM also calls on food, beverage, restaurant, and media industries to make voluntary, substantial improvements to their marketing aimed at children.[16]

Findings from my study suggest that communication strategies should encompass ideas about body image and fat stigma as well. In the years following my study, news media continue to focus on obesity as a social problem—it is commonly referred to as a "crisis" and an "epidemic" and has been framed as a triple threat to our nation by researchers and policy makers who predict that it will take a toll on our economy, health-care system, and military. For example, a 2012 study in the *American Journal of Preventive Medicine* that received a lot of media attention concluded that by 2030 42 percent of adults would be obese. The authors of this study predicted an estimated $550 billion in health-care spending between 2012 and 2030 as a result.[17]

An unintended consequence of media hype that demonizes obesity and highlights individual responsibility is fat stigma and the resultant discrimination, weight-related victimization, and fat shaming. Counter-media messages that educate youth about global diversity in body-size norms, emphasize health over beauty, and encourage youth to broaden their ideas about what it means to be beautiful are important. Counter-media messages and media-literacy curricula also need to address obesity stigma by showing how fat people are often negatively portrayed in movies and television and emphasizing the importance of treating people of all sizes with respect. Sociologist Abigail Saguy points out that a single-minded focus on body size obscures the problem of weight-based victimization.[18] The dialogue needs to be broadened to highlight the problem of obesity stigma.

As a former high school English teacher who is now married to a high school English teacher I am intimately aware of the ongoing pressures teachers face and the unrealistic expectations placed on them. This is a regular topic of conversation in my household. I understand the problematic nature of suggesting that teachers find a way to squeeze in yet another packaged curriculum. However, teaching media literacy does not have to be complicated, time consuming, or require extensive training. It can easily be incorporated into current events lessons or by way of teaching critical thinking skills.

For example, my husband led a ten-minute reader response lesson with his classes using one of the introductory chapter vignettes from this book. It sparked a discussion about the nature of teasing and bullying that occurs at their school, why fat kids get picked on, and potential strategies students and teachers can use to intervene when they witness bullying. This sort of lesson fits within the Common Core Standards and could be done using a magazine ad, television commercial, or movie clip. Child/teen development specialist Robyn Silverman offers some simple, effective ideas for teaching media literacy in her book, *Good Girls Don't Get Fat*.[19] Children and teens need to be explicitly taught how to critically examine media images, messages, and stereotypes they are inundated with daily.

Increased awareness of other avenues of influence for children and teens is also critical. I have a three-year-old son and am struck by how closely he watches me and how he mimics not just the words that come out of my mouth but my emphasis, intonation, and facial expression. Teens also learn from adults how to behave and interact with others in various contexts. The IOM asserts,

> Schools not only provide physical education and serve foods and beverages to students, but also serve as powerful role models, providing a culture that can support, rather than undermine, the efforts of children and adolescents and parents to promote healthful living.[20]

Undoubtedly, such people serve as powerful role models and shape the local culture around health, wellness, and attitudes toward people of different sizes.

Teachers are not the only adults who can offer healthy counter messages about body image and obesity. Parents, mentors, community members, and anyone who interacts with youth unwittingly and collectively teach children and teens to worry about their body size and judge others for how their bodies look through everyday conversation. Thus these potential role models need to be mindful of how to talk about body image, fat, and the way others look, realizing that when they casually comment to their spouses or friends that so-and-so has "really put on some weight" or "let themselves go," they are not only normalizing this type of discourse but modeling it; and when they obsess over their own body fat in front of youth they model that behavior and anxiety as normative.

Along those lines, it is important to remember that fat teasing, gossip, and everyday conversation about body image occurs within larger social, political, and cultural contexts "where organizations and institutions structure norms that create the possibility of marking and sharing notions of 'difference.'"[21] An important next step in understanding the social life of fat and fat stigma, in particular, is to explore the sociopolitical cultures of institutions where behaviors associated with fat stigma occur, such as schools, workplaces, and medical institutions, to get a clearer sense of how the cultures of these institutional contexts enable and cultivate marginalizing norms and behaviors.

Notes

1. Butler, 1993:69.
2. Institute of Medicine, 2005, 2012.
3. Institute of Medicine, 2012:329.
4. Institute of Medicine, 2012.
5. Institute of Medicine, 2012; Florence, Asbridge, and Veugelers, 2008; Trudeau and Shepherd, 2010.
6. Institute of Medicine, 2012:334–35.
7. Institute of Medicine, 2012.
8. US Government Accountability Office, 2014.
9. Beam *et al.*, 2010.
10. Guthrie *et al.*, 2013.
11. Beam *et al.*, 2010.
12. Ibid.
13. Best, Pearson, and Webb, 2010; Toms and Rhor, 2013.
14. Institute of Medicine, 2012.
15. Tough, 2012.
16. Institute of Medicine, 2012.
17. Finkelstein *et al.*, 2012.
18. Saguy, 2013.
19. Silverman, 2010.
20. Institute of Medicine, 2012:334.
21. Pescosolido *et al.*, 2008:432.

APPENDIX
RESEARCH METHODS

This appendix describes my research process, including how I built trust with teens, obtained permission to interview students during the school day, and navigated unanticipated challenges I encountered throughout the school year. I also describe in greater detail the methods I used to gather and analyze data.

Recruitment

I recruited fifty participants through presentations to freshman PE classes where I explained my study and handed out consent and assent forms. I focused on freshmen because they had recently made the transition into high school, where they would have to renegotiate their places within a larger adolescent social hierarchy. I also wanted to work with freshmen because students at the high school were only required to take one year of PE class, and it was standard practice for students to take PE as ninth-graders. Since part of my study involved observing and participating in PE classes, it was important that I interviewed students who would be enrolled in the physical education program.

During these presentations I explained that I study body image and asked students what they thought that meant. Responses included, "How you look," "If you like the way you look," "Your health," "What your body looks like," "Your image of your body," "Your hairstyle," and "How you dress." One girl responded by explaining that she thought the average was changing because kids were getting fatter. Some students took this opportunity to announce their personal body-image concerns. For example, in one class several boys shouted out that they were sometimes teased for being small. Some of the girls made comments about wishing they were thinner.

Both boys and girls seemed excited about my study and eager to participate. Many students asked if I would be able to take everyone who returned a signed form or if the process would be selective and some wanted to know what they could do to secure a spot in my study. My goal was fifty participants, twenty-five girls and twenty-five boys. Prior to recruitment presentations, I had been concerned about recruiting a sufficient number of participants and after the presentations, I worried that I might have attracted too many potential participants and would be faced with the difficult decision of choosing from among them. Because students' responses to the study were so positive and enthusiastic, I had initially planned to recruit from only five or six PE classes.

However, after handing out consent and assent forms to 100 students who said they wanted to participate, only a handful of signed forms were returned to me. I promptly decided to expand my recruitment efforts to all thirteen PE classes (approximately 500 students). Once I had finished recruitment presentations, I had handed out consent and assent forms to 250 teens who had said they wanted to participate. I felt certain I would have fifty students signed up soon and looked forward to beginning interviews in the next week or two. You can imagine my disappointment when, after a couple of weeks, my expanded recruitment efforts only yielded an additional fifteen to twenty signed forms.

Obtaining the remainder of signed consent and assent forms proved to be quite a challenge. I handed out the forms during PE, a class where students did not keep their backpacks with them; they dressed out for class and left their belongings in the locker rooms. I had hoped that my presence in the PE classes would serve as a reminder for students to return the signed consent and assent forms and it did. However, once students returned to the locker rooms at the end of the period to change clothes, they promptly forgot all about the forms and me. Out of sight, out of mind.

It was easy to follow up with girls because I could enter their locker room after class while they were changing and remind them. However, following up after class with boys was more difficult because I did not have access to the boys' locker room. Even if I waited outside of the locker room to ask boys for the forms, I often missed them in the throng of students rushing out the door as soon as the bell rang. A number of students also lost their signed forms or kept forgetting to bring them to school. Multiple times a day, students would see me on campus and exclaim, "Oh yeah, I forgot that form. I really want to be in your study but I can't remember to get it signed/bring it to school/take it out of my locker."

Signed forms continued to trickle in over the following two weeks. A month into the study I had recruited thirty girls and fifteen boys. I still needed an additional ten to fifteen boys and it appeared as though I had recruited all the participants I could through PE classes. I decided to take advantage of opportunistic moments when students on campus asked me who I was and what I was doing at the school. Whenever a freshman boy asked me about myself and expressed interest in what I was doing at the high school, I attempted to recruit him into the study. I also encouraged girls who had signed up to tell their guy friends about the study. Through these methods, I was able to recruit an additional five boys. At that point thirty girls and twenty boys were signed up. I decided to stop there and focus on data collection.

Data Collection and Analysis

Data collection methods included individual interviews, focus-group interviews, and daily observation throughout campus. My research was greatly facilitated by the cooperation and support of administrators and teachers at the high school. The school principal, who was writing his dissertation that year, told me that he understood the importance of having access to necessary resources for data collection and that he would provide me with anything I needed to facilitate my research.

True to his word, I was assigned an administrative assistant who called students out of class for interviews and helped me find rooms where I could conduct interviews. When the weather allowed, I conducted interviews outside, but when it was too cold or raining I was given access to the conference room or an unoccupied office. With regard to classroom observations, all of the teachers I approached were very welcoming and readily gave me permission to attend their classes whenever I wished.

I interviewed each participant twice during the course of the school year with the exception of two girls who left Desert Vista after being interviewed only one time. The first interview, which lasted about an hour, focused on body image and fat teasing. I asked participants to describe their ideal body image as well as how they felt about their bodies. I also asked about their body-image goals, what they were doing in terms of diet and exercise to achieve their goals, and how they talked about body image with their friends. Participants responded to questions about how body size affects their attraction to potential romantic partners and their personal experiences with and observations of weight-based teasing as well.

The second interview lasted approximately ninety minutes and focused on diet and exercise. I asked teens to talk about the kinds of exercise they engage in and how often, how they define exercise, and what types of exercises they perceived as more or less appropriate for girls and boys.

Participants also answered questions about PE, including what they think of their PE class, how they feel about dressing out, what kinds of things affected their motivation to participate, and how they felt about the co-ed nature of their PE classes. Questions about food consumption included discussion about what makes foods and beverages healthy or unhealthy, the types of food and beverages they consumed at school and in other contexts, reasons for eating besides hunger, where and with whom they tend to eat junk food, the degree to which their choices about what to eat and drink relate to personal body-image goals, and strategies used to limit junk food consumption.

The second interview also included questions about their families and households, such as who they lived with, what they typically ate for dinner, how often they ate together as a family, how often they ate dinner out or got take-out, what types of foods and drinks I would find in their kitchen, exercise habits of family members, and the types of activities their family engaged in together for fun. In addition, I followed up on topics that had emerged as particularly salient during the first interview. Emergent topics of importance to these teens included six-pack abs, muscle tone, and gender; perceptions of girls who are considered athletic; beliefs about body size and personal responsibility; and observations of and experiences with weight-based teasing.

At the time of the second interview, participants felt more comfortable with me because they had already been interviewed by me once before, and they had seen me on campus every day. I had also participated in most of their PE classes alongside them, and I had eaten lunch with many of them. For this reason, I cycled back to questions about teasing to obtain more in-depth information on the topic. These ninth-graders also had a better sense of the teasing culture on campus in the spring than in the fall when they were new to the high school.

I conducted six focus-group interviews with some of the participants and their friends, each lasting about an hour. Focus-group interviews were less structured than the individual interviews to allow participants to talk more openly about particular topics, such as junk food and advertising; body image and the media; teasing on campus; perceived gender differences in exercise participation and food sharing practices; and perceptions about different social cliques on campus. Study participants and their close friends comprised focus groups in order to encourage them to talk more freely. Of the six focus groups, three were all girls, two were all boys, and one included girls and boys.

I also made daily observations in various locations throughout the school, including the areas where students ate lunch, the girls' locker room, PE classes, health and life skills classes, and hallways during passing periods.

The primary goal of these observations was to explore naturally occurring conversations about body image and teasing practices among teens across contexts within the high school environment. Observation of PE classes enabled me to document gendered participation patterns as well as the ways in which teens interacted with each other. Lunchtime observations provided data on food and beverage options as well as consumption patterns, food sharing practices, and surveillance and monitoring across gendered lines. In each of these contexts I was able to observe a variety of interactions among teens, including teasing and bullying and talk about body image.

Participant observation at lunchtime and in PE classes yielded some of the most fruitful data. Occasionally, I would choose an empty table right before lunch period began and sit with whoever came to the table to eat. I experienced a variety of responses from teens who found me sitting at "their table." One day a group of girls walked over to the table where I was sitting, threw their book bags down and proceeded to say things like, "I shouldn't eat today because I feel fat" and "I need to diet but I'm hungry." When they asked who I was and I told them that I was a researcher from the university studying body image, they all laughed and talked to me about their body-image concerns for a while.

Another day I sat at an empty table and no one joined me when lunch period started. Finally, a boy timidly approached and nervously asked how I was doing. As we made small talk, I looked up to see a group of about four boys staring at us from several feet away. They eventually approached and laughingly told me that they did not know what to do when they saw a girl sitting at their table because girls never sit with them. When they asked who I was and I explained, it prompted a thoughtful conversation about body image among the group members.

After standing on the sidelines observing PE classes for a few months, I decided to dress out and actually participate alongside students. I chose to do this for several reasons. First, I wanted to experience on a visceral level how much exercise students were getting in PE classes, especially since PE was the primary or only source of regular exercise for many teens. Second, interview and observational data suggested that boys and girls participated differently in PE, with boys engaging more actively and girls participating more passively. I wanted to explore this phenomenon from the perspective of a participant in the class rather than an observer on the sidelines.

Additionally, participants said during interviews that most conversations about body image and direct teasing occurred during PE classes. As an observer at the edge of the playing field, I was too far away from students to overhear their conversations. Also, as an adult observer positioned on the sidelines, teachers were often drawn to talk to me for much of the class period, making it difficult for me to focus on observing student interaction. Physically participating in the classes allowed me to pay closer attention to what students were doing and talking about. It was also the only way I could disengage from teachers to focus on students without being rude.

Having obtained subject and parental consent, all but three individual interviews were audio recorded and all focus-group interviews were video recorded for subsequent transcription and analysis. In addition, detailed interview notes of each individual interview were taken for analysis purposes. I recorded observations through daily note taking. In all, I conducted ninety-eight individual interviews and six focus-group interviews. Interview transcripts, interview notes, and field notes were coded for thematic analysis using Atlas.ti software.

Building Trust

My previous career as a high school English teacher influenced my subsequent experience as an ethnographer in a school setting. As a teacher, I remember feeling physically, mentally, and emotionally exhausted at the end of each school day. My short-lived teaching career was fraught with stress as I struggled daily with classroom behavioral issues, problems with truancy, literacy, and failure rates for which I was held responsible. Although I knew that my role as researcher would be very different from that of teacher, I was still apprehensive about returning to the high school setting to conduct field research because my most recent experience in a high school setting had not been positive.

When I contemplated returning to the high school setting, I felt both excitement and trepidation, taking solace in the knowledge that at least this time I was a researcher and had no responsibility for managing the behavior and intellectual growth of the adolescents with whom I worked. One of my primary concerns in returning to the high school setting was how I would negotiate my role on the campus. How would students at the high school see me and how would my experiences as a former teacher color my fieldwork experience? Would I be able to shed the anxiety I felt about returning to a high school campus and more importantly, would I be able to let go of my former teacher identity in favor of a new and unfamiliar identity as researcher?

On the first morning of fieldwork my struggle with the role I was to play became apparent before I even walked out my front door. Ironically, my first struggle was at the site of my body. I stood in front of my closet at 5:45 a.m. feeling insecure about what I should wear. I did not want to dress too much like a student since I would be meeting teachers all day and I wanted them to take me seriously as a researcher. However, I also did not want to look like a teacher for fear that students would see me as an authority figure and not feel comfortable talking openly with me. I needed to choose an outfit that would make me look like someone in-between a student and a teacher.

That first day I decided to wear jeans and a striped polo style shirt with clogs. I wondered if my clothes would align me with certain groups of teens and alienate me from others. What sort of first impression would I make on teens and adults at the school? These thoughts consumed me during my twenty-five minute drive to the high school. It occurred to me that a researcher may be in much the same position as an adolescent—feeling the need to be liked by everyone in the community and being rendered very insecure by that need. I often felt like an insecure teenager throughout the school year as I worried about what people thought of me and whether or not my clothes were both "cool" and age appropriate.

As a former teacher, I was much attuned to the central role that school rules play in maintaining order among students. The hierarchy of public schools is generally such that there are two roles with regard to rules: those who are expected to enforce the rules and those who are expected to follow the rules. As a researcher, I fit neither role and wondered to what extent I would need to adhere to student rules. On my first morning at the high school one of the assistant principals gave me a tour of the school, providing me with an opportunity to ask her how some of the rules would apply to me.

She told me that the only rule she expected me to follow was dress code. Although I was given the freedom to ignore the vast majority of school rules, I knew that if I chose to do so I would align myself with authority figures rather than students. Thus, the real question for me was, "Do I want to disregard school rules and risk being thought of by students as an authority figure?" For example, no backpacks were allowed in the lunch area. I carried all of my research equipment around in a backpack and had no secure place to store it during lunch, which meant I had no choice but to break this rule. However, I decided to follow all other rules that applied to students, which meant that I did not use my cell phone, tried to arrive to classes on time, and abstained from eating or drinking in classes. I also wanted to follow the rules out of respect to adults who were responsible for maintaining order on campus.

My role as researcher in the school continued to feel somewhat ambiguous throughout the school year as both teachers and adolescents often mistook me for a student. This was something that I had also struggled with as a very young high school teacher and I spent my short tenure as a teacher working hard to exude qualities that I thought would earn me the respect of my students, such as confidence, officiousness, and a stern demeanor. These qualities served me well as a teacher and were necessary for my mental and emotional survival at the time, but I knew they would hinder me greatly in my role as a researcher. My embodied experience of being a former teacher had to be constantly renegotiated throughout the school year as I struggled to develop an identity as researcher within the school community.

Part of creating that authoritative image as a high school teacher included wearing very professional clothing. When I walked into Desert Vista on the first day wearing jeans and a casual shirt I felt naked, literally stripped of my authoritative armor. I continued to struggle with my clothing choices throughout the school year. One particularly hot day in September, I was standing outside observing a PE class when ants that had crawled inside of my clogs began biting my bare feet. When I flung off my shoes and frantically swept the ants off my feet with my hands, the PE teacher laughed and asked why I felt the need to dress so nicely, especially if I was going to observe PE classes all day long.

She wondered why I did not wear tennis shoes like the PE teachers did. I thought about her suggestion to dress more comfortably and cringed at the thought of walking around the high school campus in tennis shoes, shorts, and a t-shirt. Although I thought it was appropriate for the PE teachers to dress for exercise, for me that attire seemed entirely too casual. I wouldn't fit in with any of the teens if I dressed that way. I continued to walk this fine line between student and authority figure all year as I struggled to exude just the right image.

A likely consequence of attempting to walk the fine line between established roles at the high school was that no one knew where I fit in. One day as I walked off campus during lunch to explore the fast food restaurant across the street a teacher yelled for me to come back. As I approached her she asked to see my ID card and I explained that I was not a student at the high school but that I was a researcher from the University of Arizona. She looked skeptical, but grudgingly allowed me off campus. Before the security guards figured out who I was, they regularly asked me to present a hall pass as they saw me walking around campus during class periods. Although it was embarrassing to be continually challenged by adults on campus who thought I was a student, looking young probably helped students relate to me more easily and facilitated our interview discussions.

In addition to being mistaken for a student throughout the school year, one student asked me if I was evaluating the school and another asked if I was an "FBI spy" sent to identify students who were using and selling drugs. In fact, when I began fieldwork I worried that students would mistake me for a narc and avoid interacting with me. While this student and his friends' perception of me as an "FBI spy" did not appear to be widespread, it concerned me nonetheless. Over time, as I spent all day every day on campus among students, they seemed to relax around me regardless of whether they knew or understood my role on campus.

By virtue of the fact that I was working with a number of students representing the few high profile social cliques on campus, gaining in-group status with any of these groups proved to be much more difficult than I had originally anticipated. When I designed my study, I envisioned eating lunch with participants and their friends so that I could hear body-image discourses firsthand. I soon realized that students were taking note of whom I sat with as they made comments such as, "I saw you sitting with the Jocks/Preps yesterday." I was surprised to learn that students were actively observing me just as I was them. My movement among groups throughout the year prevented me from fully integrating into any of them. I was most widely accepted among less structured and lesser-known social groups.

Additionally, individuals associated with the high profile social cliques— the Goths/Punks, Jocks/Preps, and Mexicans—marked their membership largely through personal style choices, such as clothing, hair, makeup, and the way they talked. If my aim had been to gain acceptance among one social group instead of many, then it would have been reasonable to adopt the group's personal style in order to fit in. However, it would have seemed disingenuous and even ridiculous to constantly alter the way I dressed, wore my hair and makeup, and talked to fit in with the various social cliques on campus.

Besides, style-shifting between teacher and student discourse was challenging enough without having to constantly style-shift between discourses of the various cliques with whom I associated. As a result, I adopted a somewhat generic teenage discourse style with the most noticeable feature being frequent usage of the discourse markers "like," "um," and "you know." This one-size-fits-all teen discourse style may have further hindered my in-group status among certain cliques who actively constructed their identities in contrast to what they perceived to be mainstream teen culture.

The teachers whose classes I observed often interacted with me as a colleague, possibly because they knew that I was a former high school teacher and probably because I was the only other adult in the room. This was especially true of PE teachers who spent a great deal of class time talking to me while they supervised their students. The topics of conversation initiated by teachers usually included talk about individual students in their classes, classroom interpersonal dynamics, school politics, job-related frustrations, and, issues related to their personal lives. Two of the teachers in particular treated me as a confidante and I subsequently developed a friendship with them over the course of the school year. In addition to obtaining valuable information from the PE teachers during these conversations, I enjoyed the adult interaction.

However, I also worried that students might start to associate me with their PE teachers, which might hinder my relationships with participants who did not like PE and/or their PE teacher. At one point, I was in the girls' locker room talking to the PE teachers and afterward, as I walked by students who were dressing out, a participant asked me what I was doing in the PE teachers' office. When I told her that I was chatting with them, she said, "Ew stay away from them." This was yet another reminder that I needed to take care with the image I projected and work hard to maintain the ambiguous identity I had so carefully constructed.

I negotiated these kinds of issues around fitting in and building trust with students all year long. Ultimately, I think showing up every day, hanging out with teens at lunch, exercising alongside them in PE classes, showing a genuine interest in their lives, and letting them get to know me are what facilitated open, honest interview discussions with participants.

REFERENCES

1M Kids Stop School Lunch Due to Michelle Obama's Standards. *The Washington Times*, March 6, 2014. Retrieved from www.washingtontimes.com/news/2014/mar/6/1m-kids-stop-school-lunch-due-michelle-obamas-stan/?page=all

American Association of University Women (AAUW). 1998. *Gender Gaps: Where Schools Still Fail Our Children*. Washington, DC: American Association of University Women.

Anderson-Fye, Eileen. 2004. "A Coca-Cola Shape: Cultural Change, Body Image, and Eating Disorders in San Andrés, Belize." *Culture, Medicine, and Psychiatry* 28: 561–595.

Anderson-Fye, Eileen. 2011. "Body Images in Non-Western Cultures." In *Body Image: A Handbook of Science, Practice, and Prevention*. Edited by Thomas F. Cash and Linda Smolak, 244–252. New York: The Guilford Press.

Anderson-Fye, Eileen, Stephanie McClure, Maureen Floriano, Arundhati Bharati, and Yun Chen. Forthcoming. "Fat and Too Fat: Risk and Protection for Obesity Stigma in Three Countries." In *Fat Planet: Obesity, Culture, and Symbolic Body Capital*. Edited by Eileen P. Anderson-Fye and Alexandra Brewis. Santa Fe, NM: SAR Press; Albuquerque: University of New Mexico Press.

Bakhtin, Mikhail M. 1935 (1981). *The Dialogic Imagination: Four Essays*. Edited by Michael Holquist, translated by Caryl Emerson and Michael Holquist. Austin: University of Texas Press.

Bartky, Sandra Lee. 1988. "Foucault, Femininity, and the Modernization of Patriarchal Power." In *Feminism and Foucault: Reflections and Resistance*. Edited by Irene Diamond and Lee Quinby, 61–86. Boston: Northeastern University Press.

Bartky, Sandra Lee. 1990. *Femininity and Domination: Studies in the Phenomenology of Oppression*. New York: Routledge.

Beam, Margaret, Nicole Taylor, Jennifer Lembach, Audrey Block, and Elizabeth Vale Gandhi. 2010. "Healthy Schools Program Evaluation: Year 4 Report." Prepared for Alliance for a Healthier Generation by RMC Research Corporation, Portland, OR.

Becker, Anne. 1995. *Body, Self, and Society: The View from Fiji*. Philadelphia: University of Pennsylvania Press.

Becker, Anne. 2004. "Television, Disordered Eating, and Young Women in Fiji:

Negotiating Body Image and Identity During Rapid Social Change." *Culture, Medicine and Psychiatry* 28: 533–559.

Becker, Anne. Forthcoming. "Body Size, Social Standing, and Weight Management: The View from Fiji. In *Fat Planet: Obesity, Culture, and Symbolic Body Capital*. Edited by Eileen P. Anderson-Fye and Alexandra Brewis. Santa Fe, NM: SAR Press; Albuquerque: University of New Mexico Press.

Bernhardt, Amy M., Cara Wilking, Anna M. Adachi-Mejia, Elaina Bergamini, Jill Marijnissen, and James D. Sargent. 2013. "How Television Fast Food Marketing Aimed at Children Compares with Adult Advertisements." *PLoS ONE* 8(8): e72479.

Best, Scott, Philip J. Pearson, and Paul I. Webb. 2010. "Teachers' Perceptions of the Effects of Single-Sex and Coeducational Classroom Settings on the Participation and Performance of Students in Practical Physical Education." *Congreso de la Asociación Internacional de Escuelas Superiores de Educación Física*. 26–29: 1016–1027.

Biltekoff, Charlotte. 2013. *Eating Right in America: The Cultural Politics of Food and Health*. Durham, NC: Duke University Press.

Boero, Natalie. 2007. "All the News That's Fat to Print: The American 'Obesity Epidemic' and the Media." *Qualitative Sociology* 30(1): 41–60.

Boero, Natalie. 2012. *Killer Fat: Media, Medicine, and Morals in the American "Obesity Epidemic."* Brunswick, NJ: Rutgers University Press.

Bordo, Susan. 1993. *Unbearable Weight: Feminism, Western Culture, and the Body*. Berkeley: University of California Press.

Bordo, Susan. 1999. *The Male Body: A New Look at Men in Public and in Private*. New York: Farrar, Straus and Giroux.

Bordo, Susan. 2013. "Not Just 'a White Girl's Thing': The Changing Face of Food and Body Image Problems." In *Food and Culture: A Reader*, 3rd edition. Edited by Carole Counihan and Penny Van Esterik, 265–275. New York: Routledge. Originally published in Helen Malson and Maree Burns, Critical Feminist Approaches to Eating Dis/orders (New York: Routledge, 2009).

Bourdieu, Pierre. 1972 (1977). *Outline of a Theory of Practice*. Translated by Richard Nice. Cambridge: Cambridge University Press.

Brewis, Alexandra. 2011. *Obesity: Cultural and Biocultural Perspectives*. New Brunswick, NJ: Rutgers University Press.

Brown, Lyn Mikel. 1998. *Raising Their Voices: The Politics of Girls' Anger*. Cambridge, MA: Harvard University Press.

Brownell, Kelly D. 1994. "Get Slim with Higher Taxes." *New York Times*, December 15, 1994, A29.

Brownell, Kelly, and Katherine Horgen. 2004. *Food Fight: The Inside Story of the Food Industry, America's Obesity Crisis, and What We Can Do about It*. Chicago: Contemporary Books.

Brownell, Kelly D., Rogan Kersh, David S. Ludwig, Robert C. Post, Rebecca M. Puhl, Marlene B. Schwartz, and Walter C. Willett. 2010. "Personal Responsibility and Obesity: A Constructivist Approach to a Controversial Issue." *Health Affairs* 29(3): 379–387.

Brumberg, Joan Jacobs. 1997. *The Body Project: An Intimate History of American Girls*. New York: Vintage Books.

Bryson, Lois. 1987. "Sport and the Maintenance of Masculine Hegemony." *Women's Studies International Forum* 10(4): 349–360.

Bucholtz, Mary. 1996. "Geek the Girl: Language, Femininity, and Female Nerds." In *Gender and Belief Systems: Proceedings of the Fourth Berkeley Women and Language Conference.* Edited by Natasha Warner, Jocelyn Ahlers, Leela Bilmes, Monica Oliver, Suzanne Wertheim, and Mel Chen, 119–131. Berkeley, CA: Berkeley Women and Language Group.

Bucholtz, Mary. 1999. "'Why Be Normal?' Language and Identity Practices in a Community of Nerd Girls." *Language in Society* 28(2): 203–222.

Bucholtz, Mary. 2002. "Youth and Cultural Practice." *Annual Review of Anthropology* 31: 525–552.

Bucholtz, Mary. 2011. *White Kids: Language, Race, and Styles of Youth Identity.* New York: Cambridge University Press.

Bucholtz, Mary, and Kira Hall. 2005. "Identity and Interaction: A Sociocultural Linguistic Approach." *Discourse Studies* 7(4–5): 585–614.

Burros, Marian, and Melanie Warner. "Bottlers Agree to a School Ban on Sweet Drinks." *New York Times,* May 4, 2006, A1.

Butler, Judith. 1990. *Gender Trouble: Feminism and the Subversion of Identity.* New York: Routledge.

Butler, Judith. 1993. *Bodies That Matter: On the Discursive Limits of "Sex."* New York: Routledge.

Cameron, Deborah. 1997. "Performing Gender Identity: Young Men's Talk and the Construction of Heterosexual Masculinity." In *Language and Masculinity.* Edited by Sally Johnson and Ulrike Hanna Meinhof, 47–64. Oxford: Blackwell.

Carmona, Richard H. January 6, 2003. "Remarks to the 2003 California Childhood Obesity Conference." *US Department of Health and Human Services, Office of the Surgeon General.* Retrieved from www.surgeongeneral.gov/news/speeches/califobesity.htm

Carmona, Richard H. January 20, 2004. "Education and Training: The First Steps in Achieving National Preparedness." *US Department of Health and Human Services, Office of the Surgeon General.* Retrieved from www.surgeongeneral.gov/news/speeches/aslet01202004.htm

Centers for Disease Control and Prevention (CDC). 2012. "Youth Risk Behavior Surveillance—United States, 2011." *MMWR* 61: SS-4.

Centers for Disease Control and Prevention (CDC). n.d. "BMI Percentile Calculator for Child and Teen." Retrieved from nccd.cdc.gov/dnpabmi/Calculator.aspx

Cheshire, Jenny. 2000. "The Telling or the Tale? Narratives and Gender in Adolescent Friendship Networks." *Journal of Sociolinguistics* 4(2): 234–262.

Chriqui, Jamie, Elissa Resnick, Linda Schneider, Rebecca Schermbeck, Tessa Adcock, Violeta Carrion, and Frank Chaloupka. 2013. *School District Wellness Policies: Evaluating Progress and Potential for Improving Children's Health Five Years after the Federal Mandate. School Years 2006–07 through 2010–11.* Chicago: Bridging the Gap Program, Health Policy Center, Institute for Health Research and Policy, University of Illinois at Chicago. Retrieved from www.bridgingthegapresearch.org.

Chriqui, Jamie, Linda Schneider, Frank Chaloupka, Camille Gourdet, Amy Bruursema, Kristen Ide, and Oksana Pugach. 2010. *School District Wellness Policies: Evaluating Progress and Potential for Improving Children's Health Three Years after the Federal Mandate.* Vol. 2. Chicago: Bridging the Gap Program, Health Policy Center, Institute for Health Research and Policy, University of Illinois at Chicago. Retrieved from www.bridgingthegapresearch.org

Clark, Sheryl, and Carrie Paechter. 2007. "'Why Can't Girls Play Football?' Gender Dynamics and the Playground." *Sport, Education and Society* 12(3): 261–276.

Coates, Jennifer. 1988. "Gossip Revisited: Language in All-Female Groups." In *Women in Their Speech Communities*. Edited by Jennifer Coates and Deborah Cameron, 94–122. London: Longman.

Coates, Jennifer. 1999. "Changing Femininities: The Talk of Teenage Girls." In *Reinventing Identities: The Gendered Self in Discourse*. Edited by Mary Bucholtz, A. C. Liang, and Laurel A. Sutton, 123–144. New York: Oxford University Press.

Cockburn, Claudia, and Gill Clarke. 2002. "'Everybody's Looking At You!': Girls Negotiating the 'Femininity Deficit' They Incur in Physical Education." *Women's Studies International Forum* 25(6): 651–665.

Connell, R. W. 1983. *Which Way Is Up? Essays on Sex, Class and Culture*. Sydney, Australia: George Allen and Unwin.

Connell, R. W. 1995. *Masculinities*. Berkeley, CA: University of California Press.

Counihan, Carole. 1992. "Food Rules in the United States: Individualism, Control, and Hierarchy." *Anthropological Quarterly* 65(2): 55–66.

Craddock, Angie L., Anne McHugh, Helen Mont-Ferguson, Linda Grant, Jessica L. Barrett, Steven L. Gortmaker, and Claire Wang. 2011. "Effect of School District Policy Change on Consumption of Sugar-Sweetened Beverages among High School Students, Boston, Massachusetts, 2004–2006." *Preventing Chronic Disease* 8: A74.

Crawford, Robert. 1984. "A Cultural Account of 'Health': Control, Release, and the Social Body." In *Issues in the Political Economy of Health Care*. Edited by John McKinlay, 61–103. London: Tavistock.

Crocker, Jennifer, and Julie Garcia. 2005. "Self-Esteem and the Stigma of Obesity." In *Weight Bias: Nature, Consequences, and Remedies*. Edited by Kelly D. Brownell, Rebecca M. Puhl, Marlene B. Schwartz, and Leslie Rudd, 29–47. New York: The Guilford Press.

Daniels, Elizabeth, and Campbell Leaper. 2006. "A Longitudinal Investigation of Sport Participation, Peer Acceptance, and Self-esteem among Adolescent Girls and Boys." *Sex Roles* 55: 875–880.

Dave, Dhaval, and Inas Rashad. 2009. "Overweight Status, Self-perception, and Suicidal Behaviors among Adolescents." *Social Science and Medicine* 68: 1685–1691.

Davis, Brennan, and Christopher Carpenter. 2009. "Proximity of Fast-food Restaurants to Schools and Adolescent Obesity." *American Journal of Public Health* 99(3): 505–510.

Deaner, Robert O., David C. Geary, David A. Puts, Sandra A. Ham, Judy Kruger, Elizabeth Fles, Bo Winegard, and Terry Grandis. 2012. "A Sex Difference in the Predisposition for Physical Competition: Males Play Sports Much More than Females Even in the Contemporary US." *PLoS ONE* 7(11): e49168.

Deem, Rosemary, and Sarah Gilroy. 1998. "Physical Activity, Life-long Learning and Empowerment: Situating Sport in Women's Leisure." *Sport, Education and Society* 31(1): 89–104.

Duranti, Alessandro. 1993. "Intentions, Self, and Responsibility: An Essay in Samoan Ethnopragmatics." In *Responsibility and Evidence in Oral Discourse*. Edited by Jane H. Hill and Judith T. Irvine, 24–47. Cambridge: Cambridge University Press.

Eckert, Penelope. 1989. *Jocks and Burnouts: Social Categories and Identity in the High School*. New York: Teachers College Press.

Eckert, Penelope. 1993. "Cooperative Competition in Adolescent 'Girl Talk.'" In *Gender and Conversational Interaction*. Edited by Deborah Tannen, 32–61. New York: Oxford University Press.

Eckert, Penelope. 1996. "Vowels and Nail Polish: The Emergence of Linguistic Style in the Preadolescent Heterosexual Marketplace." In *Gender and Belief Systems: Proceedings of the Fourth Berkeley Women and Language Conference*. Edited by Natasha Warner, Jocelyn Ahlers, Leela Bilmes, Monica Oliver, Suzanne Wertheim, and Mel Chen, 183–190. Berkeley, CA: Berkeley Women and Language Group.

Eckert, Penelope, and Sally McConnell-Ginet. 1995. "Constructing Meaning, Constructing Selves: Snapshots of Language, Gender, and Class from Belten High." In *Gender Articulated: Language and the Socially Constructed Self*. Edited by Kira Hall and Mary Bucholtz, 469–507. New York: Routledge.

Eder, Donna. 1993. "'Go Get Ya a French!' Romantic and Sexual Teasing among Adolescent Girls." In *Gender and Conversational Interaction*. Edited by Deborah Tannen, 17–31. New York: Oxford University Press.

Eder, Donna, Catherine Colleen Evans, and Stephen Parker. 1995. *School Talk: Gender and Adolescent Culture*. New Brunswick, NJ: Rutgers University Press.

Eisenberg, Marla E., Dianne Neumark-Sztainer, and Mary Story. 2003. "Associations of Weight-based Teasing and Emotional Well-being among Adolescents." *Archives of Pediatrics and Adolescent Medicine* 157: 733–738.

Federal Trade Commission. 2012. *A Review of Food Marketing to Children and Adolescents—Follow-up Report*. Retrieved from www.ftc.gov/reports/review-food-marketing-children-adolescents-follow-report

Finkelstein, Eric, Olga Khaviou, Hope Thompson, Justin Trogdon, Liping Pan, Bettylou Sherry, and William Dietz. 2012. Obesity and Severe Obesity Forecasts through 2030. *American Journal of Preventative Medicine* 42(6): 563–570.

Florence, Michelle D., Mark Asbridge, and Paul J. Veugelers. 2008. "Diet Quality and Academic Performance. *Journal of School Health* 78(4): 209–215.

Foucault, Michel. 1975 (1977). *Discipline and Punish*. Edited by Alan Sheridan. New York: Vintage.

Foucault, Michel. 1980. *Power/Knowledge: Selected Interviews and Other Writings 1972–1977*. Edited by Colin Gordon, translated by Colin Gordon, Leo Marshall, John Mepham, and Kate Soper. New York: Pantheon Books.

Galst, Joann P., and Mary A. White. 1996. "The Unhealthy Persuader: The Reinforcing Value of Television and Children's Purchase-influencing Attempts at the Supermarket. *Child Development* 47: 1089–1096.

Gard, Michael, and Jan Wright. 2005. *The Obesity Epidemic: Science, Morality and Ideology*. London: Routledge.

Garrett, Robyne. 2004a. "Gendered Bodies and Physical Identities." In *Body Knowledge and Control: Studies in the Sociology of Physical Education and Health*. Edited by John Evans, Brian Davies, and Jan Wright, 140–156. London: Routledge.

Garrett, Robyne. 2004b. "Negotiating a Physical Identity: Girls, Bodies and Physical Education." *Sport, Education and Society* 9(2): 223–237.

Gay Alliance. 2012. "Safe Zone Training Programs." Retrieved from www.gayalliance.org/safezonet.html

Gill, Rosalind, Karen Henwood, and Carl McLean. 2005. "Body Projects and the Regulation of Normative Masculinity." *Body and Society* 11(1): 37–62.

Goffman, Erving. 1963. *Stigma: Notes on the Management of Spoiled Identity*. Englewood Cliffs, NJ: Prentice Hall.

Goodwin, Marjorie Harness. 1990. *He-Said-She-Said: Talk As Social Organization Among Black Children*. Bloomington: Indiana University Press.

Goodwin, Marjorie Harness. 1999. "Constructing Opposition within Girls' Games." In *Reinventing Identities: The Gendered Self in Discourse*. Edited by Mary Bucholtz, A. C. Liang, and Laurel A. Sutton, 388–409. New York: Oxford University.

Goodwin, Marjorie Harness. 2002. "Building Power Asymmetries in Girls' Interaction." *Discourse and Society* 13(6): 715–730.

Greenhalgh, Susan. 2015. *Fat-Talk Nation: The Human Costs of America's War on Fat*. Ithaca and London: Cornell University Press.

Gremillion, Helen. 2005. "The Cultural Politics of Body Size." *Annual Reviews in Anthropology* 34: 13–32.

Griffiths, Lucy J., and Angie S. Page. 2008. "The Impact of Weight-related Victimization on Peer Relationships: The Female Adolescent Perspective." *Obesity* 16(Suppl. 2): S39–S44.

Grilo, Carlos, Denise Wilfley, Kelly D. Brownell, and Judith Rodin. 1994. "Teasing, Body Image, and Self-esteem in a Clinical Sample of Obese Women." *Addictive Behaviors* 19(4), 443–450.

Grogan, Sarah, and Helen Richards. 2002. "Body Image: Focus Groups with Boys and Men." *Men and Masculinities* 4(3): 219–232.

Gumpertz, John. 1982a. *Discourse Strategies*. Cambridge: Cambridge University Press.

Gumpertz, John. 1982b. *Language and Social Identity*. Cambridge: Cambridge University Press.

Gumpertz, John. 1992. "Contextualization and Understanding." In *Rethinking Context: Language as an Interactive Phenomenon*. Edited by Alessandro Duranti and Charles Goodwin, 229–252. Cambridge: Cambridge University Press.

Guthrie, Joanne F., Constance Newman, Katherine Ralston, Mark Prell, and Michael Ollinger. June 2013. "Nutrition Standards for Competitive Foods in Schools: Implications for Foodservice Revenues, EIB-114." *US Department of Agriculture, Economic Research Service*.

Hancox, Robert J., and Richie Poulton. 2006. "Watching Television Is Associated with Childhood Obesity, but Is It Clinically Important?" *International Journal of Obesity* 30: 170–175.

Hardin, Marie, and Jennifer Greer. 2009. "The Influence of Gender-role Socialization, Media Use and Sports Participation on Perceptions of Gender-Appropriate Sports." *Journal of Sport Behavior* 32(2): 207–226.

Hargreaves, Jennifer. 1986. "Where's the Virtue? Where's the Grace? A Discussion of the Social Production of Gender Relations in and through Sport." *Theory, Culture and Society* 3(1): 109–121.

Hargreaves, Jennifer. 1993. *Sporting Females: Critical Issues in the History and Sociology of Women's Sports*. New York: Routledge.

Harriger, Jennifer, Rachel Calogero, David Witherington, and Jane Ellen Smith. 2010. "Body Size Stereotyping and Internalization of the Thin-Ideal in Preschool-Age Girls." *Sex Roles* 63: 609–620.

Hebdige, Dick. 1979. *Subculture: The Meaning of Style*. London: Methuen.

Heilman, Elizabeth. 1998. "The Struggle For Self: Power and Identity in Adolescent Girls." *Youth and Society* 30: 182–208.

Hill, Jane H. 2008. *The Everyday Language of White Racism*. Oxford: Wiley-Blackwell.

Holub, Shayla, Cin Cin Tan, and Sanobar Patel. 2011. "Factors Associated with Mothers' Obesity Stigma and Young Children's Weight Stereotypes." *Journal of Applied Developmental Psychology* 32: 118–126.

Horgen, Katherine B., and Kelly D. Brownell. 2002. "Confronting the Toxic Environment: Environmental and Public Health Actions in a World Crisis. In *Handbook of Obesity Treatment*. Edited by Thomas A. Wadden and Albert J. Stunkard, 95–106. New York: The Guilford Press.

Hrushka, Daniel J. Forthcoming. From Thin to Fat and Back Again: A Dual Process Model of the Big Body Mass Reversal. In *Fat Planet: Obesity, Culture, and Symbolic Body Capital*. Edited by Eileen P. Anderson-Fye and Alexandra Brewis. Santa Fe, NM: SAR Press; Albuquerque: University of New Mexico Press.

Huff, Joyce. 2001. "A 'Horror of Corpulence': Interrogating Bantingism and Mid-Nineteenth Century Fat-Phobia." In *Bodies Out of Bounds: Fatness and Transgression*. Edited by Jana Evans Braziel and Kathleen LeBesco, 39–59. Berkeley: University of California Press.

Hymes, Dell. 1974. *Foundations in Sociolinguistics: An Ethnographic Approach*. Philadelphia: University of Pennsylvania Press.

Institute of Medicine (IOM). 2005. *Preventing Childhood Obesity: Health in the Balance*. Washington, DC: The National Academies Press.

Institute of Medicine (IOM). 2012. *Accelerating Progress in Obesity Prevention: Solving the Weight of the Nation*. Washington, DC: The National Academies Press.

Institute of Medicine (IOM). 2013. *Educating the Student Body: Taking Physical Education and Physical Activity to School*. Washington, DC: The National Academies Press.

Irvine, Judith. 1996. "Shadow Conversations: The Indeterminacy of Participant Roles." In *Natural Histories of Discourse*. Edited by Michael Silverstein and Greg Urban, 131–159. Chicago: University of Chicago Press: 131–159.

Jacoby, Sally, and Elinor Ochs. 1995. "Co-Construction: An Introduction." *Research on Language and Social Interaction* 28(3): 171–183.

Jeanes, Ruth. 2011. "'I'm Into High Heels and Make Up but I Still Love Football': Exploring Gender Identity and Football Participation with Preadolescent Girls." *Soccer & Society* 12(3): 402–420.

Johnson, Sally, and Frank Finlay. 1997. "Do Men Gossip? An Analysis of Football Talk on Television." In *Language and Masculinity*. Edited by Sally Johnson and Ulrike Hanna Meinhof, 130–143. Oxford: Blackwell.

Katz, David L., Tracy Fox, Francine R. Kaufman, Marlene B. Schwartz, and Margo G. Wootan. 2013. "Policy and System Changes in Marketing Foods to Children." *Childhood Obesity* 9(6): 477-483.

Kehler, Michael. 2010. "Negotiating Masculinities in PE Classrooms: Boys, Body Image, and 'Want[ing] to Be in Good Shape.'" In *Boys' Bodies: Speaking the Unspoken*. Edited by Michael Kehler and Michael Atkinson, 153–175. New York: Peter Lang Publishing.

Kiesling, Scott. 2002. "Playing the Straight Man: Displaying and Maintaining Male Heterosexuality in Discourse. In *Language and Sexuality: Contesting Meaning in Theory and Practice*. Edited by Kathryn Campbell-Kibler, Robert J. Podesva, Sarah Roberts, and Andrew Wong, 249–266. Stanford, CA: CSLI Publications.

Klomsten, Anne Torhild, Herb Marsh, and Einar Skaalvik. 2005. "Adolescents'

Perceptions of Masculine and Feminine Values in Sport and Physical Education: A Study of Gender Differences." *Sex Roles* 52(9/10): 625–636.

Koivula, Nathalie. 1995. "Ratings of Gender Appropriateness of Sports Participation: Effects of Gender-Based Schematic Processing." *Sex Roles* 33(7/8): 543–557.

Koivula, Nathalie. 2001. "Perceived Characteristics of Sports Categorized as Gender-Neutral, Feminine and Masculine." *Journal of Sport Behavior* 24(4): 377–393.

Krane, Vikki, Precilla Choi, Shannon Baird, Christine Aimar, and Kerrie Kauer. 2004. "Living the Paradox: Female Athletes Negotiate Femininity and Muscularity." *Sex Roles* 50(5/6): 315–329.

Kubik, Martha Y., Leslie A. Lytle, and Mary Story. 2005. "Schoolwide Food Practices Are Associated with Body Mass Index in Middle School Students." *Archives of Pediatrics and Adolescent Medicine* 159: 1111–1114.

Kwan, Samantha. 2009. "Individual Versus Corporate Responsibility: Market Choice, the Food Industry, and the Pervasiveness of Moral Models of Fatness." *Food, Culture, and Society* 12(4): 478–495.

Kwan, Samantha, and Jennifer Graves. 2013. *Framing Fat: Competing Constructions in Contemporary Culture.* New Brunswick, NJ: Rutgers University Press.

Lawrence, Regina G. 2004. "Framing Obesity: The Evolution of News Discourse on a Public Health Issue." *The Harvard International Journal of Press/Politics* 9(3): 56–75.

Lehmkuhl, Heather, Laura Nabors, and Emily Iobst. 2010. "Factors Influencing Preschool Age Children's Acceptance of Models Presented As Overweight." *International Journal of Pediatric Obesity* 5: 19–24.

Lenhart, Clare M., Alexandra Hanlon, Youjeong Kang, Brian P. Daly, Michael D. Brown, and Freda Patterson. 2012. "Gender Disparity in Structured Physical Activity and Overall Activity Level." *Adolescence: Evaluation of Youth Risk Behavior Surveillance Data.* ISRN Public Health 2012, Article ID 674936, 8 pages.

Let's Move: 1.6M Paying Students Stop School Lunch—"Challenges with Palatability." *CBS News*, March 4, 2014. Retrieved from http://cnsnews.com/news/article/ ali-meyer/let-s-move-16m-paying-students-drop-school-lunch-challenges-palatability

Lévi-Strauss, Claude. 1966. *The Savage Mind.* Chicago: University of Chicago Press.

Linn, Susan. 2004. *Consuming Kids: The Hostile Takeover of Childhood.* New York: The New Press.

Macklem, Gayle. 2003. *Bullying and Teasing: Social Power in Children's Groups.* New York: Kluwer Academic/Plenum Publishing.

Margulies, Allison, Randy Floyd, and Robin Hojnoski. 2008. "Body Size Stigmatization: An Examination of Attitudes of African American Preschool-Age Children Attending Head Start." *Journal of Pediatric Psychology* 33(5): 487–496.

McClure, Stephanie. 2013. *"It's Just Gym": Physicality and Identity among African American Adolescent Girls.* PhD dissertation, Case Western Reserve University, Cleveland, OH.

McClure, Stephanie. Forthcoming. "Symbolic Body Capital of an 'Other' Kind: African American Females as a Bracketed Subunit in the Calculus of Female Body Valuation." In *Fat Planet: Obesity, Culture, and Symbolic Body Capital.* Edited by Eileen P. Anderson-Fye and Alexandra Brewis. Santa Fe, NM: SAR Press; Albuquerque: University of New Mexico Press.

Mead, George H. 1934. *Mind, Self, and Society.* Chicago: University of Chicago Press.

Mendoza-Denton, Norma. 1996. "'Muy Macha': Gender and Ideology in Gang-Girls' Discourse about Makeup." *Ethnos* 61(1–2): 47–63.

Mendoza-Denton, Norma. 1999a. "Fighting Words: Latina Girls, Gangs, and Language Attitudes." In *Speaking Chicana: Voice, Power, and Identity*. Edited by D. Letticia Galindo and María Dolores Gonzales, 40–56. Tucson: University of Arizona Press.

Mendoza-Denton, Norma. 1999b. "Turn-Initial *No*: Collaborative Opposition Among Latina Adolescents." In *Reinventing Identities: The Gendered Self in Discourse*. Edited by Mary Bucholtz, A. C. Liang, and Laurel A. Sutton, 273–292. New York: Oxford University Press.

Mendoza-Denton, Norma. 2008. *Homegirls: Language and Cultural Practice among Latina Youth Gangs*. Oxford: Blackwell Publishing.

Mills, Carol B., and Amy Carwile. 2009. "The Good, the Bad, and the Borderline: Separating Teasing from Bullying." *Communication Education* 58(2): 276–301.

National Association for Sport and Physical Education (NASPE) and American Heart Association (AHA). 2010. "Shape of the Nation Report: Status of Physical Education in the USA." Reston, VA: NASPE.

Nestle, Marion. 2002. *Food Politics*. Berkeley, CA: University of California Press.

Neumark-Sztainer, Dianne, Mary Story, and Loren Faibisch. 1998. "Perceived Stigmatization among Overweight African-American and Caucasian Adolescent Girls." *Journal of Adolescent Health* 23: 264–270.

Neumark-Sztainer, Dianne, Mary Story, Cheryl Perry, and Mary A. Casey. 1999. "Factors Influencing Food Choices of Adolescents: Findings from Focus-group Discussions with Adolescents." *Journal of the American Dietetic Association* 99(8): 929–937.

Nichter, Mimi. 2000. *Fat Talk: What Girls and Their Parents Say about Dieting*. Cambridge, MA and London: Harvard University Press.

Nichter, Mark, and Mimi Nichter. 1991. "Hype and Weight." *Medical Anthropology*. 13(3): 249–284.

Nichter, Mimi, and Nancy Vuckovic. 1994. "Fat Talk: Body Image among Adolescent Girls." In *Many Mirrors: Body Image and Social Relations*. Edited by Nicole Sault, 109–131. New Brunswick, NJ: Rutgers University Press.

Oliver, Eric J. 2006. *Fat Politics: The Real Story Behind America's Obesity Epidemic*. Oxford and New York: Oxford University Press.

Parker, Sheila, Mimi Nichter, Mark Nicther, Nancy Vuckovic, Colette Sims, and Cheryl Ritenbaugh. 1995. "Body Image and Weight Concerns among African American and White Adolescent Females: Differences That Make a Difference." *Human Organization* 54(2): 103–114.

Pascoe, C. J. 2007. *Dude, You're a Fag: Masculinity and Sexuality in High School*. Berkeley: University of California Press.

"Pentagon Attacks Obesity with New Food Choices." *Reuters*, February 9, 2012. Retrieved from www.reuters.com/article/2012/02/09/us-usa-military-obesity-idUSTRE8180RV20120209

Pescosolido, Bernice A., Jack K. Martin, Annie Lang, and Sigrun Olafsdottir. 2008. "Rethinking Theoretical Approaches to Stigma: A Framework Integrating Normative Influences on Stigma (FINIS)." *Social Science and Medicine* 67: 431–440.

Pomerantz, Anita. 1984. "Agreeing and Disagreeing with Assessments: Some Features of Preferred/Dispreferred Turn Shapes." In *Structures of Social Action: Studies in Conversation Analysis*. Edited by J. Maxwell Atkinson and John Heritage, 57–101. Cambridge: Cambridge University Press.

Pope, Harrison G., Katharine A. Phillips, and Roberto Olivardia. 2000. *The Adonis Complex: The Secret Crisis of Male Body Obsession*. New York: The Free Press.

Powell, Lisa M., Jennifer L. Harris, and Tracy Fox. 2013. "Food Marketing Expenditures Aimed at Youth: Putting the Numbers in Context." *American Journal of Preventative Medicine* 45(4): 453–461.

Puhl, Rebecca, and Janet Latner. 2007. "Obesity, Stigma, and the Health of the Nation's Children." *Psychological Bulletin* 133(4): 557–580.

Puhl, Rebecca, Joerg Luedicke, and Cheslea Heuer. 2011. "Weight-based Victimization toward Overweight Adolescents: Observations and Reactions of Peers. *Journal of School Health* 81(11): 696–703.

Puhl, Rebecca M., Jamie Lee Peterson, and Joerg Luedicke. 2013. "Weight-Based Victimization: Bullying Experiences of Weight Loss Treatment-Seeking Youth." *Pediatrics* 131: e1–e9.

Ritenbaugh, Cheryl. 1982. "Obesity As a Culture-Bound Syndrome." *Culture, Medicine, and Psychiatry* 6: 347–361.

Rubin, Lisa, Mako Fitts, and Anne Becker. 2003. "'Whatever Feels Good in My Soul': Body Ethics and Aesthetics among African American and Latina Women." *Culture, Medicine and Psychiatry* 27: 49–75.

Ryan, Travis A., and Todd G. Morrison. 2009. "Factors Perceived to Influence Young Irish Men's Body Image Investment: A Qualitative Investigation." *International Journal of Men's Health* 8(3): 213–234.

Ryan, Travis A., Todd G. Morrison, and Cormac Ó Beaglaoich. 2010. "Adolescent Males' Body Image: An Overview of Research on the Influence of Mass Media." In *Boys' Bodies: Speaking the Unspoken*. Edited by Michael Kehler and Michael Atkinson, 21–50. New York: Peter Lang Publishing.

Sabo, Don, and Phil Veliz. 2008. *Go Out and Play: Youth Sports in America*. East Meadow, NY: Women's Sports Foundation.

Saguy, Abigail. 2013. *What's Wrong with Fat?* New York: Oxford University Press.

Saguy, Abigail, and Kjerstin Gruys. 2010. "Morality and Health: News Media Constructions of Overweight and Eating Disorders." *Social Problems* 57(2): 231–250.

Saguy, Abigail, Kjerstin Gruys, and Shanna Gong. 2010. "Social Problem Construction and National Context: News Reporting on 'Overweight' and 'Obesity' in the United States and France." *Social Problems* 57(4): 586–610.

Schlosser, Eric. 2001. *Fast Food Nation: The Dark Side of the All-American Meal*. New York: Houghton Mifflin.

Schwartz, Hillel. 1986. *Never Satisfied: A Cultural History of Diets, Fantasies, and Fat*. New York: Free Press.

Schwartz, Marlene, and Kelly D. Brownell. 2007. "Actions Necessary to Prevent Childhood Obesity: Creating the Climate for Change. *Journal of Law, Medicine, and Ethics* 35(1) 78–89.

Sheikh, Farah. 2014. "Fed Up: The State of School Lunch As Told by Those Who Actually See It." *DoSomething.org* Retrieved from www.dosomething.org/campaigns/fed-up

Silverman, Robyn. 2010. *Good Girls Don't Get Fat: How Weight Obsession is Messing Up Our Girls and How We Can Help Them Thrive Despite it*. Ontario, Canada: Harlequin.

Simmons, Rachel. 2002. *Odd Girl Out: The Hidden Culture of Aggression in Girls*. New York: Houghton Mifflin Harcourt Publishing.

Slater, Amy, and Marika Tiggermann. 2010. "'Uncool to do Sport': A Focus Group Study of Adolescent Girls' Reasons for Withdrawing from Physical Activity." *Psychology of Sport and Exercise* 11: 619–626.

Sobal, Jeffery. 1995. "The Medicalization and Demedicalization of Obesity." In *Eating Agendas: Food and Nutrition as Social Problems*. Edited by Donna Maurer and Jeffery Sobal, 67–90. New York: Walter de Gruyter.

Sobo, Elisa. 1994. "The Sweetness of Fat: Health, Procreation, and Sociability in Rural Jamaica." In *Many Mirrors: Body Image and Social Meaning*. Edited by Nicole Sault, 132–154. New Brunswick, NJ: Rutgers University Press.

Stearns, Peter. 2002. *Fat History: Bodies and Beauty in the Modern West*. New York: New York University Press.

Story, Mary, Karen M. Kaphingst, and Simone A. French. 2006. "The Role of Schools in Obesity Prevention." *The Future of Children* 16: 109–142.

Story, Mary, Karen M. Kaphingst, Ramona Robinson-O'Brien, and Karen Glanz. 2008. "Creating Healthy Food and Eating Environments: Policy and Environmental Approaches." *Annual Review of Public Health* 29: 253–272.

Strauss, Richard S., and Harold A. Pollack. 2003. "Social Marginalization of Overweight Children." *Archives of Pediatric and Adolescent Medicine* 157: 746–752.

"Surgeon General to Cops: Put Down the Donuts." 3 *CNN*, March 3, 2003. Retrieved from www.cnn.com/2003/HEALTH/02/28/obesity.police/

Taber, Daniel R., Jamie F. Chriqui, Lisa M. Powell, and Frank J. Chaloupka. 2012. "Banning All Sugar-sweetened Beverages in Middle Schools." *Archives of Pediatrics and Adolescent Medicine* 166: 256–262.

Tannen, Deborah. 1990. *You Just Don't Understand: Women and Men in Conversation*. New York: Ballentine Books.

Taylor, Nicole L. 2011. "'Guys, She's Humongous!': Gender and Weight-Based Teasing in Adolescence." *Journal of Adolescent Research* 26(2): 178–199.

Taylor, Wendell, Bettina Beech, and Sharon Cummings. 1997. "Increasing Physical Activity Levels among Youth: A Public Health Challenge." In *Health-Promoting and Health-Compromising Behaviors among Minority Adolescents*. Edited by Dawn K. Wilson, Wendell C. Taylor, and James R. Rodrigue, 107–127. Washington, DC: American Psychological Association.

Terry-McElrath, Yvonne M., Lindsey Turner, Anna Sandoval, Lloyd D. Johnston, Frank J. Chaloupka. 2014. "Commercialism in US Elementary and Secondary School Nutrition Environments: Trends from 2007 to 2012." *JAMA Pediatrics* 168(3): 234–242.

Theberge, Nancy. 1997. "'It's Part of the Game:' Physicality and the Production of Gender in Women's Hockey." *Gender and Society* 11: 69–87.

Thompson, J. Kevin, Sylvia Herbozo, Susan Himes, and Yuko Yamamiya. 2005. "Attributions and Weight-Based Prejudice." In *Weight Bias: Nature, Consequences, and Remedies*. Edited by Kelly D. Brownell, Rebecca M. Puhl, Marlene B. Schwartz, and Leslie Rudd, 137–149. New York: The Guilford Press.

Thorne, Barry. 1992. "Girls and Boys Together ... But Mostly Apart: Gender Arrangements in Elementary School." In *Education and Gender Equality*. Edited by Julia Wrigley, 115–130. Milton Park, UK: RoutledgeFalmer.

Thorne, Barry. 1993. *Gender Play: Girls and Boys in School*. New Brunswick, NJ: Rutgers University Press.

Toms, Marc and Linda E. Rohr. 2013. "Increasing Enjoyment in Physical Education through Gender Segregated Classes." *Physical & Health Education Nexus* 4(3): 1–15.

Tough, Paul. 2012. *How Children Succeed: Grit, Curiosity, and the Hidden Power of Character*. New York: Houghton Mifflin Harcourt Publishing.

Trainer, Sarah. 2013. *Local Interpretations of Global Trends: Body Concerns and Self-Projects Enacted by Young Emirati Women.* PhD dissertation, The University of Arizona, Tucson, AZ.

Trainer, Sarah. Forthcoming. "Glocalizing Beauty: Weight and Body Image in the New Middle East." In *Fat Planet: Obesity, Culture, and Symbolic Body Capital.* Edited by Eileen P. Anderson-Fye and Alexandra Brewis. Santa Fe, NM: SAR Press; Albuquerque: University of New Mexico Press.

Trudeau, François, and Roy J. Shephard. 2010. "Relationships of Physical Activity to Brain Health and the Academic Performance of School Children." *American Journal of Lifestyle Medicine* 4: 138–150.

US Department of Agriculture, Food and Nutrition Service. January 26, 2012. "Nutrition Standards in the National School Lunch and School Breakfast Programs." Final Rule. *Federal Register: Rules and Regulations* 77(17): 4088–4167.

US Government Accountability Office. 2005. *School Meal Programs: Competitive Foods Are Widely Available and Generate Substantial Revenues for Schools.* (Publication No. GAO-05-563). Washington, DC: USGPO.

US Government Accountability Office. 2014. *School Lunch: Implementing Nutrition Changes Was Challenging and Clarification of Oversight Requirements Is Needed.* (Publication No. GAO-14-104). Washington, DC: USGPO.

Vartanian, Lenny R., Marlene B. Schwartz, and Kelly D. Brownell. 2007. "Effects of Soft Drink Consumption on Nutrition and Health: A Systematic Review and Meta-analysis." *American Journal of Public Health* 97: 667–675.

Veit, Helen Zoe. 2013. *Modern Food, Moral Food: Self-Control, Science, and the Rise of Modern American Eating in the Early Twentieth Century.* Chapel Hill, NC: University of North Carolina Press.

Wadden, Thomas A., Kelly D. Brownell, and Gary D. Foster. 2002. "Obesity: Responding to the Global Epidemic." *Journal of Consulting and Clinical Psychology* 70(3): 510–525.

Wescott, Robert F., Brendan M. Fitzpatrick, and Elizabeth Phillips. 2012. "Industry Self-Regulation to Improve Student Health: Quantifying Changes in Beverage Shipments to Schools." *American Journal of Public Health* 102(10): 1928–1935.

Wex, Marianne. 1979. *Let's Take Back Our Space: "Female" and "Male" Body Language as a Result of Patriarchal Structures.* Berlin: Frauenliteraturverlag Hermine Fees.

Willis, Paul, Simon Jones, Joyce Canaan, and Geoff Hurd. 1990. *Common Culture: Symbolic Work at Play in the Everyday Cultures of the Young.* Buckingham: Open University Press.

Wolf, Naomi. 1991. *The Beauty Myth: How Images of Beauty Are Used Against Women.* New York: William Morrow and Co.

Yon, Bethany A. and Rachel K. Johnson. 2014. "Dietary Patterns and Sugar-Sweetened Beverage Consumption among Adolescents and Adults." *Current Nutrition Reports* 3: 43–50.

Young, Iris. 1980. "Throwing Like a Girl: A Phenomenology of Feminine Body Comportment Motility and Spatiality." *Human Studies* 3: 137–156.

INDEX